AF656373

SRE with AIOps

Building resilient systems with AIOps, ML-driven observability, and agentic AI

Sunny Behl

Giridhar Kanikarapu

www.bpbonline.com

First Edition 2026

ISBN: 978-93-78542-343

LIMITS OF LIABILITY AND DISCLAIMER OF WARRANTY

Distributors:

BPB PUBLICATIONS
20, Ansari Road, Darya Ganj
New Delhi-110002
Ph: 23254990/23254991

DECCAN AGENCIES
4-3-329, Bank Street,
Hyderabad-500195
Ph: 24756967/24756400

MICRO MEDIA
Shop No. 5, Mahendra Chambers,
150 DN Rd. Next to Capital Cinema,
V.T. (C.S.T.) Station, MUMBAI-400 001
Ph: 22078296/22078297

To View Complete BPB Publications Catalogue Scan the QR Code:

Published by Manish Jain for BPB Publications, 20 Ansari Road, Darya Ganj, New Delhi-110002 and Printed by him at Repro India Ltd., Rewari.

www.bpbonline.com

Dedicated to

Every SRE engineer who has ever fought fires at 3 AM.

This book is the intelligence that fights alongside you.

About the Authors

- **Sunny Behl** is the director and head of AIOps and digital production management at a major global financial institution, serving over 200 million customer accounts across more than 160 countries. With more than 20 years of experience transforming large-scale IT organizations, Sunny brings rare depth across AIOps, cloud-native platforms, site reliability engineering, DevOps, and agile methodologies.

  He is the holder of five US patents granted by the **United States Patent and Trademark Office (USPTO)**, three for automated AIOps platform management and two for microservices anomaly detection. These patents reflect Sunny's commitment to translating engineering insight into intellectual innovation.

  A Splunk certified power user and SRE-certified professional via the DevOps institute, Sunny also holds a bachelor of engineering in electronics and communication and a post graduate program in artificial intelligence and machine learning. He is based in Irving, Texas, where he plays a pivotal role in Citigroup's technology and business enablement strategy.

- **Giridhar Kanikarapu** is a distinguished technology leader at a global financial institution with over 13 years of experience driving digital transformation across industries, including travel management, healthcare, and retail banking. He holds a master's degree in computer science and brings deep expertise in cloud computing, artificial intelligence, and modern software engineering practices.

  In this role, Giridhar leads strategic technology modernization initiatives with a strong focus on site reliability engineering, AIOps, resilient production support, and scalable cloud-native architectures. He is known for delivering forward-looking solutions that leverage AI and cloud technologies to improve system reliability, accelerate innovation, and boost organizational agility. With a cross-industry perspective, he bridges legacy banking systems with next-generation digital capabilities, enabling enterprises to thrive in a rapidly evolving technology landscape.

About the Reviewers

- **Sangharsh Agarwal** is a passionate site reliability and DevOps engineer with extensive professional experience in designing, building, and operating large-scale cloud-native platforms. He specializes in **site reliability engineering** (**SRE**), DevOps automation, cloud infrastructure, CI/CD pipelines, observability, and platform engineering. Sangharsh has deep expertise in modern cloud technologies, including Kubernetes, Docker, infrastructure as code, and automated delivery pipelines.

  He began his career as a software developer working with C++ and Python developer and later transitioned into DevOps and SRE, focusing on building reliable, scalable, and secure systems for modern SaaS platforms.

  Sangharsh actively contributes to the evolution of reliability engineering practices and is an advocate for integrating DevOps, SRE, security, and compliance into a unified operational framework for next-generation cloud platforms. He frequently writes and shares insights with the engineering community on topics such as SRE practices, automation, observability, and AI-driven operations.

  He is currently working as a senior site reliability engineer at Adobe, where he focuses on building scalable cloud infrastructure, modern CI/CD systems, and reliability platforms for large-scale SaaS products.

- **Parag Bhardwaj** is a senior product manager and principal architect specializing in multi-cloud governance, FinOps, and AI-driven enterprise systems. With more than two decades of experience spanning cloud architecture, automation, cost optimization, and large-scale operational transformation, he is recognized for bringing clarity, structure, and measurable impact to complex technical environments.

  An MBA in adaptive leadership and a B.Tech in information technology form the foundation of his multidisciplinary expertise. Parag is an IEEE Senior Member, a published author, and a trusted technical reviewer known for blending hands-on engineering depth with strategic product leadership.

  He is the author of two industry-focused books: *Azure FinOps Essentials: A Practical Guide to Cloud Cost Management and Optimization*, and *FinOps for Snowflake: A Practical Guide to Financial Governance and Optimization*

Parag's professional work spans cloud governance modernization, cost-optimization frameworks, automation-driven reliability, and cross-functional adoption of governance as a service. He is known for elevating product quality through rigorous QA leadership and enabling teams through empathetic, structured communication.

Beyond his enterprise leadership roles, Parag is actively building his insurance venture and is deeply committed to mentoring, teaching advanced technical concepts, and supporting family and group logistics across borders. His interests include AI systems, linear algebra, data modeling, financial planning, and simplifying complex regulatory landscapes for real-world decision-making.

His career reflects a consistent theme: transforming complexity into clarity, empowering teams, and architecting systems that scale with purpose.

Acknowledgements

Writing a book is never a solitary endeavor. Behind every chapter lies a constellation of mentors, colleagues, friends, and family whose contributions, visible and invisible, have made this work possible. I am deeply grateful to each of them.

First and foremost, I want to express my heartfelt gratitude to my family members, whose unwavering belief in the value of knowledge and hard work has been the foundation of everything I have achieved. Their encouragement throughout this journey and throughout my life is a gift I can never fully repay.

I owe an enormous debt of gratitude to my co-author, Giridhar Kanikarapu, whose sharp intellect, collaborative spirit, and deep technical expertise elevated this book beyond what I could have produced alone. Working with him has been both a privilege and a pleasure.

My profound thanks go to my colleagues and teams at a leading global financial institution, whose real-world challenges and collective brilliance inspired many of the frameworks and insights in this book. The problems we solved together under pressure, at scale, and often in the dark of incident bridges, are the raw material from which these chapters are built. Special mention to the AIOps and production management technology teams, who have been the true proving ground for the ideas presented here.

I am grateful to the broader SRE and AIOps community, the practitioners, researchers, open-source contributors, and authors whose work I have studied, referenced, and been inspired by over the years. Giants like Google's SRE team, whose foundational thinking shaped an entire discipline, and the innovators are continuously pushing the boundaries of intelligent automation.

I would sincerely like to thank the team at BPB Publications for their professionalism, guidance, and patience throughout the publishing process. Their commitment to technical excellence and their support in shaping this manuscript into its final form have been invaluable.

Finally, to every reader who picks up this book, thank you for investing your time in these ideas. My greatest hope is that the frameworks and insights shared here help you build systems that are not merely reliable but truly intelligent.

Preface

In the early years of my career, I watched brilliant engineers spend their nights chasing phantom alerts, manually correlating logs, and performing the same diagnostic rituals over and over again, not because they lacked skill, but because the tools and systems they operated demanded it. Reliability was won through heroism. That always struck me as unsustainable. This book is my attempt to offer a better way.

The convergence of **site reliability engineering** (SRE) and **artificial intelligence for IT operations** (**AIOps**) is not simply a technological trend; it is a fundamental shift in how we think about production systems. For decades, reliability was a reactive discipline: something broke, an engineer investigated, and a fix was applied. Today, the complexity of distributed cloud-native systems has outgrown the human capacity for manual triage. The volume of telemetry, the speed of deployments, and the interconnectedness of microservices demand a new operating model, one where intelligence is embedded in the fabric of operations itself.

This book was born from that conviction. Over more than twenty years of leading IT operations and AIOps initiatives, including building patent-holding platforms at a major global financial institution that serve over 200 million customer accounts globally, I have seen firsthand what happens when machine learning, intelligent automation, and sound SRE principles are brought together. Incidents that took hours to diagnose are resolved in seconds. Alert noise that burned out entire teams is silenced by smart correlation. Systems that once required constant human intervention begin to heal themselves. The transformation is real, and it is available to any organization willing to make the journey.

This book is structured to guide you through that journey, not as an abstract academic exercise, but as a practitioner's roadmap drawn from hard-won experience. It is divided into four sections. The first lays the foundational principles of SRE and introduces AIOps as a strategic capability. The second shows how to apply intelligence to eliminate operational toil across incident, change, and problem management. The third goes deeper into the platform's intelligent core, advanced anomaly detection, causal inference, chaos engineering, and the AIOps-powered SRE assistant. The final section looks ahead, exploring generative AI chatbots, enterprise-scale adoption, and the emerging frontier of autonomous operations and agentic AI.

Each chapter is written to be both conceptually clear and immediately actionable. You will find architectural patterns you can adapt, frameworks you can operationalize, and technical depth you can build upon, whether you are an SRE practitioner, a cloud architect, an IT operations leader, or a technology executive setting the strategic direction for your organization.

A brief word on what this book does not attempt to do: it is not a product manual for any single AIOps platform, nor is it a comprehensive machine learning textbook. It is an engineering practitioner's guide, one that takes the reader from foundational concepts to the frontier of intelligent operations, with enough technical depth to be genuinely useful and enough strategic perspective to be genuinely transformative.

The future of SRE is not more engineers fighting more fires. It is smarter systems, powered by intelligence, that prevent the fires from starting, and extinguish the ones that do before any human has to be woken up. I hope this book helps you build that future. The book is divided into 13 chapters:

Chapter 1: SRE Principles Driving Modern Operations- This chapter sets the practical tone for the entire book. This chapter demystifies SRE, not as a buzzword but as a disciplined, outcome-driven approach to modern operations. Readers will explore SLOs, SLIs, error budgets, and the relentless pursuit of toil reduction as strategic levers for balancing innovation and reliability.

Chapter 2: AIOps Tools for SRE- This chapter positions AIOps as a strategic enabler of SRE goals. Readers learn to evaluate core AIOps capabilities, from anomaly detection to intelligent alerting, and build a compelling business case for adoption within their reliability culture. The chapter bridges vision and execution.

Chapter 3: AIOps Knowledgebase- This chapter explores the architecture of observability-driven intelligence. It introduces the unified data model for ingesting logs, metrics, and traces, and explains how automated service discovery and dependency mapping create a dynamic system blueprint, the single pane of glass for SRE teams.

Chapter 4: Intelligent Incident Management for SREs- This chapter reimagines incident response through the lens of AI. This chapter covers advanced alert correlation, noise reduction, predictive incident prevention, automated triage, and streamlined postmortem analysis, reducing cognitive load and accelerating resolution at every stage of the incident lifecycle.

Chapter 5: Streamlining Change and Problem Management- This chapter introduces AIOps-driven techniques for assessing change risk, performing canary analysis, and predicting impact on SLOs. Readers gain tools to make change safer, smarter, and more predictable, and to automate problem identification and root cause resolution.

Chapter 6: Path to Productivity and Reliability- This chapter quantifies the value of toil elimination. Through metrics like freed-up engineering time and improved availability, readers learn to measure the ROI of intelligent operations. Real-world case studies demonstrate how AIOps-enabled SRE practices drive both productivity and reliability.

Chapter 7: Advanced Anomaly Detection- This chapter takes anomaly detection from static thresholds to dynamic intelligence. This chapter introduces autoencoders, isolation forests, and time series modeling to detect deviations in real-time, and shows how to integrate anomaly detection directly into error budget strategies.

Chapter 8: Causal Inference and Efficient Root Cause Analysis- This chapter makes root cause analysis faster and smarter using causal inference. Readers explore intelligent event grouping, probabilistic RCA, and automated post-incident workflows, moving from reactive diagnostics to predictive remediation and dramatically reducing downtime.

Chapter 9: Intelligent SRE Assistant- This chapter introduces the AIOps-powered assistant as an always-on, context-aware collaborator for SRE teams. This chapter covers how to build and operationalize an intelligent assistant that surfaces relevant insights, recommends actions, and automates repetitive diagnostic workflows.

Chapter 10: Chaos Engineering and Reliability Testing- This chapter introduces chaos engineering as a proactive reliability discipline. The chapter explores fault injection, blast radius control, and integrating chaos experiments with AIOps platforms, using controlled failure to validate SLOs and build confidence in system resilience.

Chapter 11: Generative AI-powered SRE Chatbot- This chapter explores the architecture of conversational AIOps agents. Readers learn how generative AI can automate incident response, runbook execution, and postmortem analysis through natural language, and it introduces the concept of agentic AI as an autonomous collaborative partner for SREs.

Chapter 12: Scaling AIOps Across the Enterprise- This chapter explores readers through scaling AIOps from a pilot to enterprise-wide adoption. Topics include organizational design, change management, cross-team collaboration, training and upskilling SRE teams, and measuring the business-wide impact of intelligent operations.

Chapter 13: Future Trends in SRE and AIOps- This chapter serves as a strategic roadmap for the next decade of intelligent operations. The chapter explores autonomous remediation, predictive governance, agentic AI swarms, and the evolving role of LLMs in SRE workflows, transitioning SREs from mechanics to decision architects.

Code Bundle and Coloured Images

Please follow the link to download the
Code Bundle and the ***Coloured Images*** of the book:

https://rebrand.ly/rnht3hi

The code bundle for the book is also hosted on GitHub at
https://github.com/bpbpublications/SRE-with-AIOps.
In case there's an update to the code, it will be updated on the existing GitHub repository.

We have code bundles from our rich catalogue of books and videos available at **https://github.com/bpbpublications.** Check them out!

Errata

We take immense pride in our work at BPB Publications and follow best practices to ensure the accuracy of our content to provide an indulging reading experience to our subscribers. Our readers are our mirrors, and we use their inputs to reflect and improve upon human errors, if any, that may have occurred during the publishing processes involved. To let us maintain the quality and help us reach out to any readers who might be having difficulties due to any unforeseen errors, please write to us at: **errata@bpbonline.com**

Your support, suggestions and feedback are highly appreciated by the BPB Publications' Family.

Piracy

If you come across any illegal copies of our works in any form on the internet, we would be grateful if you would provide us with the location address or website name. Please contact us at **business@bpbonline.com** with a link to the material.

If you are interested in becoming an author

If there is a topic that you have expertise in, and you are interested in either writing or contributing to a book, please visit **www.bpbonline.com**. We have worked with thousands of developers and tech professionals, just like you, to help them share their insights with the global tech community. You can make a general application, apply for a specific hot topic that we are recruiting an author for, or submit your own idea.

Reviews

Please leave a review. Once you have read and used this book, why not leave a review on the site that you purchased it from? Potential readers can then see and use your unbiased opinion to make purchase decisions. We at BPB can understand what you think about our products, and our authors can see your feedback on their book. Thank you!

For more information about BPB, please visit **www.bpbonline.com**.

Join our Discord space

Join our Discord workspace for latest updates, offers, tech happenings around the world, new releases, and sessions with the authors:

https://discord.bpbonline.com

Table of Contents

Chapter 1
SRE Principles Driving Modern Operations

Introduction

This chapter examines the key concepts behind **site reliability engineering** (**SRE**) and its impact on today's technology operations. In the past decade, technology has moved from stable, separate systems to complex, cloud-based setups. These changes mean updates happen more often, and there is a higher risk of things going wrong. Today, SRE plays a bigger role than ever. It brings engineering and daily operations together, making sure technology truly helps the business reach its goals instead of just being a set of tools or a buzzword.

Structure

In this chapter, we will cover the following topics:

- Importance of SRE executives
- Strategic imperative for SRE
- Core principles of SRE
- SLIs, SLOs, and error budgets
- Balancing reliability with innovation
- Relentless pursuit of toil reduction
- Strategic risk management in SRE
- Leading the SRE transformation

Objectives

By the end of this chapter, readers will gain a comprehensive understanding of why SRE has become a strategic imperative. They will be equipped to apply key SRE principles to enhance system reliability and performance, and to use SLIs, SLOs, and error budgets as tools for guiding engineering and product decisions. Readers will learn to recognize and avoid common reliability pitfalls, balance innovation velocity with operational resilience, and identify and eliminate toil through structured automation. Additionally, they will be prepared to foster a culture of controlled risk and continuous learning, and to lead SRE adoption as a cross-functional business initiative.

Importance of SRE executives

In today's digital-first landscape, reliability is no longer just a technical concern; it is a business-critical priority. As systems grow more complex and customer expectations rise, the consequences of downtime extend far beyond engineering teams. They impact revenue, reputation, compliance, and competitive advantage. This shift has elevated SRE from an operational function to a strategic discipline that belongs in the boardroom.

The following points highlight why SRE is now central to executive decision-making and organizational resilience:

- Downtime now poses significant risks to a company's finances, reputation, and compliance, not just technical operations.
- Customers expect fast digital experiences, and their loyalty can change quickly.
- Rapid innovation offers a competitive edge, provided it does not compromise system stability.

This chapter introduces SRE as a practical, business-focused discipline. It leverages metrics, automation, and cultural alignment to achieve scalable reliability without hindering innovation. It lays the foundation for creating self-optimizing, self-healing systems through **artificial intelligence for IT operations** (**AIOps**).

Strategic imperative for SRE

Three main forces shape the modern operational environment:

- **Market forces driving change**:
    - o **Architectural complexity**: Monoliths have been replaced by microservices, containers, serverless functions, and multi-cloud deployments. While this increases agility, it also multiplies the potential points of failure.
    - o **Customer-centric competition**: In today's digital markets, the user experience is a core part of the product. Metrics such as latency, availability, and performance have become business indicators that can directly impact revenue and customer loyalty.
    - o **Regulatory and compliance pressures**: Industries such as finance, healthcare, and critical infrastructure must comply with strict regulations like the **General Data Protection Regulation** (**GDPR**) and the **Health Insurance Portability and**

Accountability Act (HIPAA), which require high reliability and strong data protection. In these sectors, reliability is a legal necessity; downtime or data loss can lead to significant penalties and reputational harm.

- **Cost of downtime**: For a global e-commerce company, an hour of downtime during a busy period can mean millions in lost sales. Similarly, system failure at a financial institution can result in substantial regulatory fines and long-term reputational damage. Industry data underscores these risks:
    - When IT systems go down, the costs add up fast. On average, a company can lose around $5,600 per minute of downtime.
    - 93% of companies report that one hour of downtime costs over $100,000.
    - In regulated sectors, penalties for non-compliance can exceed the direct cost of the outage.
- **Reasons for traditional ITIL-only approaches falling short**: Traditional **Information Technology Infrastructure Library (ITIL)** approaches are often too slow and process-heavy for modern cloud-native environments; SRE modernizes these practices by:
    - Embedding engineering practices into operations.
    - Using data-driven decision-making instead of relying solely on process compliance.
    - Automating tasks to reduce human error and operational toil.

SRE as a strategic lever

For **Chief Technology Officers (CTOs)** and IT leaders, SRE is not just about keeping the lights on; it is about enabling safe, sustainable innovation:

- **For the C-suite**: SRE provides a measurable, contractual framework for balancing risk and innovation.
- **For operations leaders**: The SRE model offers a scalable way to handle complexity without needing more staff.
- **For SRE teams**: The SRE approach fosters an empowered culture, enabling engineers to solve underlying issues instead of just treating symptoms.

Core principles of SRE

SRE is built on a set of interconnected principles that create a culture and architecture capable of delivering reliability at scale:

- **Availability**: The foundation of trust; availability is the most visible measure of reliability. It defines whether users can access a service when they need it. In SRE, availability is not about chasing perfection; it is about aligning uptime targets with business value and user expectations:

- **Definition**: The percentage of time a service is operational and accessible.
- **Strategic view**: The goal is not to randomly chase five nines but to align uptime targets with business value. Every system has its own specific reliability requirements. For example, a payment gateway usually demands a high uptime of approximately 99.999%, while an internal HR portal can operate satisfactorily with a slightly lower target of around 99.5%.
- **KPIs**: Uptime percentage, **mean time between failures (MTBF)**, **mean time to recovery (MTTR)**, and any breaches of **Service Level Agreements (SLAs)**. Keeping track of metrics can help ensure success and highlight areas that need improvement.

  Understanding the strategic importance of availability helps organizations prioritize reliability efforts where they matter most. The following figure illustrates how different availability targets align with business value across various systems and use cases:

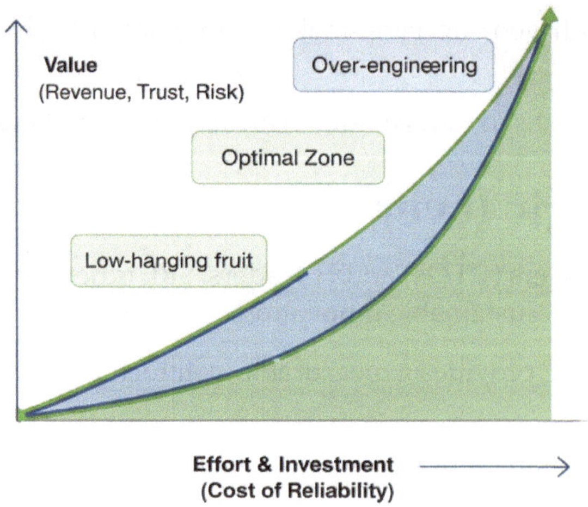

Figure 1.1: Business value of availability

- **Latency**: The invisible dealbreaker; even when systems are available, slow response times can erode user trust. Latency measures how quickly a system reacts to requests, and in high-performing environments, it is treated as a critical component of user experience:
  - **Definition**: The time it takes for a system to respond to a request.
  - **Strategic view**: Even if a service is available, slow responses can damage user trust and engagement.

    o **KPIs**: P95/P99 response time, **time to first byte** (**TTFB**), transaction completion time, and user abandonment rate.

While availability ensures that a system can be accessed, latency determines how usable and satisfying that access is. The following figure highlights the hidden business impact of latency, showing how even slight delays can significantly affect user engagement and operational outcomes:

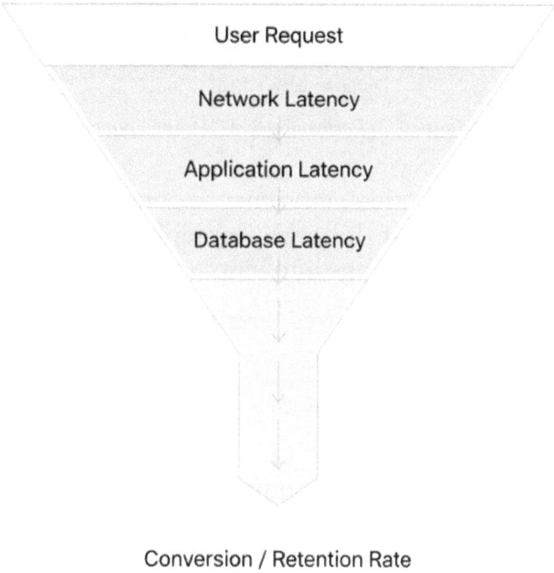

Figure 1.2*: The latent cost of latency*

- **Performance**: Sustaining throughput under load; performance ensures that systems can handle expected and peak workloads without degradation. It reflects the system's ability to maintain consistent behavior under stress, which is essential for scalability and user satisfaction:
    o **Definition**: The capacity of a system to manage both regular and maximum workloads effectively, without a decrease in performance.
    o **Strategic view**: Performance is about consistency under stress.
    o **KPIs**: Throughput (transactions/sec), resource utilization %, error rate under load, and capacity headroom %.

Performance is the backbone of scalable and responsive systems. While latency affects individual user interactions, performance determines how well a system holds up under increasing demand. The following figure illustrates the relationship between performance and latency, showing how throughput and responsiveness interact as load increases:

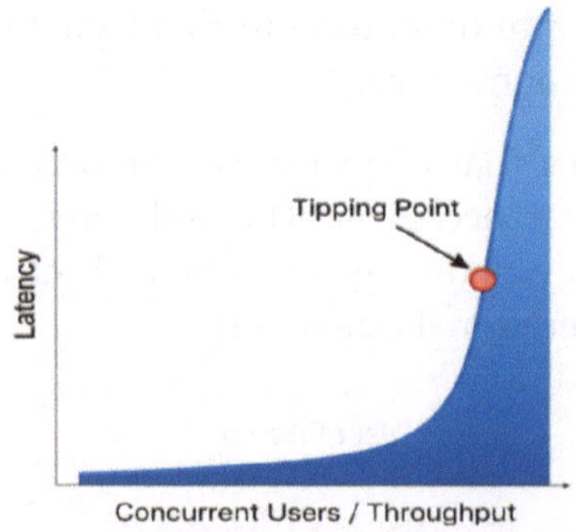

***Figure 1.3**: Performance vs. latency curve*

- **Efficiency**: Doing more with less; efficiency is about delivering reliable performance at the lowest sustainable cost. It enables organizations to optimize resource usage, reduce waste, and reinvest savings into innovation and resilience:
  - **Definition**: Delivering required performance and reliability at the lowest sustainable cost.
  - **Strategic view**: Efficiency is a profit lever; savings on infrastructure can be reinvested in innovation.
  - **KPIs**: Cost per transaction, resource utilization efficiency, and idle resource percentage.

  Efficiency bridges the gap between performance and sustainability. It ensures that systems not only deliver results but do so with optimal resource usage. The following figure illustrates how cost scales with utilization, emphasizing the importance of balancing performance demands with infrastructure efficiency:

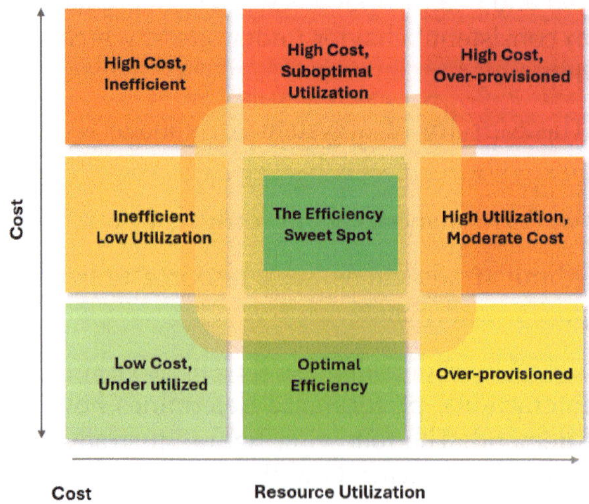

***Figure 1.4**: Cost vs. utilization*

- **Change management**: Deploying without fear; frequent and safe deployments are a hallmark of modern operations. Change management in SRE focuses on minimizing risk during releases, enabling teams to innovate confidently without compromising stability:
  - o **Definition**: Deploying frequently and safely.
  - o **Strategic view**: The ability to deploy without destabilizing systems is a competitive advantage.
  - o **KPIs**: Change failure rate, deployment frequency, **mean time to detect** (**MTTD**) post-change issues, and rollback rate.

  Change management is not just about deploying updates; it is about doing so with confidence and control. The ability to release frequently without compromising system stability is a key differentiator in modern operations. The following figure illustrates the risk dynamics associated with different types of changes, helping teams assess and manage deployment impact effectively:

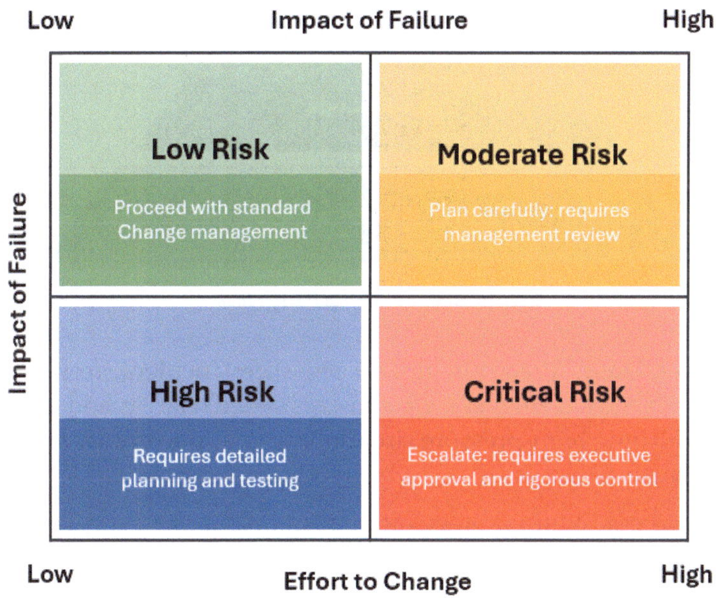

Figure 1.5: The change risk matrix

- **Monitoring and observability**: Seeing the truth in real-time; monitoring alerts teams to issues, while observability helps them understand root causes. Together, they form the nervous system of modern operations, enabling proactive detection and faster resolution of incidents:
  - o **Definition**: Monitoring tells you something is wrong, while observability helps you understand why.

- o **Strategic view**: Observability is the nervous system of modern operations; without it, you are operating blindly.
- o **KPIs**: Alert accuracy percentage, signal-to-noise ratio, time to identify root cause, and coverage of critical services.

In modern operations, visibility is everything. Monitoring provides the alerts, but observability delivers the insights needed to act. Together, they empower teams to detect issues early and resolve them efficiently. The following figure outlines the layers of the observability stack, showcasing how different components contribute to a comprehensive understanding of system health:

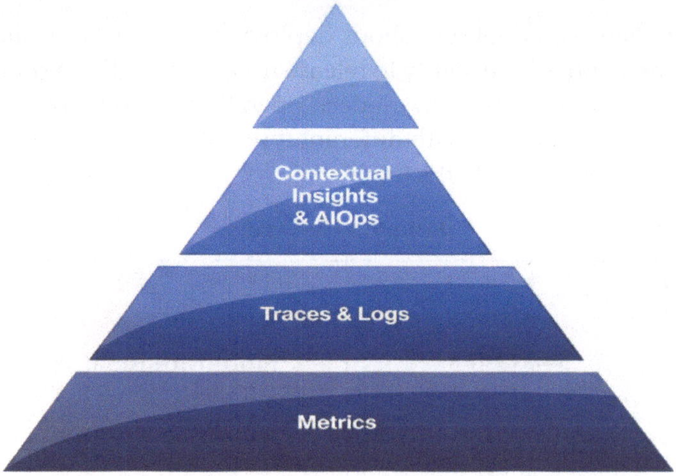

Figure 1.6: The observability stack

- **Emergency response**: Precision under pressure; incident response is a defining moment for reliability teams. SRE emphasizes speed, clarity, and coordination during emergencies, turning high-pressure situations into opportunities to reinforce trust and improve systems:
  - o **Definition**: The ability to respond to incidents quickly and effectively.
  - o **Strategic view**: Incident response is a critical leadership moment that can either build or erode trust.
  - o **KPIs**: **Mean time to acknowledge (MTTA)**, MTTR, customer impact duration, and postmortem completion rate.

Emergency response is where reliability is truly tested. In high-stakes moments, precision, speed, and coordination are essential to minimize impact and restore trust. The following figure illustrates the continuous lifecycle of incident management, emphasizing how each phase, from detection to resolution, contributes to operational resilience:

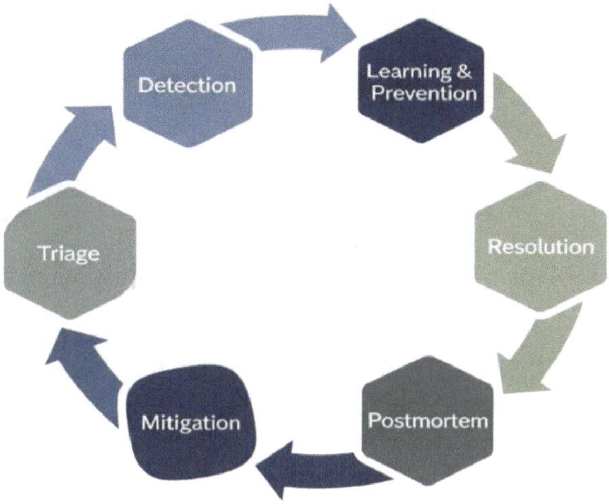

***Figure 1.7**: The continuous incident lifecycle*

The leadership takeaway is that these principles are mutually reinforcing. High availability depends on effective change management. Low latency requires strong performance engineering. Efficiency gains are unlocked through observability and automation. Emergency response is faster when monitoring is precise. Treat them as strategic levers; each one can be tuned to balance reliability, cost, and innovation velocity.

SLOs, SLIs, and error budgets

In high-performing organizations, reliability is a quantifiable commitment expressed through **service level indicators** (**SLIs**), **service level objectives** (**SLOs**), and error budgets. These concepts act as a contract between engineering and the business, guiding decisions and balancing innovation with stability.

- **SLIs**: Measuring what matters; reliability begins with measurement, and SLIs are the foundation. SLIs quantify how well a system performs from the user's perspective, offering a data-driven lens into availability, latency, and other critical behaviors. Without meaningful SLIs, teams risk optimizing for internal metrics that fail to reflect the actual user experience:
  - **Definition**: Quantitative metrics that reflect system reliability and performance from the user's viewpoint.
  - **Examples**: **Application Performance Index** (**Apdex**), request success rate, P95 or P99 latency, error rate, availability, and saturation.
  - **Strategic insight**: SLIs must be user-centric. A system might appear healthy internally while users experience poor performance. The best SLIs reflect the user's experience.

- **SLOs**: Defining acceptable reliability; once SLIs are established, SLOs define what *good enough* looks like. These targets are not arbitrary; they are negotiated thresholds that balance user expectations with engineering feasibility. SLOs transform reliability from a vague aspiration into a measurable commitment that guides operational decisions:
    - **Definition**: A target threshold for an SLI over a set time period, defining what *good enough* looks like.
    - **Example**: 99.9% of requests must complete within 500ms over a rolling 30-day period.
    - **Strategic insight**: SLOs are negotiated targets that balance user expectations with engineering feasibility.
- **Error budgets**: Quantifying risk and enabling innovation; error budgets represent the allowable margin of failure within an SLO. They provide a structured way to manage risk, enabling teams to innovate confidently when reliability is strong and to slow down when systems are under stress. More than a metric, error budgets are a governance tool that connects reliability to business agility:
    - **Definition**: The allowable margin of failure, which is the difference between perfect reliability and your SLO.
    - **Example**: An error budget is calculated by subtracting the SLO from 100% to 99.9% SLO translates to a 0.1% error budget, which equates to approximately 43 minutes of acceptable downtime per month.
    - **Strategic insight**: Error budgets empower teams to make data-driven decisions between reliability and innovation. In mature SRE environments, reliability is not left to interpretation; it is defined, measured, and managed through a structured trio: SLIs, SLOs, and error budgets. These elements form the backbone of reliability engineering, enabling teams to align technical performance with user expectations and business outcomes. The following figure illustrates how these components interact to guide decision-making, balance risk, and support continuous delivery:

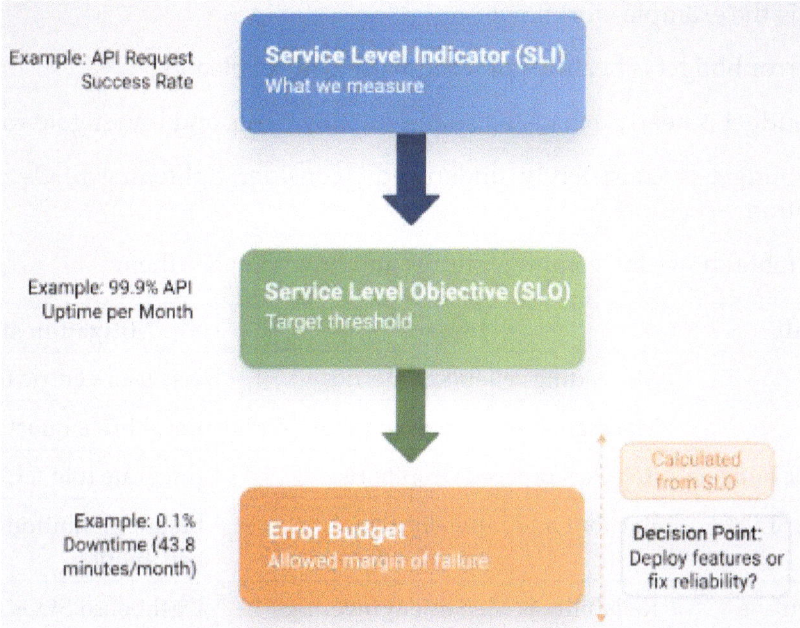

Figure 1.8: *SLIs, SLOs, and error budget in action*

SRE decision framework

To make reliability actionable, SRE teams use a structured workflow that connects user experience metrics to engineering decisions. This approach ensures that service quality is continuously measured, aligned with business goals, and used to guide development velocity. The following steps outline how SLIs, SLOs, and error budgets are applied in day-to-day operations to balance innovation with stability

- **Define SLIs that reflect user experience**: Start by identifying the key indicators that best represent how users perceive the service, such as latency, availability, or error rates.
- **Set SLOs based on historical data and business goals**: Use past performance and strategic priorities to establish realistic and meaningful targets for each SLI.
- **Monitor error budget burn in real-time**: Track how much of the error budget is consumed to understand whether the system is operating within acceptable limits.
- **Use budget status to guide release decisions**: Let the current error budget health influence whether to proceed with deployments, pause them, or investigate issues.
- **Review and recalibrate quarterly**: Regularly revisit SLIs and SLOs to ensure they remain aligned with evolving user expectations and business needs.

The following is the example workflow:

- If the error budget is healthy | proceed with feature releases
- If the budget is nearly exhausted | pause deployments and investigate root causes
- If the budget is consistently underused | consider tightening SLOs or increasing innovation velocity

The following table shows the common pitfalls and how to avoid them:

Pitfall	Impact	Mitigation strategy
Vanity SLIs	Misleading reliability metrics	Use user-centric indicators
Static SLOs	Misaligned with evolving workloads	Recalibrate quarterly
Ignored error budgets	Releases proceed despite risk	Integrate into CI/CD gating
Overly tight SLOs	Burnout and false alarms	Balance ambition with feasibility
Lack of executive visibility	Reliability is seen as engineering-only	Dashboard SLOs for leadership

Table 1.1*: Common pitfalls in SRE practice and how to address them*

Let us discuss the leadership takeaway. SLOs, SLIs, and error budgets are not just technical constructs; they are strategic instruments. They enable organizations to:

- Quantify reliability in business terms
- Make risk visible and manageable
- Align engineering velocity with customer expectations
- Empower teams to innovate without compromising trust

When used well, they transform reliability from a defensive posture into a competitive advantage.

Balancing reliability with innovation

Achieving the right balance between reliability and innovation is a strategic challenge for every organization. The pressure to innovate is constant, but every new deployment carries risk. SRE manages this tension by treating reliability and innovation not as opposing forces but as coequal priorities, managed through data, automation, and shared accountability.

Reliability innovation trade-off

Every organization must decide how much risk it is willing to tolerate in pursuit of speed. That decision should be:

- Quantified through error budgets
- Aligned across engineering, product, and business teams
- Revisited regularly based on performance and outcomes

The strategic insight is that reliability is not the absence of failure; it is the ability to fail gracefully, recover quickly, and learn continuously.

Balancing reliability and innovation is a strategic decision that requires cross-functional alignment and continuous evaluation. The following figure illustrates how organizations can use SRE principles, such as error budgets and SLOs, to navigate this trade-off and make informed decisions about acceptable risk in pursuit of velocity:

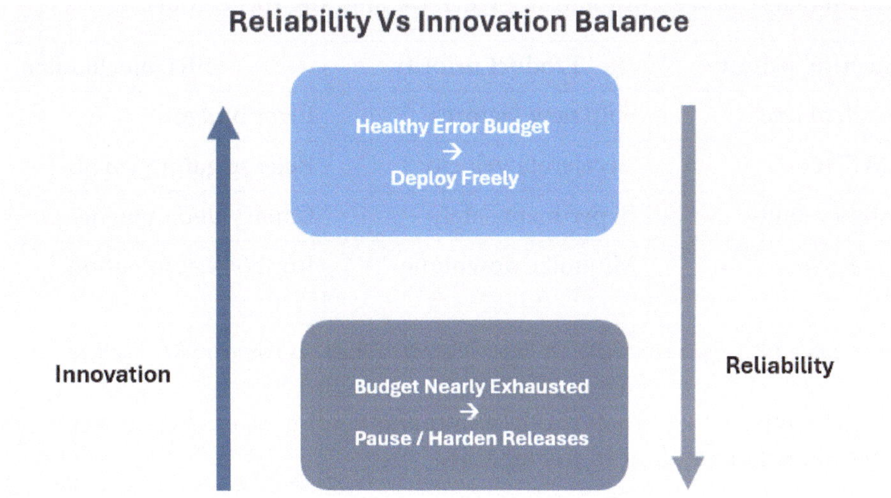

Figure 1.9: Reliability vs. innovation tradeoff

Using error budgets to guide innovation velocity

Error budgets are the governor of the innovation engine. They allow teams to:

- Proceed with releases when reliability is strong
- Slow down when risk is elevated
- Justify decisions with data, not gut instinct

For example, a global **software as a service** (**SaaS**) provider used error budget burn rates to throttle deployments during peak traffic windows. This reduced customer-impacting incidents by 35% and improved stakeholder trust in engineering decisions.

The following are the best practices:

- Integrate error budget checks into CI/CD pipelines
- Visualize budget burn in dashboards accessible to product teams
- Use budget status to prioritize reliability work vs. feature delivery

Aligning engineering and product goals

Innovation without reliability leads to customer churn, while reliability without innovation leads to stagnation. To harmonize innovation and reliability, organizations must bridge the gap between engineering priorities and product objectives. The following table illustrates how SRE mechanisms serve as a common framework for aligning these goals:

Engineering priority	Product priority	SRE mechanism
Reduce incident rate	Ship new features	Error budgets
Improve MTTR	Accelerate velocity	Release gating via SLOs
Increase observability	Experiment safely	Canary deployments
Automate recovery	Minimize downtime	Runbook automation

Table 1.2: Alignment of engineering and product priorities through SRE practices

The leadership insight is that when product and engineering teams co-own reliability goals, innovation becomes safer and more sustainable.

Building a culture of controlled risk

High-performing SRE organizations embrace controlled risk, the idea that failure is inevitable, but its impact can be minimized through preparation and automation.

The following are the cultural traits:

- Blameless postmortems
- Proactive chaos testing
- Continuous learning loops
- Shared accountability for uptime and velocity

For example, a fintech firm introduced release readiness reviews that included SRE, product, and QA leads. These reviews used SLO compliance and error budget status to greenlight or defer releases, and the result was 50% fewer hotfixes and a 20% increase in deployment frequency.

The following table lists the KPIs that reflect balance:

KPI	Indication
Error budget burn rate	Reliability health vs. risk exposure
Deployment frequency	Innovation velocity
Change failure rate	Stability of releases
MTTR	Resilience and recovery speed
Customer impact duration	Business cost of instability

***Table 1.3**: KPIs reflecting a culture of controlled risk*

Tip: **Track these KPIs together, not in isolation, to understand the proper balance between reliability and innovation.**

The leadership takeaway is that balancing reliability with innovation is not a compromise; it is a capability, and it requires:

- Clear metrics
- Shared ownership
- Intelligent automation
- A culture that values learning over blame

When reliability becomes a strategic enabler of innovation, organizations can move faster, scale smarter, and build trust with every release.

Relentless pursuit of toil reduction

In every mature operations environment, there is a moment when the team realizes they are spending more time reacting than engineering. The dashboards are lit up, the alerts are noisy, and the same manual steps are repeated day after day. This is not just inefficiency; it is operational debt, and it has a name toil.

Toil is the quiet thief of engineering time. It does not crash systems or trigger escalations, but it slowly erodes morale, velocity, and innovation. The most effective SRE leaders treat toil not as a nuisance but as a strategic threat, and they pursue its elimination with discipline and urgency.

Recognizing toil

Toil is not always predictable; it hides in routine tasks, legacy scripts, and tribal knowledge. You will find it in:

- The midnight Slack ping to restart a stuck service
- The manual steps are buried in a wiki page for incident triage
- The engineer who is the only one who knows how to fix that thing
- The recurring ticket to rotate logs or clean up disk space
- The alert that fires every day but never leads to action

What these tasks have in common is that they do not scale, do not teach, and do not improve the system. They are operational dead weight.

Toil as a strategic risk

Toil is not just a time sink; it is a reliability risk. Manual work introduces variability as it delays response. It distracts engineers from proactive improvements, and over time, it creates a brittle environment where only a few people know how things really work.

For leaders, the cost of toil shows up in:

- Slower incident resolution
- Higher attrition among ops teams
- Missed opportunities for automation
- Reduced capacity for innovation

Let us discuss the real-world example. A global payments company found that 40% of its SRE time was spent on repetitive diagnostics during incidents. By automating those steps, they cut MTTR by half and reallocated two full-time engineers to platform resilience work.

Practical framework for toil elimination

Toil reduction is not a one-time fix; it is a continuous discipline. Here is a pragmatic approach used by high-performing teams. Follow the steps:

1. **Surface the work**:
    a. Ask engineers to log every recurring task for two weeks
    b. Include incident response, maintenance, and monitoring actions
    c. Do not filter; capture everything

2. **Score and prioritize**: For each task, assess:
    a. **Frequency**: How often does it occur?
    b. **Duration**: How long does it take?
    c. **Impact**: What happens if it is delayed or skipped?
    d. **Automatability**: Can it be scripted or triggered?
3. **Automate ruthlessly**:
    a. Start with high-frequency, low-complexity tasks
    b. Use scripting, runbooks, and event-driven automation
    c. Track time saved and reinvest it in engineering improvements

The following figure outlines how high-performing teams systematically identify, assess, and automate recurring operational tasks to reclaim engineering capacity and improve reliability:

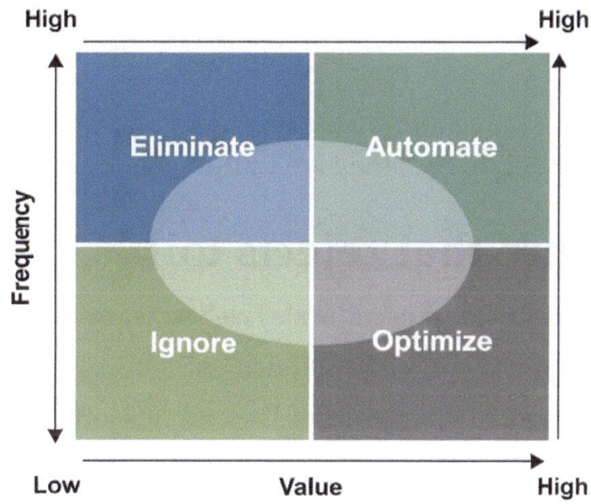

Figure 1.10: Toil prioritization matrix

Automation that actually works

Not all automation is created equal. The best toil-killing solutions are:

- **Self-healing**: Enabled by AIOps, self-healing systems autonomously detect failures and perform corrective actions, such as restarting services or applying fixes, without manual intervention.
- **Runbook-driven**: Convert tribal knowledge into executable workflows
- **Signal-aware**: Suppress noisy alerts and surface actionable ones
- **Infrastructure as code (IaC)**: Eliminate manual provisioning and drift

For example, a retail tech firm used event-driven automation to resolve 70% of disk space alerts without human intervention. The result is fewer escalations, faster recovery, and happier engineers.

Tracking meaningful progress in reliability engineering

Toil reduction should be tracked like any other strategic initiative. The following metrics help teams assess progress toward reliability, efficiency, and operational maturity:

Metric	Operational insight
Percentage of manual tasks automated	Progress in eliminating repetitive work
MTTR	Impact of automation on recovery speed
Alert noise ratio	Signal-to-noise improvement
SRE time allocation	Shift from reactive to proactive work
Onboarding time	Ease of ramp-up for new engineers

***Table 1.4**: KPI for measuring toil reduction and reliability gains*

Tip: **Report toil reduction alongside reliability and velocity metrics. It shows that your team is not just keeping the lights on; they are building a better system.**

Building a culture that rejects toil

Toil elimination is not just technical; it is cultural. The best teams:

- Celebrate automation wins in retros and demos
- Encourage engineers to automate themselves out of a job
- Allocate sprint time for engineering improvements
- Treat toil as a form of technical debt

The executive insight is that toil is often invisible at the leadership level. Expose toil, evaluate its impact, and drive it out. Every hour saved is an hour reinvested in resilience, scale, and innovation.

Strategic risk management in SRE

In the fast-paced world of engineering, risk is not an anomaly; it is an inherent part of the process. Each new deployment, architectural shift, or scaling choice brings with it a degree of unpredictability. The real issue is not the presence of risk, but rather an organization's capacity to effectively manage it.

SRE provides a structured approach to assessing and overseeing risk. This is achieved through tools like error budgets, SLOs, and realistic reliability goals. These mechanisms do not eradicate risk; instead, they illuminate it, making it something that can be discussed and acted upon.

Error budgets as reliability signal

An error budget is the allowable margin of failure defined by your SLO. It is the difference between perfect reliability and what you have agreed is good enough.

For example, for an SLO of 99.8% availability over a month, the error budget is 0.2%, which allows for up to about 1 hour and 27 minutes of downtime in that period.

However, error budgets are more than math. They are a governance tool:

- Healthy budget | deploy freely
- Budget nearing exhaustion | pause, investigate, stabilize
- Budget exceeded | freeze changes, prioritize recovery

Refer to the following figure:

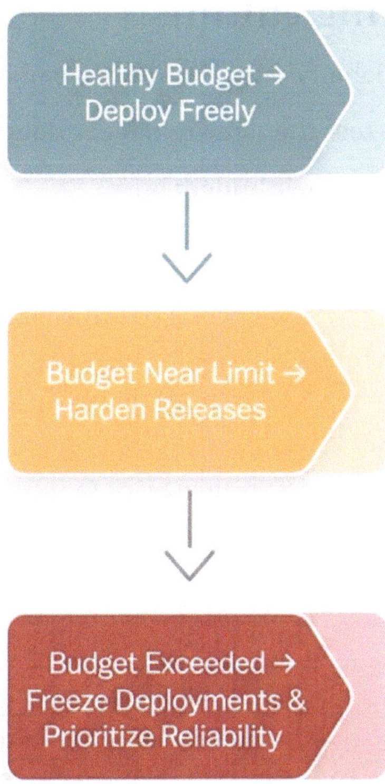

***Figure 1.11**: Error budget decision flow*

Pragmatic reliability begins with business alignment

Chasing perfect reliability is a seductive trap. Every extra nine minutes of uptime costs exponentially more in engineering time, infrastructure spend, and opportunity cost. To make reliability a strategic advantage, leaders must resist the pursuit of perfection and instead focus on what delivers meaningful business value. The following insights illustrate how pragmatic reliability can unlock innovation, optimize engineering capacity, and preserve customer trust:

- **Strategic insight**: The goal is not perfection. The goal is reliability that aligns with business value.
- **Real-world example**: A B2B SaaS company reduced its SLO from 99.99% to 99.9% after analyzing customer impact. The change freed up 20% of engineering capacity for feature development, with zero increase in churn.
- **Leadership takeaway**: Reliability is a business decision, not a purity test. The correct target is the one that protects user trust without stalling innovation.

Risk-aware engineering culture

Error budgets and pragmatic reliability only work when embedded in culture. That means:

- **Transparency**: Everyone sees the same reliability data
- **Accountability**: Teams own their budget burn
- **Collaboration**: Product and engineering make decisions together
- **Learning**: Budget breaches trigger retros, not blame

Let us discuss the case vignette. A fintech firm used error budget dashboards in sprint planning. When burn rates spiked, they deferred risky releases and invested in observability. This has led to a reduction in incidents by 30% and enabled more rapid recovery.

The following table lists KPIs that reflect strategic risk management:

KPI	Strategic Insight
Error budget burn rate	Reliability margin vs. risk exposure
Deployment frequency	Innovation velocity
Change failure rate	Stability of releases
MTTR	Resilience and recovery speed
SLO compliance trend	Reliability trajectory over time

Table 1.5: Strategic risk management KPIs

Tip: Track these KPIs together to understand whether your organization is moving fast responsibly, not just moving fast.

Strategic risk management in SRE is not about avoiding failure; it is about failing smart. Error budget gives teams the confidence to innovate within safe boundaries. Pragmatic reliability targets ensure that engineering effort is invested where it matters most. Together, they create a culture where risk is not feared; it is governed.

When reliability becomes a negotiated, measurable, and shared responsibility, organizations unlock the ability to scale, ship, and learn, without losing trust.

Leading the SRE transformation

SRE is not a toolset; it is a mindset, and like any cultural shift, it demands leadership, clarity, and sustained momentum. Whether you are modernizing legacy systems or scaling cloud-native platforms, the SRE transformation is not just about uptime; it is about engineering excellence, operational resilience, and business agility.

This chapter offers a pragmatic roadmap for leaders who want to embed SRE principles into their organization, not as a side initiative, but as a core operating model.

Establishing why before how

Before rolling out SRE practices, leaders must answer: Why now? What problem are we solving? What value will reliability unlock?

Organizations frequently encounter the following challenges:

- A growing number of incidents
- Slow recovery from outages
- Unreliable release processes
- Operations teams experiencing high levels of burnout
- Loss of customers due to system instability

The leadership insight is that the SRE transformation succeeds when it is framed as a business enabler, not just a technical upgrade.

Build a cross-functional coalition

SRE is not an Ops-only initiative. It touches product, engineering, QA, and even finance. Successful rollouts involve:

- **Executive sponsorship**: To fund and protect the initiative
- **Product alignment**: To embed reliability into delivery

- **Platform engineering**: To build automation and observability
- **Change agents**: To evangelize and coach across teams

Let us discuss the case vignette. A global bank launched its SRE program with a triad: CTO, head of product, and head of infrastructure. This alignment accelerated adoption and avoided turf wars.

Define your maturity model

Not every team needs full-blown SRE on day one. A maturity model helps leaders set expectations and track progress.

The following table lists example maturity stages:

Stage	Characteristics
Reactive	Manual Ops, frequent firefighting
Aware	Basic monitoring, some automation
Proactive	SLOs defined, error budgets tracked
Predictive	Automated recovery, chaos testing
Adaptive	Reliability embedded in product strategy

***Table 1.6**: SRE maturity stages*

Tip: Use maturity stages to guide coaching, tooling, and investment, not to grade teams.

Building a roadmap

A successful SRE rollout is iterative. Here is a proven phased approach:

1. **Foundations**:
    a. Define SLOs and SLIs
    b. Audit operational toil
    c. Establish error budget tracking
    d. Build observability dashboards
    e. Implement **continuous integration and continuous deployment** (CI/CD) pipelines
2. **Automation and enablement**:
    a. Automate high-toil tasks
    b. Integrate SRE practice into CI/CD

   c. Launch blameless postmortems
   d. Train product teams on reliability metrics

3. **Scale and embed**:
   a. Expand SRE roles across domains
   b. Introduce chaos engineering
   c. Align reliability with business KPIs
   d. Share wins across the org

Sustain momentum through culture

SRE transformation is not a sprint; it is a cultural shift. Sustain momentum by:

- Celebrating automation wins
- Sharing postmortem learnings org-wide
- Recognizing engineers who reduce toil
- Embedding reliability into **objectives and key results** (**OKRs**) and planning cycles

The executive insight is that the resilient culture is the foundation of lasting SRE success.

Conclusion

SRE is a leadership discipline focused on transforming reliability into a strategic advantage. It goes beyond simply maintaining system uptime, aiming instead to build systems that are inherently resilient, scalable, and capable of rapid recovery.

The next chapter explores the impact of **artificial intelligence** (**AI**) and **machine learning** (**ML**) on SRE, exploring advancements from predictive incident response to autonomous remediation. The future of reliability will be AI-augmented, data-driven, and highly adaptive, rather than solely human-led.

Join our Discord space

Join our Discord workspace for latest updates, offers, tech happenings around the world, new releases, and sessions with the authors:

https://discord.bpbonline.com

Chapter 2
AIOps Tools for SRE

Introduction

In today's digital operations, traditional rule-based automation alone is no longer enough to ensure reliability at scale. AIOps, as an advanced form of automation, leverages AI and ML to address limitations of conventional approaches. **Artificial intelligence for IT operations** (**AIOps**) emerged as a critical capability for SRE teams seeking to move beyond reactive firefighting. By harnessing ML, advanced analytics, and intelligent automation, AIOps platforms empower organizations to detect critical issues, cut through alert fatigue, and remediate incidents before they impact users. This chapter positions AIOps as a reliability accelerator. It moves beyond tool comparisons and focuses on outcomes: reduced **mean time to recovery** (**MTTR**), improved signal-to-noise ratio, and better alignment with **service level objectives** (**SLOs**). It also outlines how to evaluate platforms, justify investment, and embed AIOps into the daily rhythm of SRE teams.

Structure

In this chapter, we will cover the following topics:

- Understanding AIOps in the SRE context
- Core functions of AIOps platforms
- Mapping AIOps features to reliability goals
- Building a business case for AIOps adoption
- Leading AIOps implementation in SRE teams
- Core components of the AIOps ecosystem
- Practical workflows and real-world examples

Objectives

By the end of this chapter, readers will gain a comprehensive understanding of the role AIOps plays within the SRE framework, particularly in enabling scalable reliability. The chapter explores the essential functions of AIOps platforms, such as anomaly detection, intelligent alerting, event correlation, and automated incident response, and how these capabilities align with key SRE metrics like MTTR and the error budget. It emphasizes the transition from reactive to proactive operations through AIOps and guides readers in building a quantifiable business case for its adoption by linking technical improvements to strategic outcomes. Additionally, the chapter provides insights into leading successful AIOps implementation, covering aspects like data readiness, organizational change management, and integration into existing SRE workflows. Finally, it offers criteria for evaluating and selecting the most suitable tools, libraries, and technologies within the AIOps ecosystem to meet specific reliability objectives.

Understanding AIOps in the SRE context

AIOps stands for artificial intelligence for IT operations, where AI serves as the mechanism that enables operational intelligence. The goal is not to automate everything; it is to automate the right things. AIOps is not a replacement for SRE; it is an **accelerant** and a **force multiplier** that scales the SRE's capabilities to meet the complexity of modern, cloud-native systems.

SRE's data challenge

The collaboration between AIOps and SRE is necessitated by the explosion of telemetry data in modern environments (microservices, multi-cloud, Kubernetes). This complexity creates two core challenges for SREs:

- **Alert fatigue (Noise vs. signal)**: A single system failure can trigger hundreds of alerts across logs, metrics, and traces. SREs are overwhelmed with noise, leading to burnout and the risk of ignoring actual critical issues (the cry wolf problem).
- **Slow root cause analysis (RCA)**: The complexity and distributed nature of services make manually correlating disparate events across different tools a time-consuming, error-prone effort. This directly inflates MTTR, making it difficult to maintain SLOs.

Strategic insight with the AIOps value proposition

AIOps platforms apply ML and statistical models to a broad spectrum of operational data, including logs, metrics, traces, and events, to pinpoint anomalies, correlate incidents, and guide remediation actions. For SREs, this means:

- Fewer false positives
- Accelerated root cause identification
- Smarter incident response

However, the efficacy of an AIOps implementation is entirely dependent on its alignment with defined reliability goals. To be effective, the tools must be calibrated to the organization's specific SLOs, error budgets, and overarching business priorities. Without this critical tuning, an AIOps platform risks becoming another source of noise, generating alerts that are disconnected from actual business or user impact.

The fundamental value of AIOps lies in its ability to transform raw telemetry data into actionable, automated responses. *Figure 2.1* illustrates how the AIOps platform ingests observability data to automatically detect, diagnose, and either resolve or efficiently escalate incidents to SREs:

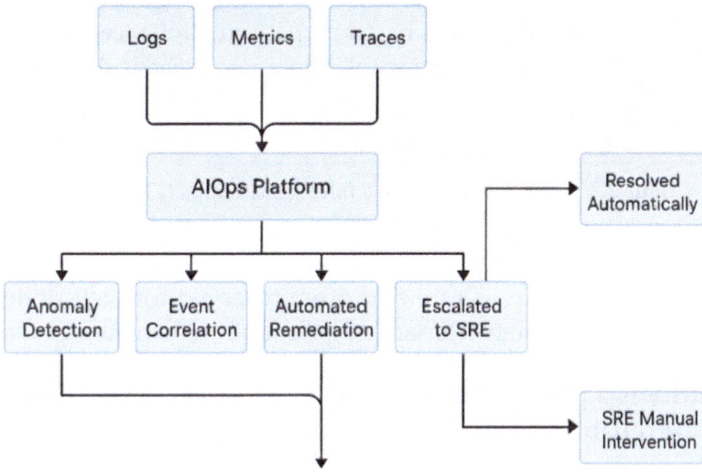

***Figure 2.1**: AIOps-enabled incident management workflow*

The following table lists the common misconceptions:

Misconception	Reality
AIOps fully automates and replaces engineers	It enhances human decision-making
AIOps is plug-and-play	It requires tuning and training
AIOps is only for large enterprises	It scales across environments

***Table 2.1**: Distinguishing AIOps myths from operational reality*

Note: **AIOps is not a toolset; it is a mindset shift. It requires cultural alignment, data hygiene, and a clear understanding of what reliable means in context.**

From automation to autonomy

AIOps is not a binary switch; it is a spectrum of operational intelligence. Understanding where your organization sits on this spectrum helps set realistic expectations and guide implementation strategy.

The journey to full AIOps adoption is typically defined by increasing levels of autonomy, moving from simple scripted responses to advanced, self-healing systems. *Table 2.2* outlines these different stages of the AIOps maturity spectrum and their corresponding impact on SRE functions:

Intelligence level	Description	SRE impact
Basic automation	Scripted actions triggered by predefined rules (e.g., restart service on failure)	Reduces toil but limited adaptability
Assisted intelligence	AI suggests actions based on pattern recognition and historical data	Enhances decision-making and speeds diagnosis
Autonomous operations	Systems self-heal and optimize without human intervention	Enables proactive reliability and frees up engineering time

Table 2.2: *The AIOps operational intelligence maturity spectrum*

Most organizations begin with assisted intelligence, using AIOps to surface insights and recommend actions. Full autonomy is rare and often reserved for well-understood, low-risk scenarios. The goal is not to eliminate human judgment but to elevate it.

Note: **AIOps maturity is a journey. SRE leaders must assess where they are, where they want to be, and what reliability outcomes justify the leap.**

Core functions of AIOps platforms

AIOps platforms are not built to impress; they are built to reduce noise, surface patterns, and accelerate decisions. The most effective ones do not overwhelm teams with dashboards. They operate in the background, efficiently correlating data and surfacing actionable insights for engineers. At their core, these platforms perform a handful of essential functions. Each one maps directly to a reliability challenge.

Anomaly detection that actually detects

While traditional monitoring tools flood teams with alerts, AIOps adds critical context by applying statistical and machine learning models to distinguish meaningful deviations from routine fluctuations. Not all increases are cause for concern. Not every dip is a crisis. The goal is to distinguish signal from noise.

Some platforms use time series modeling. Others rely on clustering or neural networks. The method matters less than the outcome: fewer false positives, faster identification of real issues, and less cognitive load on the team.

For example, a payment processing platform uses AIOps to monitor transaction latency. When the system detects a sudden spike outside of normal patterns, it triggers an alert and initiates automated diagnostics, helping the SRE team respond before users notice a slowdown.

Intelligent alerting and noise suppression

Alert fatigue is real. When a large number of alerts fire simultaneously, critical signals are easily lost, increasing the risk of missing important incidents. AIOps platforms reduce alert volume by correlating related events, suppressing duplicates, and prioritizing based on impact. This is not just about filtering; it is about understanding. If a database failure triggers ten downstream alerts, the platform should know that and surface the root cause, not the symptoms.

For example, during a network outage, hundreds of alerts may be generated across different services. AIOps correlates these events, identifies the root cause, and surfaces a single actionable incident for the SRE team to address.

Event correlation and root cause analysis

Incidents rarely happen in isolation. AIOps tools group related events, trace dependencies, and highlight probable causes. This is not magic; it is math. However, when done well, it feels like intuition.

Instead of scrolling through logs or jumping between dashboards, engineers get a focused view: what happened, why it happened, and what to do next.

For example, following a service outage, the AIOps platform analyzes system logs and traces, identifies a recent configuration change as the likely cause, and presents this insight to the SRE team for immediate action.

Predictive insights and risk modeling

The best incidents are the ones that never happen altogether. AIOps platforms can forecast potential failures based on historical patterns, usage trends, and system behavior. This allows teams to act before thresholds are breached or services degrade.

It is not about being perfect; it is about being prepared. Predictive modeling turns hindsight into foresight.

For example, by analyzing usage patterns, an AIOps platform predicts when storage capacity will be exhausted and recommends scaling actions before users are impacted.

Automated incident response and remediation

AIOps platforms can go beyond detection and alert by orchestrating automated responses to known issues. This includes restarting failed services, scaling resources, rolling back deployments, or executing predefined runbooks. By automating routine remediation tasks, SREs can reduce MTTR and free up time for higher-value engineering work.

For example, upon detecting a memory leak in a microservice, the AIOps platform autonomously restarts the compromised container and alerts the SRE team. Concurrently, an actionable item is generated for the development team to implement a permanent fix for the memory leak. This approach ensures minimal disruption and proactive resolution.

Mapping AIOps features to reliability goals

The true value of AIOps lies not in the sophistication of its machine learning algorithms, but in its measurable impact on your SLOs and the overall error budget. For an SRE, the platform's utility is judged by how much it improves the speed, accuracy, and efficiency of the reliability process.

A successful AIOps strategy must have a direct and measurable impact on the reliability indicators that define SRE performance. This means aligning its outcomes with metrics like error budgets, availability, and MTTR.

AIOps impact on core SRE metrics

The essential SRE goals defined by time-based metrics are drastically improved by specific AIOps functions. This relationship moves the conversation from tool capabilities to business outcomes. The true measure of AIOps's success is its demonstrable effect on SLOs and key time-based metrics. *Table 2.3* details the direct, functional mapping of core AIOps capabilities to essential SRE goals and their corresponding metrics, illustrating how intelligent automation drives quantifiable improvements in reliability and efficiency:

Reliability goal	Core metric	AIOps function that contributes	Reliability impact
Prediction and prevention	Error budget preservation	Predictive insights and risk modeling	Turns historical data into foresight, allowing for intervention before an SLO is breached, thus preserving the error budget
Detection speed	MTTD	Proactive deviation flagging	Automatically distinguishes signal from noise and flags genuine deviations instantly, dramatically minimizing the time an incident goes unnoticed
Diagnosis speed	MTTA	Intelligent alerting and event correlation	Reduces alert volume and presents a single, enriched, prioritized incident view, cutting down on triage and handover time for the on-call team

Reliability goal	Core metric	AIOps function that contributes	Reliability impact
Recovery speed	MTTR	Event correlation and automated RCA	Provides a probable root cause (e.g., a specific code change or system dependency) at the moment of alert, eliminating hours of manual investigation
Operational efficiency	Toil reduction	Automated incident response and remediation	Automates routine fixes (like restarts and rollbacks) so SREs can focus on engineering

***Table 2.3**: Mapping AIOps functions to core SRE reliability goals and metrics*

From reactive response to proactive resilience

Mapping AIOps features to reliability goals highlights a shift in the SRE posture: the move from being primarily reactive (responding to failures) to becoming increasingly proactive (preventing failures) and ultimately predictive. The core value of AIOps is realized through specific capabilities that directly address the most critical, time-consuming challenges for SRE teams. These capabilities ensure SREs can better manage their time and their error budget:

- **Preserving the error budget through predictive insights**: A critical SRE mandate is managing the error budget, the tolerance for failure over a given period. Traditional monitoring only tells you when you have spent some of your budget.
    - **AIOps elevate this by predicting spending.** Using time series analysis and forecasting models, AIOps can extrapolate current consumption rates (e.g., sustained high latency) and predict the exact moment the SLO is likely to be violated.
    - **The outcome**: This capability creates a time buffer, a mean time to intervention, where SREs can execute planned scaling or mitigating actions to preserve the remaining budget.
- **Accelerating incident resolution with intelligent correlation**: The combined metrics of MTTA and MTTR directly reflect the cost of an outage. Slow diagnosis (high MTTA) and slow repair (high MTTR) are the primary drivers of financial loss and user dissatisfaction.
    - **AIOps's correlation engine is the solution**: It transforms a flood of hundreds of disparate events (logs, metrics, and traces) into a single, cohesive narrative. By using topological awareness and time series clustering, it identifies the *patient zero* event and the cascading dependencies.

- **The outcome**: The SRE receives an alert that is not just *Server X is down*, but *Deployment Y on Server X caused CPU saturation, which impacted Service Z*, with all necessary logs and runbooks attached. This direct, enriched context can slash MTTR by up to 50% or more.

- **Eliminating toil with automated remediation**: SRE is philosophically committed to reducing toil. While basic automation handles simple tasks, AIOps handles complex, contextual automation, which is the next frontier of toil reduction.
  - **AIOps's role**: Once an AIOps platform has accurately identified the root cause and the level of impact, it can trigger sophisticated automated runbooks. These actions aren't simple restarts; they can involve rollback procedures, database connection pool resizing, or resource rebalancing.
  - **The outcome**: The system heals itself from well-known failure modes, allowing the SRE team to focus their intellectual capital on designing robust systems and engineering away from the next class of potential failures.

The ultimate goal of AIOps is to create a closed-loop feedback system that continuously learns and improves system reliability. *Figure* 2.2 visualizes this continuous cycle, showing how diverse data streams are processed by the AIOps platform to drive key functions, from anomaly detection to predictive insights, leading directly to automated remediation, reduced toil, and measurable improvements in system reliability:

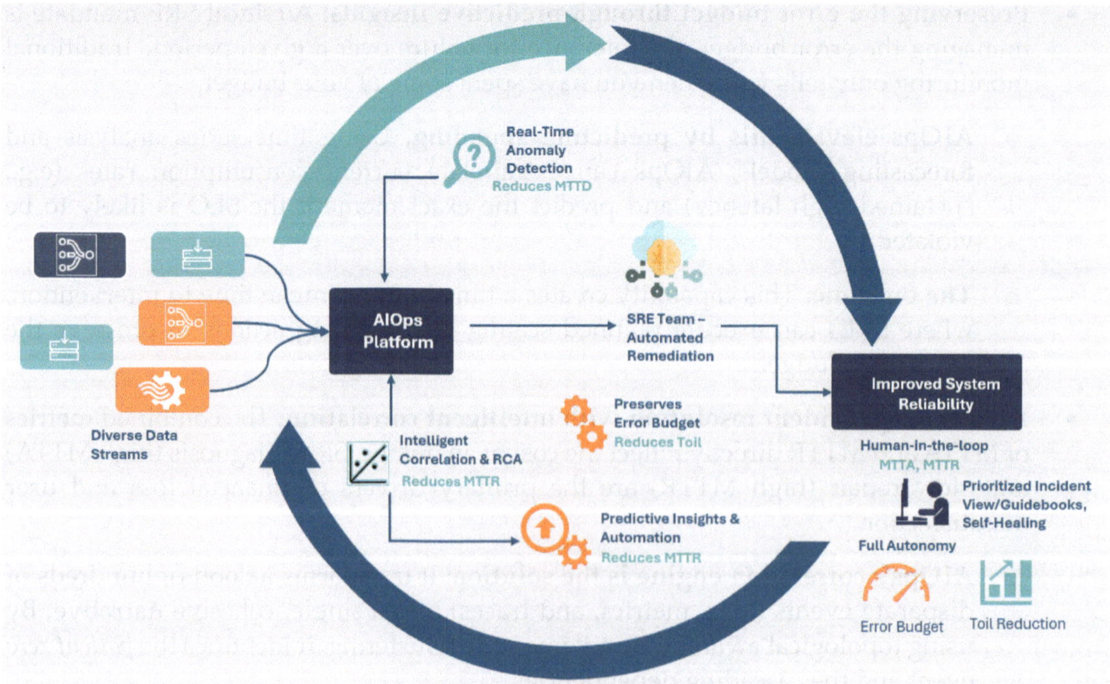

Figure 2.2: AIOps reliability feedback loop

Building a business case for AIOps adoption

AIOps may be technically compelling, but without a clear business rationale, it risks being dismissed as just another tool. To secure buy-in from leadership, finance, and even skeptical engineers, SRE leaders must translate technical benefits into business outcomes.

Frame reliability as a business enabler

Start by shifting the narrative. Reliability is not just a technical metric; it is a customer experience metric. Every minute of downtime is a lost opportunity, a damaged brand, or a missed revenue moment. AIOps helps protect those moments:

- To secure buy-in from leadership and finance, SRE leaders must translate the technical benefits of AIOps into measurable business outcomes. When pitching AIOps, do not lead with features; lead with impact and quantifiable results, such as we can reduce MTTR by 40%, which means fewer customer complaints and faster recovery.
- We can prevent incidents before they happen, preserving our error budget and avoiding SLA penalties.
- We can reduce alert fatigue, improving engineer morale and retention.

These are outcomes that resonate beyond engineering.

Quantify the cost of inaction

AIOps adoption is often delayed, not because it lacks value, but because the cost of not adopting it is poorly understood. To build a compelling business case, leaders must illuminate the hidden toll of reactive operations. This requires quantifying the cost of the status quo by detailing several areas where inaction creates significant financial and operational leakage, including:

- **Operational inefficiency**: Without AIOps, SRE teams spend excessive time on manual triage, redundant alerts, and repetitive remediation. This is not just a productivity issue; it is a resource drain.
    - **Example**: Consider a scenario where an engineer allocates 10 hours weekly to repetitive incident analysis. At an average cost of $100 per hour, this results in over $52,000 annually in effort, per engineer, on toil alone.
    - **Impact**: This time could be redirected toward reliability engineering, system hardening, or feature delivery.
- **Extended downtime and MTTR**: Every minute of downtime costs money. Without intelligent correlation and automated remediation, MTTR remains high, and outages linger. The financial impact of this extended downtime can be directly quantified.

- **Example**: A SaaS platform with $5,000/hour revenue loses $83 per minute during an outage. If AIOps can reduce MTTR from 45 minutes to 20, that is a savings of $2,083 per incident.
- **Impact**: Multiply by incident frequency, and the financial case becomes undeniable.

- **Alert fatigue and burnout**: High alert volumes without prioritization lead to desensitization. Engineers begin ignoring alerts, increasing the risk of missing critical signals. The practical consequences of high alert volume are significant and often hidden.
  - **Example**: A team receiving 1,000 alerts per week, with a 70% false positive rate, wastes hundreds of hours annually. Worse, it contributes to burnout, attrition, and knowledge loss.
  - **Impact**: Replacing an engineer can cost $30,000 to $50,000 in hiring, onboarding, and lost productivity.
- **Missed predictive opportunities**: Without predictive modeling, organizations operate in hindsight. They react to failures instead of preventing them.
  - **Example**: A storage system fails due to capacity exhaustion. AIOps could have forecasted the trend and triggered scaling days earlier.
  - **Impact**: The outage affects customer SLAs, triggers penalties, and damages brand trust, costs that are hard to quantify but deeply felt.
- **SLO breaches and SLA penalties**: Error budgets are finite. When incidents go undetected or unresolved, SLOs are breached. For external-facing services, this can mean SLA violations.
  - **Example**: A breach of SLA uptime guarantees may incur penalties of 5 to 10% of the monthly contract value.
  - **Impact**: For a $1M/year contract, that is $8,300/month in potential penalties.
- **Lost competitive advantage**: In fast-moving markets, reliability is a differentiator. Companies that fail to evolve their operations risk falling behind.
  - **Example**: A competitor with AIOps delivers faster recovery, fewer outages, and better customer experience.
  - **Impact**: Customers notice, churn increases, and market share erodes.

Note: The cost of inaction is not just technical debt, it is financial leakage, talent attrition, and strategic risk. AIOps has become essential for ensuring reliability in contemporary operational environments.

Align with strategic priorities

AIOps can be positioned as an enabler for broader organizational objectives, such as digital transformation, customer experience, and operational efficiency. When presenting the case for AIOps, it is helpful to relate its benefits to these strategic priorities.

For example:

- **Scaling cloud infrastructure**: AIOps supports reliability without requiring proportional increases in staffing.
- **Supporting continuous operations**: AIOps enables timely responses to issues, even outside regular working hours.
- **Advancing platform engineering**: AIOps provides the intelligence necessary to make self-service operations safer and more effective.

Proposals that clearly connect AIOps to executive priorities are more likely to gain support and progress efficiently.

Prove value quickly

A business case should emphasize quick wins and tangible results, not require justification for a large-scale, multi-year investment.

SRE leaders should propose a focused pilot, for example:

1. Choose a high-noise service with frequent incidents.
2. Measure baseline metrics (MTTD, MTTR, alert volume).
3. Deploy AIOps in a limited scope.
4. Track improvements over 30 to 60 days.

Then present the results. If MTTR drops by 50%, that is your business case.

Include the hidden return on investment

Not all returns are obvious. AIOps deliver value in ways that do not show up on a balance sheet, but still matter:

- **Engineer productivity**: Less time spent on manual triage means more time for innovation.
- **Team morale**: Fewer 2 AM pages mean happier, more engaged engineers.
- **Knowledge retention**: AIOps captures patterns and context that might otherwise be lost when team members leave.

These soft benefits often become hard advantages over time.

Leading AIOps implementation in SRE teams

Securing the budget is only the first milestone; successful AIOps adoption depends on effective leadership within SRE teams. This transition is not merely a technical deployment but a significant organizational shift that requires managing data quality, team trust, and the evolution of the SRE role itself.

Phase 1: Establish data readiness and governance

AIOps tools are only as good as the data fed into them. Before selecting a vendor or deploying code, SRE leaders must ensure the data pipeline is robust, consistent, and adheres to strict quality standards. This phase is often underestimated but is the bedrock of any successful AIOps initiative.

- **The data hygiene mandate with standardization as the key**:
    - **Challenge**: Disparate data sources, inconsistent formats, and missing metadata lead to garbage in, garbage out for AIOps algorithms.
    - **Actionable guidance**: Mandate uniformity across all observability data (logs, metrics, traces, events). Establish clear standards for:
        - **Log formats**: Implement structured logging (e.g., JSON) with consistent fields for service name, environment, transaction ID, and severity.
        - **Metric naming conventions**: Enforce consistent prefixes and labels (e.g., `service_name_http_requests_total`).
        - **Trace context propagation**: Ensure consistent context (e.g., `trace_id`, `span_id`) across all services using Open Telemetry or similar standards.
    - **Leadership role**: Drive accountability for data quality across development and operations teams. This often requires cross-functional workshops and established guidelines that are integrated into CI/CD pipelines.
- **Data aggregation and normalization as the unified observability fabric**:
    - **Challenge**: Data silos prevent AIOps platforms from seeing the complete picture, leading to incomplete correlations and missed insights.
    - **Actionable guidance**: Implement a strategy to centralize and normalize all observability data into a single platform or data lake (e.g., Elasticsearch, Splunk, an object storage with query capabilities). This involves:
        - **Robust data ingestion pipelines**: Using agents (e.g., Fluentd, Filebeat, Open Telemetry Collector) to reliably stream data.

    - **Schema enforcement and transformation**: Standardizing data structures before it hits the AIOps engine, enriching it with contextual metadata (e.g., owner, team, business service).
  - **Leadership role**: Advocate for the necessary infrastructure and tools to build this unified data layer. Highlight how this consolidation not only benefits AIOps but also improves overall observability for all engineers.
- **Accurate topology mapping context is king**:
  - **Challenge**: AIOps cannot intelligently correlate events or perform accurate root cause analysis without knowing how services and infrastructure components are related.
  - **Actionable guidance**: Implement and maintain dynamic service dependency mapping. This can be achieved through:
    - **Service mesh**: Leveraging tools like Istio or Linkerd to automatically discover and map service communications.
    - **Configuration management databases (CMDBs)**: Ensuring CMDBs are up-to-date and integrated with deployment pipelines.
    - **Automated discovery tools**: Utilizing AIOps platforms' native discovery capabilities or third-party tools that actively map infrastructure and application dependencies.
  - **Leadership role**: Emphasize that continuous, accurate topology mapping is a shared responsibility, not a one-time project. It is a living document essential for both AIOps and human incident responders.

Phase 2: Manage organizational change and trust

The introduction of AIOps, especially in its assisted or autonomous forms, changes the SRE's day-to-day work, which can breed skepticism or resistance. Leadership must actively foster trust in the new intelligence layer and communicate the evolving role of SREs. To successfully manage this transition and foster adoption, SRE leadership must focus on three core principles that prioritize trust, transparency, and role evolution:

- **The human in the loop principle**:
  - **Challenge**: Instantaneous, unverified automation can lead to catastrophic errors and a complete loss of trust in the system.
  - **Actionable guidance**: Begin with an *assisted intelligence* model. AIOps should *suggest* actions (e.g., probable root cause is that database connection pool exhaustion, and the recommended action is to restart service X with increased memory allocation), but require an SRE to approve and execute.

   - **Gradual ramp up**: As confidence and accuracy grow, gradually introduce partial automation, then full automation for well-understood, low-risk scenarios.
 - **Leadership role**: Set clear expectations; communicate that AIOps is about augmentation, not immediate replacement. Champion small successes, celebrate accurate suggestions, and visibly learn from any incorrect ones.
- **Transparency and explainability**:
 - **Challenge**: SREs are engineers who need to understand *why* something is happening. A *black box* AIOps platform, even if accurate, will be met with skepticism.
 - **Actionable guidance**: Demand and leverage explainability features. An effective AIOps platform should be able to:
   - **Show evidence**: Point to the specific logs, metrics, or traces that led to a correlation or a root cause deduction.
   - **Highlight anomalous patterns**: Visually represent the baseline and the deviation that triggered an alert.
   - **Visualize dependencies**: Show the chain of events across the service topology.
 - **Leadership role**: Foster a culture of inquiry. Encourage SREs to *debug* the AIOps platform and provide feedback on its accuracy. Use explainability to train SREs on new incident patterns and system behaviors that AIOps identifies.
- **Evolving the SRE role from firefighter to architect of automation**:
 - **Challenge**: SREs may fear that AIOps will diminish their importance or eliminate their jobs.
 - **Actionable guidance**: Redefine and elevate the SRE's evolving role. Position them as:
   - **Data scientists for operations**: SREs will be refining the models, curating data sets for training, and identifying new patterns for AIOps to learn.
   - **Automation architects**: Designing and implementing the automated runbooks and self-healing mechanisms that AIOps orchestrates.
   - **System optimizers**: Leveraging AIOps insights to proactively improve system design and prevent future incidents, rather than just reacting to them.
 - **Leadership role**: Invest in training and upskilling. Provide opportunities for SREs to learn about machine learning fundamentals, data engineering, and

automation frameworks. Celebrate those who champion and contribute to the AIOps platform.

Phase 3: Strategize tooling and deployment

The deployment strategy should prioritize proving value quickly in low-risk, high-noise areas, building momentum, and demonstrating tangible ROI.

- **The pilot project selection target high impact low risk areas**:
  - **Challenge**: Starting with a mission-critical, highly complex service can lead to long implementation times and high failure risk.
  - **Actionable guidance**: Choose a pilot service that is:
    - **High noise**: Generates a large volume of alerts, causing alert fatigue.
    - **Frequent incidents**: Experiences recurring, well-understood incidents.
    - **Contained**: Has limited critical dependencies, making its impact manageable.
    - **Measurable**: Has clear baseline metrics for MTTA, MTTD, MTTR, and alert volume.
  - **Leadership role**: Champion the pilot. Dedicate resources, protect the team from distractions, and actively track the pilot's success metrics.
- **Define and track AIOps success metrics**:
  - **Challenge**: Without clear, measurable goals, it is hard to demonstrate the value of AIOps.
  - **Actionable guidance**: Beyond core SLOs, track metrics directly related to AIOps impact:
    - **Alert reduction ratio**: Percentage decrease in the number of *actionable* alerts presented to SREs.
    - **Correlation accuracy**: Percentage of incidents where AIOps correctly grouped related events and identified the primary cause.
    - **MTTD or MTTR improvement**: Quantifiable reduction in detection and resolution times for incidents within the AIOps scope.
    - **Toil reduction percentage**: Hours saved from manual incident investigation and remediation.
  - **Leadership role**: Establish these metrics *before* implementation, continuously monitor them, and use them to communicate progress and justify scaling the initiative.

- **Integration over replacement harmony with existing workflows**:
  - **Challenge**: Forcing SREs to abandon familiar tools for a completely new, unproven stack creates friction and resistance.
  - **Actionable guidance**: Ensure the AIOps platform integrates seamlessly with existing critical SRE tools:
    - **Incident management systems**: Push correlated incidents directly to PagerDuty, Opsgenie, or similar tools.
    - **ITSM or ticketing systems**: Create tickets (e.g., Jira, ServiceNow) for longer-term remediation or post-mortems.
    - **Collaboration platforms**: Send incident summaries and updates to Slack or Microsoft Teams channels.
    - **Runbook automation**: Trigger existing automated runbooks or scripts.
  - **Leadership role**: Prioritize integration capabilities during tool selection. Emphasize that AIOps is an enhancement layer, not a disruptive overhaul of established, effective workflows.

Note: AIOps implementation is a change management challenge first and a technical challenge second. Successful adoption requires a measured, trustworthy approach that focuses on augmenting, not replacing, the expertise of the SRE team.

Successfully implementing AIOps is not a single deployment but a phased, iterative journey that touches technology, process, and culture. *Figure 2.3* illustrates the recommended approach, emphasizing that success flows sequentially from a strong foundation of data quality (**Phase 1**) through managing human trust and roles (**Phase 2**), before moving to measurable tooling and deployment (**Phase 3**):

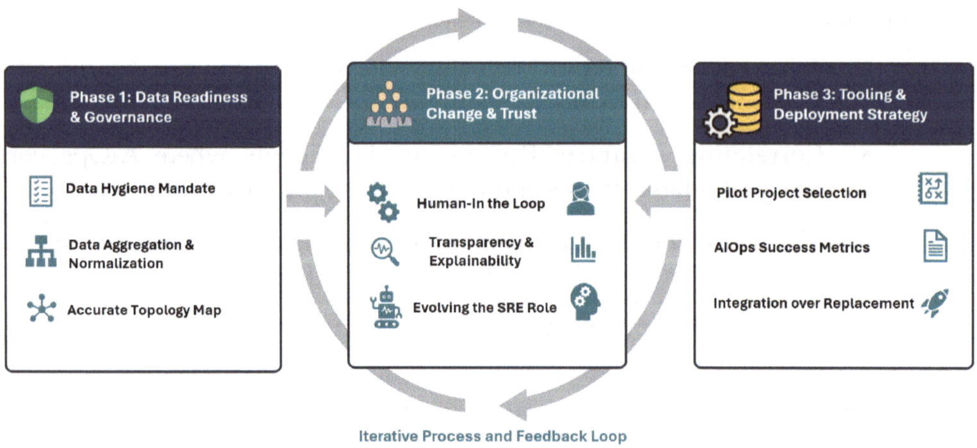

Figure 2.3: AIOps implementation framework

Core components of the AIOps ecosystem

AIOps is not a single product; it is an intricate ecosystem of platforms, frameworks, and open-source libraries that enable intelligent operations. Understanding this diverse landscape helps SRE teams evaluate options and select tools that align precisely with their reliability goals. The AIOps ecosystem can be segmented into five core component areas:

- **Data ingestion and observability**: AIOps critically depend on rich, high-quality data. Observability platforms provide the raw signals, such as logs, metrics, and traces, that serve as the essential feed for AIOps engines.
  - **Examples**:
    - **Prometheus**: A leading open-source system for time series metrics collection and real-time alerting.
    - **Grafana**: A versatile open-source visualization and dashboarding tool for telemetry data.
    - **OpenTelemetry**: A vendor-neutral set of **application programming interfaces** (**APIs**), **software development kits** (**SDKs**), and tools for generating, collecting, and exporting distributed tracing, metrics, and logs.
    - **Elastic Stack (ELK)**: A powerful combination of Elasticsearch (search and analytics), Logstash (data processing), and Kibana (visualization) for log aggregation and search capabilities.
  - **Why it matters**: Without clean, consistent, and comprehensive telemetry, AIOps algorithms cannot deliver accurate or reliable insights. Robust data hygiene is the absolute foundation of operational intelligence.
- **Machine learning and analytics libraries**: For SRE teams with specific, advanced requirements or those building custom AIOps capabilities, ML frameworks provide the fundamental building blocks for sophisticated anomaly detection, clustering, and predictive modeling.
  - **Examples**:
    - **TensorFlow and PyTorch**: Dominant open-source deep learning frameworks for advanced anomaly detection and complex pattern recognition.
    - **Scikit-learn**: A widely used Python library offering a broad range of classical ML algorithms for tasks like clustering, classification, and regression.
    - **Statsmodels**: A Python module that provides classes and functions for the estimation of many different statistical models, crucial for time series analysis.

        - **River**: An online machine learning library designed for streaming data, enabling real-time model updates.
    - **Why it matters**: These libraries empower SRE teams to experiment with and deploy bespoke models, precisely tailored to their unique infrastructure, application behaviors, and specific reliability challenges.
- **Enterprise AIOps platforms**: These are full-stack solutions designed to ingest, process, and correlate vast amounts of telemetry, applying machine learning to deliver actionable insights and automate workflows at scale. They typically integrate seamlessly with existing observability tools, **IT service management (ITSM)** systems, and various cloud platforms.
    - **Examples**:
        - **Dynatrace**: Combines comprehensive observability with AI-driven root cause analysis and predictive insights.
        - **Moogsoft**: Specializes in advanced event correlation and intelligent noise reduction for large-scale, complex environments.
        - **BigPanda**: Focuses on alert correlation and streamlined incident automation for hybrid infrastructures.
        - **ServiceNow AIOps**: Integrates deeply with ITSM workflows for automated remediation, governance, and service-aware operations.
    - **Why it matters**: These platforms provide robust, end-to-end capabilities, making them suitable for organizations seeking a unified approach to anomaly detection, alert suppression, and automated remediation across their operations.
- **Intelligent automation and orchestration**: These tools translate AIOps insights into tangible actions, orchestrating automated workflows that significantly reduce toil and accelerate incident response and remediation.
    - **Examples**:
        - **StackStorm**: An open-source, event-driven automation platform with highly customizable workflows (*If X happens, then do Y*).
        - **Ansible**: A powerful open-source tool for infrastructure automation, configuration management, and application deployment, ideal for remediation tasks.
        - **PagerDuty automation actions**: Capabilities within PagerDuty to trigger automated scripts or runbooks directly during an incident response.
    - **Why it matters**: Automation and orchestration engines are critical for closing the loop between detection and resolution, transforming insights into immediate, effective actions.

- **Business and service integration**: This final layer connects AIOps insights and automated actions with the human and business processes that govern service management. These tools ensure that the intelligence derived from the ecosystem is integrated into ITSM, collaboration, and governance workflows, providing the context necessary for both SREs and business stakeholders.

  To operationalize business and service integration within the AIOps stack, organizations rely on a set of tools that bridge automated insights with human workflows and governance processes. Common examples include:

  - **ITSM platforms (e.g., ServiceNow, Jira Service Management)**: Used for automated incident ticketing, change management, and **configuration management database** (**CMDB**) updates based on AIOps findings.
  - **Collaboration tools (e.g., Slack, Microsoft Teams)**: Channels for pushing correlated incident summaries and real-time updates for quick, transparent human coordination.
  - **PagerDuty**: Acts as the central nervous system for alerting, on-call management, and triggering automated actions based on the enriched AIOps incidents.
  - **Why it matters**: This layer turns technical insights into business context, ensuring that AIOps drives measurable improvements in SLOs or SLAs and integrates smoothly into established organizational processes.

Note: The AIOps ecosystem is incredibly diverse, meaning there is no one-size-fits-all solution.

SRE leaders should adopt a strategic approach:

- Start with business outcomes, not just tool features. Define what problems AIOps needs to solve.
- Evaluate integration capabilities with existing observability, ITSM, and collaboration systems.
- Consider scalability, explainability, and ease of automation when selecting platforms.
- Always pilot before committing to enterprise-wide adoption, proving value in contained environments.

Figure 2.4 illustrates the layered architecture that underpins intelligent operations in an AIOps ecosystem. Each layer builds upon the previous to enable end-to-end automation and actionable insights.

***Figure 2.4**: A layered approach to intelligent operations*

Practical workflows and real-world examples

AIOps truly demonstrates its value through practical applications, transforming reactive operations into proactive, intelligent processes. This section illustrates common AIOps workflows, showcasing how the tools and principles discussed previously translate into tangible benefits for SRE teams:

- **Proactive anomaly detection and predictive alerting workflow**: This workflow focuses on anticipating issues before they escalate into service-impacting incidents. By analyzing historical and real-time operational data, AIOps identifies deviations from normal behavior, allowing teams to act preemptively.
  - **The problem**: Traditional monitoring often alerts only *after* a threshold is breached, meaning an issue is already impacting performance or users. SRE teams are constantly reacting to events rather than preventing them.
  - **The AIOps solution**: Machine learning algorithms continuously analyze metrics (CPU usage, latency, error rates), logs, and traces to establish baselines and detect

subtle anomalies that human eyes might miss. This enables the prediction of potential failures, triggering alerts before critical thresholds are crossed.

- **Real-world impact and benefits**:
  - **Reduced MTTR**: Issues are addressed before they become major incidents.
  - **Increased uptime and service reliability**: Proactive intervention prevents outages.
  - **Reduced alert fatigue**: Alerts are more meaningful, often indicating a developing problem rather than a fully-fledged crisis.

The following figure is a simple workflow diagram for proactive anomaly detection and predictive alerting:

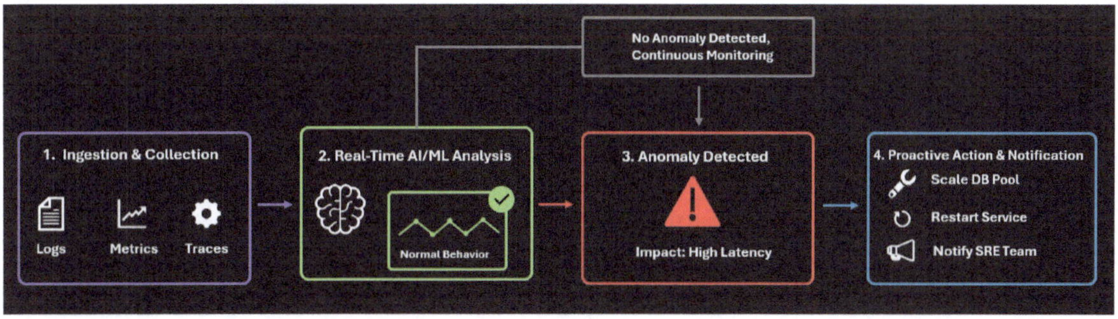

Figure 2.5: Proactive anomaly detection workflow

- **Intelligent event correlation and root cause analysis workflow**: This workflow addresses the problem of alert fatigue by transforming a massive volume of raw events into a small number of actionable incidents:
  - **The problem**: Modern systems generate thousands of monitoring events per minute. Without AIOps, SREs are overwhelmed by a tsunami of alerts, often missing the critical signal amidst the noise. Multiple alerts from dependent services (e.g., a database failing causes 50 downstream microservices to alert) are treated as separate incidents, drastically slowing down diagnosis.
  - **The AIOps solution**: A dedicated correlation engine uses ML algorithms (like clustering, causal inference, and topological analysis) to analyze all incoming events, group related signals, suppress duplicates, and pinpoint the **probable root cause** (**PRC**) by leveraging the service topology map.
  - **Real-world impact or benefits**:
    - **Significant alert reduction**: Reduces the daily volume of actionable alerts by 80 to 95%.

    - **Faster MTTD**: SREs are immediately notified of the *actual* incident, not just the symptoms.
    - **Higher quality incidents**: Incidents are enriched with context (PRC, impacted services, relevant logs or metrics), accelerating human investigation.

The following figure shows how AIOps streamlines event correlation and root cause analysis. The workflow begins with ingesting large volumes of logs, metrics, traces, and alerts, then applies machine learning algorithms to suppress noise and group related signals. Using service topology, the system identifies the probable root cause and finally enriches the incident with actionable insights, reducing alert fatigue and accelerating resolution.

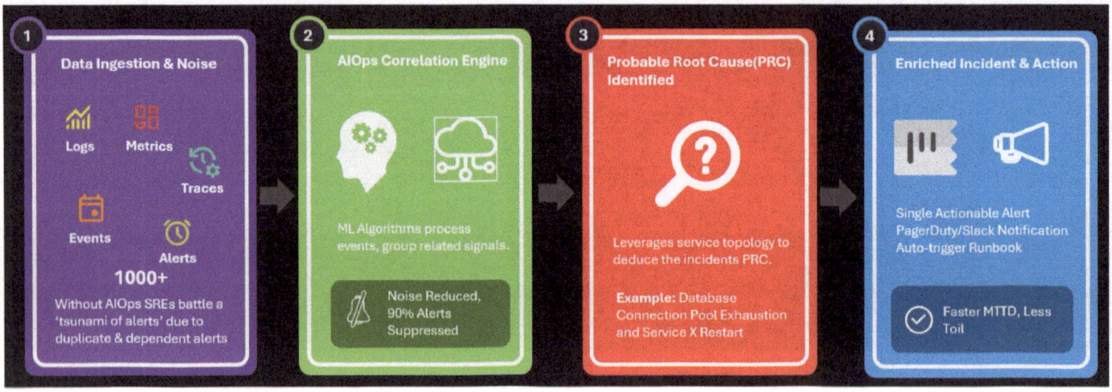

Figure 2.6: Intelligent event correlation and root cause analysis workflow

- **Automated remediation and self-healing workflow**: This workflow represents the ultimate goal of AIOps: closing the loop between insight and action by automatically fixing the problem. This capability significantly reduces MTTR and frees SREs from repetitive, low-value work (toil).
    - **The problem**: Once an incident's root cause is known, SREs still must manually execute a series of steps (e.g., restart a container, clear a queue, scale up a resource). These are repetitive, time-consuming, and error-prone tasks that delay full-service recovery.
    - **The AIOps solution**: By integrating the AIOps correlation engine with an automation or orchestration platform (like StackStorm or Ansible), the system can trigger pre-defined, verified runbooks immediately upon identifying a known, low-risk root cause. This is the assisted intelligence model evolving into partial or full autonomy.
    - **Real-world impact or benefits**:
        - **Drastic MTTR reduction**: Recovery happens in seconds or minutes, not hours, for common incidents.

- **Reduced toil**: SREs are liberated from routine firefighting and can focus on higher-value reliability engineering tasks.
- **Increased system resilience**: The system heals itself, making it inherently more robust.

The following figure depicts an AIOps-driven automated remediation and self-healing workflow. The sequence begins with anomaly detection and probable root cause identification by the AIOps engine. Based on predefined conditions, an automated runbook is triggered through orchestration tools such as StackStorm or Ansible to execute corrective actions. Post-execution, system health is validated using telemetry checks and behavioral baselines, ensuring that normal operating conditions are restored. Finally, the enriched incident record is updated with mediation details, enabling auto-closure and reducing MTTD and MTTR to sub-minute levels.

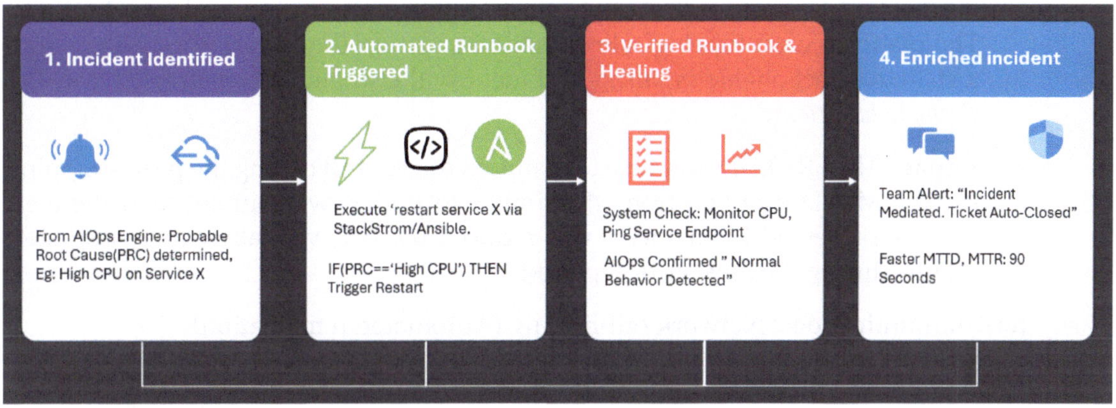

Figure 2.7: Automated remediation and self-healing workflow

Real-world AIOps examples

The practical workflows we have outlined are: proactive detection, intelligent correlation, and automated remediation, which are currently implemented across various industries.

Here are a few real-world examples that demonstrate the tangible business value of AIOps:

- **Financial services**: Preventing fraud and outages (Proactive detection):
  - **Scenario**: A major investment bank experienced frequent, intermittent transaction failures caused by memory leaks that were hard to spot amidst normal traffic. Traditional monitoring only alerted when the system was already redlining.
  - **AIOps solution**: They implemented an AIOps platform (e.g., Dynatrace) to run time series analysis on application metrics (heap size, garbage collection frequency). The ML model established a baseline for normal resource degradation

and began flagging a subtle, slow creep in memory usage 48 hours before any human-visible performance degradation occurred.

- **Impact**: The bank shifted from reacting to customer-reported failures to proactive maintenance. These reduced critical outages related to application performance by 40% and saved an estimated $5 million annually in lost transaction fees and regulatory fines.

- **E-commerce or retail**: Managing peak season traffic (Intelligent correlation):
  - **Scenario**: An online retail platform handling seasonal traffic spikes struggled with alert overload, receiving thousands of notifications during peak hours, overwhelming the NOC team and leading to missed critical alerts.
  - **AIOps solution**: They deployed an event correlation platform (e.g., Moogsoft or BigPanda) to ingest all alerts from their logging, monitoring, and security tools. The platform used topological correlation to group thousands of raw alerts into just 10 to 15 actionable *situations* and identify the single root cause (e.g., *Web Tier Cache Exhaustion*).
  - **Impact**: The SRE team was able to maintain full control during the peak shopping season. MTTD dropped from 15 minutes to under two minutes, and the alert volume presented to engineers was reduced by 98%, virtually eliminating alert fatigue during the most critical period.

- **Telecommunications**: Network self-healing (Automated remediation):
  - **Scenario**: A global telecom provider dealt with constant, repetitive failures of specific regional network switches (e.g., high latency, connection drops) that required an engineer to log in and manually reboot the device. This consumed hundreds of hours of engineering time monthly (toil).
  - **AIOps solution**: They coupled their AIOps platform (for root cause identification) with an automation engine (e.g., StackStorm / Ansible). When the AIOps engine detected the specific signature of the *known faulty switch,* it automatically triggered an Ansible runbook to remotely execute the verified reboot procedure and verify the connection health afterward.
  - **Impact**: They achieved 90% automation for this class of recurring network incidents. The MTTR dropped from 25 minutes to less than two minutes. This not only saved engineer time (toil reduction) but also significantly improved the quality of service for millions of customers.

Note: These examples illustrate that AIOps's value extends far beyond the IT department. It directly impacts customer experience, protects brand reputation, and drives measurable financial savings by converting reactive spending into strategic reliability investment.

Conclusion

This chapter established AIOps not as an optional tool, but as a reliability accelerator and a fundamental necessity for modern SRE teams operating on a scale. We moved beyond the hype to focus on measurable outcomes, implementation strategy, and the practical application of intelligent operations. We began by clarifying that AIOps is a mindset shift first, a move from basic automation to a spectrum of assisted and autonomous intelligence. The technical core lies in five essential functions: anomaly detection, intelligent alerting, root cause analysis, predictive insights, and automated remediation. Crucially, we mapped these functions directly to the core SRE metrics, demonstrating a clear path to measurable reliability improvement.

Finally, we explored the rich AIOps ecosystem, demonstrating that whether through proprietary Enterprise platforms or tailored solutions built with open-source ML libraries, the goal remains the same: transforming a flood of raw telemetry into actionable, contextual intelligence. The three workflows, like proactive detection, intelligent correlation, and automated self-healing, showcase the tangible path to operational resilience.

The next chapter will explore how to build the essential foundation for AIOps by creating a unified observability data model through consistent ingestion of logs, metrics, and traces, coupled with automated service discovery, to deliver a single pane of glass that transforms raw data into clear, actionable insights for SRE teams.

CHAPTER 3
AIOps Knowledgebase

Introduction

In the domain of intelligent operations, data serves as the fundamental resource, yet true value emerges only when it is transformed into actionable insight. This chapter examines how SRE teams can design a knowledgebase that converts fragmented telemetry into unified, contextual intelligence. By constructing a dynamic system blueprint through automated service discovery and dependency mapping, organizations enable a comprehensive, real-time view that supports informed and proactive decision-making. The AIOps knowledgebase is not merely a repository of information; it functions as the central nervous system of reliability, orchestrating intelligence across every operational layer.

Structure

In this chapter, we will cover the following topics:

- Building unified observability data models
- Ingesting logs, metrics, and traces
- Automated service discovery and dependency mapping
- Creating a single pane of glass for SRE teams
- Delivering actionable insights to SRE teams
- Practical workflows and real-world examples

Objectives

By the end of this chapter, readers will gain a practical framework for architecting the AIOps knowledgebase. This includes mastering how to unify observability data (logs, metrics, and traces), automate service discovery and dependency mapping, and visualize system components to create the single pane of glass necessary for SRE teams to transition from reactive troubleshooting to proactive reliability engineering. Mastering this foundation will enable readers to dramatically reduce alert noise, accelerate RCA, and establish the structural integrity required for all advanced AIOps functions to deliver measurable reliability improvements.

Building unified observability data models

In the world of AIOps, data is the lifeblood, but without structure, it is just noise. SRE teams need more than raw telemetry; they need a unified observability data model that transforms fragmented signals into coherent intelligence. This model ensures that when an alert fires from a metric (like high CPU), the AIOps engine can immediately associate it with the relevant traces (showing the user request path) and logs (providing debug detail) because they share a common set of identifiers like trace ID, service name, and environment tag. This section explores how to architect such a model, ensuring that logs, metrics, and traces are not just collected, but contextualized, correlated, and actionable.

Strategic insight

A unified observability data model is not a monolithic schema; it is a dynamic framework that harmonizes disparate telemetry sources. It enables AIOps platforms to correlate events, detect anomalies, and surface insights with precision. For SREs, this means:

- Faster incident detection and diagnosis
- Reduced cognitive load
- Improved signal-to-noise ratio

However, building this model requires intentional design. It is not just about ingesting everything; it is about ingesting the right things in the right way. *Table 3.1* details the essential components of a robust, unified data model, outlining the design requirements and the direct SRE impact of each component:

Component	Description	SRE impact
Schema normalization	Standardizes data formats across logs, metrics, and traces	Enables consistent parsing and correlation across services
Metadata enrichment	Adds contextual tags (e.g., service name, environment, owner)	Improves searchability and root cause analysis
Time series alignment	Synchronizes timestamps across telemetry types	Facilitates accurate event sequencing and anomaly detection
Source attribution	Identifies origin of data (e.g., container ID, host, region)	Supports dependency mapping and impact analysis
Retention strategy	Defines how long data is stored and at what granularity	Balances cost with diagnostic depth and historical analysis

***Table 3.1**: Essential components for a unified observability data model*

Common misconceptions

When building the unified data model, SRE teams frequently encounter misleading advice regarding data strategy. Ignoring these pitfalls can cripple the AIOps platform's ability to provide actionable insights. *Table 3.2* clarifies the three most critical misconceptions that often undermine the successful implementation of the knowledgebase:

Misconception	Reality
Just collect everything	Volume without structure leads to noise, not insight
Logs are enough	Metrics and traces provide critical context for performance and causality
Schema is optional	Without normalization, AIOps engines struggle to correlate and analyze

Table 3.2: Common misconceptions in AIOps data collection

Design principles for SRE teams

Successfully building and operating the AIOps knowledgebase relies on adhering to specific, non-negotiable standards throughout the data pipeline. These principles ensure that the telemetry is not only collected but is fit for purpose, enabling correlation and machine learning analysis. The following five core design principles must be adopted by SRE teams to guarantee the quality and utility of the unified observability data model:

- **Start with use cases, not tools**: Do not let vendor capabilities dictate your model. Begin with reliability goals: What incidents do you want to detect faster? What patterns do you want to surface?
- **Enforce structured logging**: Move from free-text logs to structured formats (e.g., JSON). Include consistent fields: `timestamp`, `service_name`, `environment`, `trace_id`, and `severity`.
- **Standardize metric naming**: Use clear, hierarchical naming conventions (e.g., `service_name.http_requests_total`). This enables aggregation, filtering, and alerting with precision.
- **Ensure trace context propagation**: Use distributed tracing standards (e.g., OpenTelemetry) to propagate `trace_id` and `span_id` across services. This is essential for end-to-end visibility.
- **Centralize and normalize**: Aggregate telemetry into a unified platform or data lake. Apply schema enforcement and enrich data with business context (e.g., impacted customer segment, SLA tier).

Real-world example

A global e-commerce platform struggled with fragmented observability, logs in one system, metrics in another, and traces missing entirely. After implementing a unified data model:

- They standardized logging across services using JSON schemas.
- Metrics were centralized in Prometheus with consistent labels.
- Traces were collected via OpenTelemetry and visualized in Jaeger.
- Metadata enrichment added business context (e.g., order ID, customer tier).

As a result, MTTR dropped by 35%, and incident correlation accuracy improved by 60%.

Figure 3.1 illustrates the architectural blueprint for this model, depicting how telemetry flows through standardized pipelines to create a coherent, actionable intelligence layer:

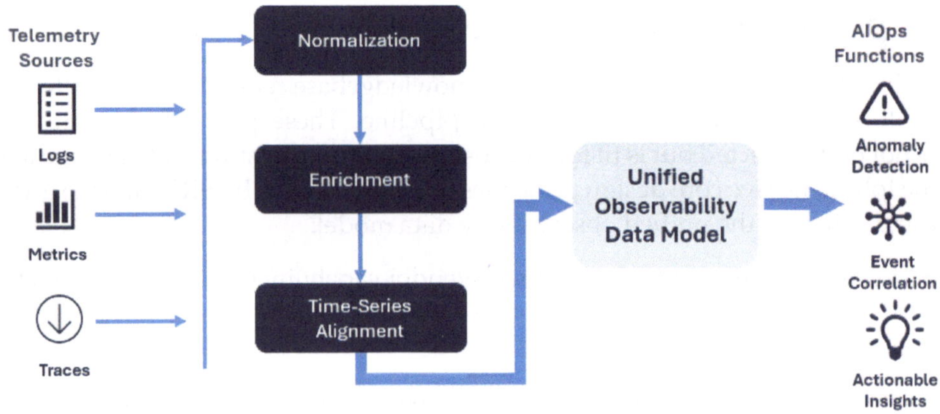

***Figure 3.1**: Unified observability data model architecture*

Leadership takeaway is that a unified observability data model is not a luxury; it is a prerequisite for effective AIOps. It transforms telemetry into intelligence, enabling SRE teams to detect, diagnose, and resolve incidents with speed and confidence. Leaders must champion data hygiene, enforce standards, and invest in the infrastructure that turns raw signals into reliable insights.

Ingesting logs, metrics, and traces

Telemetry is the raw signal of system behavior, but without disciplined ingestion, it becomes an unmanageable torrent. AIOps thrive on structured, high-quality data streams, and the ingestion layer is where this transformation begins. This section explores how SRE teams can design ingestion pipelines that capture logs, metrics, and traces efficiently, normalize them for consistency, and enrich them for context.

Strategic insight

Ingestion is not a passive act of *collect everything*. It is an intentional process that balances completeness with relevance. The goal is to ensure that every byte ingested contributes to operational clarity, not noise. For SREs, this means:

- Real-time visibility into system health
- Context-rich telemetry for faster diagnosis
- Scalable pipelines that handle dynamic workloads without bottlenecks

Core principles of telemetry ingestion

For the AIOps knowledgebase to function effectively, the underlying data ingestion pipelines must adhere to strict engineering standards. Without these foundational design choices, even the most advanced machine learning algorithms will fail to deliver reliable insights. *Table 3.3* summarizes the four core principles that govern effective telemetry ingestion and explains why each is critical to the success of an AIOps implementation:

Principle	Why it matters
Standardization	Consistent formats enable correlation and analytics across diverse sources
Contextualization	Metadata tags (service name, environment, trace ID) turn raw data into actionable intelligence
Scalability	Pipelines must handle spikes during incidents without dropping critical signals
Security and compliance	Sensitive data must be masked or encrypted during transit and storage

Table 3.3: Core principles of telemetry ingestion

For the AIOps knowledgebase to build a complete, contextual picture of system health, it must successfully unify the three pillars of modern observability: Logs, Metrics, and Traces.

The following breakdown details the distinct roles, best practices, and practical applications for each of these foundational telemetry types, which together form a comprehensive narrative of system behavior:

- **Logs**: The narrative of events:
  - **Role**: Logs capture discrete events, warnings, transactions—that form the narrative of system behavior.

- **Best practices**:
  - Use structured logging (e.g., JSON) with consistent fields: **`timestamp`**, **`service_name`**, **`severity`**, **`trace_id`**.
  - Implement log rotation and retention policies to prevent storage bloat.
- **Tools**: Fluentd, Logstash, Filebeat for aggregation; Elasticsearch or Splunk for indexing and search.
- **Example**: A payment gateway uses structured logs to trace transaction failures, enriched with customer ID and region for impact analysis.

- **Metrics**: The pulse of performance:
  - **Role**: Metrics provide quantitative signals, CPU utilization, latency, and error rates that indicate system health.
  - **Best practices**:
    - Adopt consistent naming conventions (e.g., **`service_name.http_requests_total`**).
    - Use labels for dimensions like environment, region, and version.
  - **Tools**: Prometheus for collection and alerting; Grafana for visualization.
  - **Example**: An e-commerce platform monitors **`checkout_latency_seconds`** to detect performance degradation during peak traffic.
- **Traces**: The map of dependencies:
  - **Role**: Traces reveal the journey of a request across distributed services, exposing bottlenecks and failure points.
  - **Best practices**:
    - Implement context propagation using OpenTelemetry standards.
    - Capture critical spans (e.g., database queries, API calls) for meaningful insights.
  - **Tools**: Jaeger or Zipkin for distributed tracing; OpenTelemetry Collector for ingestion.
  - **Example**: A microservices-based application uses tracing to identify a slow database query causing cascading latency across services.

Architecting the ingestion pipeline

A unified data model is only as effective as the pipeline that feeds it. Telemetry ingestion must be treated as a critical engineering function, not merely a data collection task, to ensure consistency, scalability, and integrity. The following design considerations and workflow steps are essential for architecting a robust pipeline, as illustrated conceptually in *Figure 3.2*, the telemetry ingestion pipeline, to reliably transform raw data into a normalized format ready for AIOps analysis:

- **Design considerations**:
    - **Edge processing**: Apply enrichment and filtering at the source to reduce downstream load and cost.
    - **Streaming vs. batch**: Use streaming for real-time insights (alerts, anomaly detection); use batch for historical analysis and trend identification.
    - **Fault tolerance**: Ensure pipelines can buffer and retry during network disruptions to prevent the loss of critical signals during an incident.
- **Workflow**:
    - Collect telemetry using agents (Fluentd, OpenTelemetry Collector).
    - Normalize and enrich data with metadata tags.
    - Stream to a centralized observability platform or data lake.
    - Apply schema enforcement before feeding into AIOps engines.

The effectiveness of a unified data model depends entirely on the robustness of its ingestion pipeline. This pipeline must be engineered with precision to ensure that telemetry is consistently normalized, enriched, and delivered at scale without compromising integrity. It is not a passive data collection mechanism but a critical reliability function that underpins every AIOps capability. *Figure 3.2* illustrates the conceptual architecture of the telemetry ingestion pipeline, highlighting the flow from edge processing and normalization to centralized aggregation and schema enforcement, which collectively prepare data for advanced analytics and machine learning:

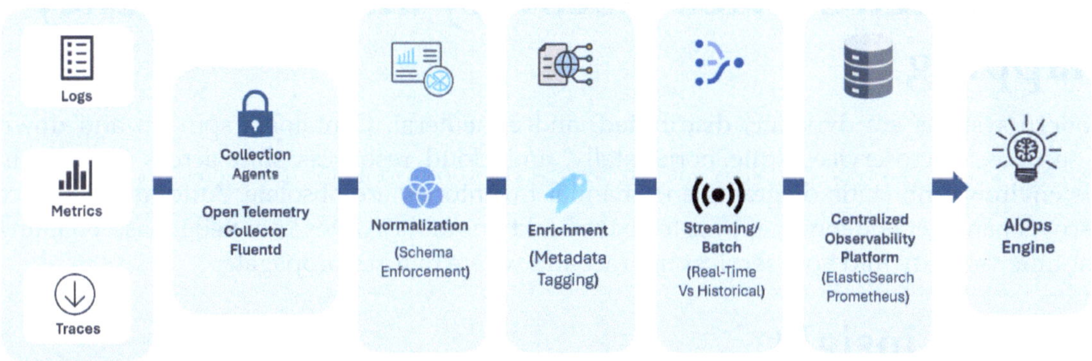

Figure 3.2*: Telemetry ingestion pipeline*

Common misconceptions

Even with robust design principles in place, SRE teams must actively guard against pervasive misconceptions that can undermine the integrity and value of the AIOps knowledgebase. These faulty assumptions lead to unnecessary costs and alert fatigue. *Table 3.4* clarifies the most frequent ingestion pitfalls, contrasting the common, yet misguided, belief with the operational reality:

Misconception	Reality
Collect everything for completeness	Excessive ingestion without filtering leads to noise and cost overruns
Logs alone are enough	Metrics and traces provide critical performance and dependency context
Batch ingestion is sufficient	Real-time streaming is essential for proactive incident prevention

***Table 3.4**: Common misconceptions in telemetry ingestion*

Leadership takeaway

Telemetry ingestion is the foundation of operational intelligence. Leaders must prioritize:

- **Data hygiene**: Enforce standards for logs, metrics, and traces.
- **Pipeline resilience**: Design for scale and fault tolerance.
- **Contextual enrichment**: Ensure every signal carries business and operational context.

Without disciplined ingestion, AIOps becomes guesswork. With it, SRE teams gain the clarity and confidence to act decisively.

Automated service discovery and dependency mapping

Modern systems are dynamic, distributed, and ephemeral. Containers spin up and down in seconds, microservices scale horizontally, and cloud resources shift across regions. In this environment, static diagrams and manual inventories are obsolete. Automated service discovery and dependency mapping form the backbone of the AIOps knowledgebase, enabling real-time visibility into how services interact and where failures propagate.

Strategic insight

You cannot manage what you cannot see. For SRE teams, understanding service topology is critical for:

- **Root cause analysis**: Pinpointing the origin of cascading failures.
- **Impact assessment**: Identifying which services and customers are affected.
- **Change management**: Predicting the blast radius of deployments.

Automated discovery ensures that this visibility is continuous, accurate, and actionable. For example, a cascading failure may begin with an upstream API timeout, which causes a queue backlog in the dependent service, eventually leading to database connection exhaustion and degraded performance across multiple microservices. Without automated discovery, this failure chain remains hidden, delaying diagnosis and increasing MTTR.

Core capabilities

Translating the strategic need for continuous visibility into a functional AIOps knowledgebase requires platforms to execute specific, foundational tasks. *Table 3.5* details the core capabilities required for automated service discovery and dependency mapping, explaining the function of each and its direct impact on SRE operational efficiency:

Capability	Description	SRE impact
Dynamic service discovery	Identifies services and components as they appear in the environment	Eliminates manual updates and stale inventories
Dependency mapping	Captures relationships between services, databases, APIs, and infrastructure	Enables correlation engines to trace failure chains
Topology visualization	Presents a real-time map of service interactions	Improves situational awareness during incidents

***Table 3.5**: Core capabilities for automated discovery*

Techniques for automated discovery

Achieving dynamic, continuous service discovery requires leveraging advanced techniques that can operate effectively in ephemeral, cloud-native environments where services may not have traditional static IP addresses or configurations. The following four techniques represent the modern methods SRE teams can employ to maintain an accurate, real-time map of their service topology for the AIOps knowledgebase:

- **Service mesh integration**: Tools like Istio or Linkerd intercept service-to-service traffic, providing granular visibility into communication patterns.
    - **Benefit**: Native support for dynamic environments and zero-code instrumentation.

- **eBPF-based observability**: **Extended Berkeley Packet Filter (eBPF)** hooks into the Linux kernel to capture network and system calls without intrusive agents.
  - o **Benefit**: Lightweight, high-fidelity telemetry for containerized workloads.
- **Configuration management databases (CMDB)**: Modern CMDBs integrate with CI/CD pipelines to maintain accurate inventories.
  - o **Benefit**: Provides a single source of truth for service ownership and metadata.
- **AIOps native discovery**: Enterprise AIOps platforms often include built-in discovery engines that scan APIs, logs, and orchestration layers.
  - o **Benefit**: Seamless integration with correlation and RCA workflows.

The following figure illustrates the architecture for automated service discovery and dependency mapping in modern AIOps environments. It highlights the key techniques, service mesh, eBPF-based observability, CMDB integration, and AIOps-native discovery, that feed into a real-time topology map, forming the foundation for intelligent correlation and impact analysis.

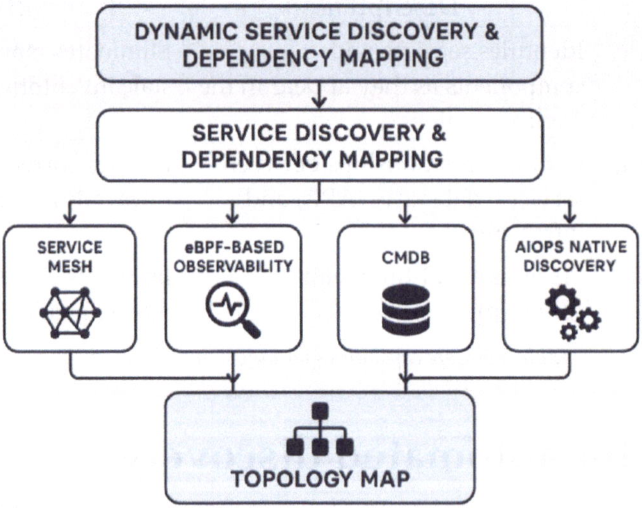

Figure 3.3: Dynamic service discovery and dependency mapping

Challenges and solutions

While the automation of service discovery is essential, it introduces specific challenges related to the dynamic nature of cloud environments and data management. SRE teams must proactively design systems to address these issues to maintain the integrity of the AIOps knowledgebase. *Table 3.6* outlines the primary challenges in automated discovery and provides actionable solutions to ensure the topology map remains accurate and useful over time:

Challenge	Solution
Ephemeral infrastructure	Use service mesh and orchestration hooks to capture transient components
Data Silos	Centralize discovery outputs into the unified observability model
Accuracy over time	Implement continuous scanning and CI/CD integration to keep maps current

Table 3.6: Challenges and solutions in automated service discovery

Real-world example

A global SaaS provider deployed Istio for service mesh observability and integrated its telemetry with an AIOps platform. The result:

- Real-time topology maps updated with every deployment.
- Incident correlation improved by 70%, as the platform could trace cascading failures across microservices.
- MTTR dropped by 40%, thanks to precise impact analysis and automated remediation triggers.

Leadership takeaway

Automated service discovery and dependency mapping are not optional, they are essential for operational resilience. Leaders must:

- Invest in technologies that provide continuous, real-time visibility.
- Mandate integration with CI/CD pipelines to ensure accuracy.
- Treat topology as a living artifact, not a static diagram.

Without this foundation, AIOps cannot deliver meaningful insights. With it, SRE teams gain the clarity to act decisively and prevent outages before they escalate.

Creating a single pane of glass for SRE teams

In complex, distributed environments, visibility is often fragmented; logs in one tool, metrics in another, traces scattered across dashboards. This siloed approach forces SREs to context-switch during incidents, wasting precious time and increasing cognitive load. The single pane of glass concept solves this by consolidating observability and AIOps insights into a unified interface, enabling faster decisions and proactive reliability management.

Strategic insight

A single pane of glass is not just a dashboard; it is a decision-support system. It integrates telemetry, topology, and actionable intelligence into one cohesive view. For SRE teams, this means:

- Reduced MTTR through contextualized alerts and automated diagnostics.
- Improved situational awareness during high-severity incidents.
- Streamlined workflows by embedding collaboration and remediation tools.

Core design principles

Building a truly effective single pane of glass requires moving beyond simple dashboard consolidation; it requires intentional design focused on the user's workflow and cognitive load. *Table 3.7* details the core design principles that ensure the unified interface provides contextual intelligence, rather than just more data:

Principle	Why it matters
Role-based views	Tailor dashboards for different personas (SRE, DevOps, Security) to avoid information overload
Contextual intelligence	Combine telemetry with dependency maps and business impact data for meaningful insights
Integration over replacement	Embed existing tools (ITSM, runbooks, collaboration platforms) rather than forcing a new stack
Real-time updates	Ensure dashboards reflect live system state, not stale snapshots

Table 3.7: Core design principles for the single pane of glass

Key features of an effective single pane

The single pane of glass must deliver more than simple monitoring; it must be engineered to provide context, correlation, and intelligence directly into the SRE workflow. The following four features are mandatory for transforming a static dashboard into a dynamic, decision-support system:

- **Unified telemetry visualization**:
    - Combine logs, metrics, and traces in correlated views.
    - For example, clicking on a latency spike reveals related logs and trace spans instantly.
- **Dynamic topology overlay**:
    - Display service dependencies alongside telemetry.

    - For example, highlight impacted services during an outage and show blast radius.
- **Incident context and recommendations**:
    - Integrate AIOps insights for root cause analysis and remediation suggestions.
    - For example, *Probable root cause: Database connection pool exhaustion. Recommended action: Increase pool size.*
- **Collaboration and workflow integration**:
    - Push incident summaries to Slack or Teams.
    - Auto-create tickets in ServiceNow or Jira with enriched context.

Common misconceptions

The single pane of glass is a crucial component of the AIOps knowledgebase, but its effectiveness is often hampered by misunderstandings about its purpose and scope. *Table 3.8* identifies and refutes common misconceptions, clarifying that this interface is a comprehensive decision-support system, not merely a collection of simple dashboards:

Misconception	Reality
A single pane is just a dashboard	It is a decision-making hub that integrates telemetry, topology, and automation
More widgets are equal to better visibility	Clutter reduces clarity; focus on actionable intelligence
It replaces existing tools	It should complement and integrate, not disrupt established workflows

Table 3.8: Common misconceptions about a single pane of glass and their realities

Real-world example

A global fintech company implemented a single pane of glass using Grafana integrated with its AIOps platform:

- Logs, metrics, and traces were visualized in correlated panels.
- Service topology overlays highlighted impacted microservices during incidents.
- Automated remediation runbooks could be triggered directly from the dashboard.

Impact

As a result of working from a single, contextual interface, engineers experienced a 45% reduction in MTTR and a significant drop in alert fatigue.

The following figure illustrates how a unified interface consolidates telemetry, topology, and AIOps insights into a single, actionable view for SRE teams. It emphasizes integration with existing observability tools, ITSM platforms, and collaboration channels to streamline workflows and accelerate incident response.

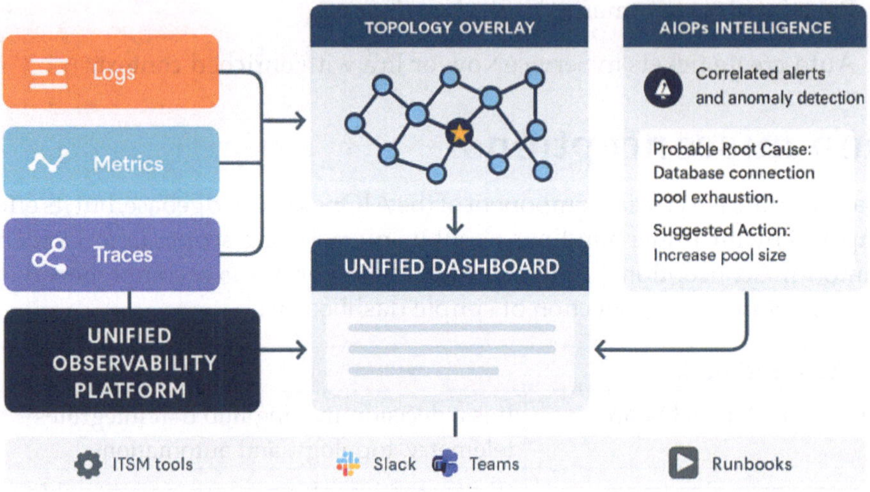

Figure 3.4: *Single pane of glass architecture*

Delivering actionable insights to SRE teams

Data without context is noise. Dashboards without intelligence are decoration. The true value of an AIOps knowledgebase lies in its ability to transform raw telemetry into actionable insights, such as clear, prioritized, and contextual recommendations that empower SRE teams to act decisively. This section explores how to design and operationalize insight delivery so that it drives measurable reliability outcomes.

Strategic insight

Actionable insights bridge the gap between observability and operational excellence. They answer three critical questions for SREs:

1. What happened? (Detection)
2. Why did it happen? (Diagnosis)
3. What should we do next? (Remediation)

When these answers are surfaced in real-time, enriched with context, and integrated into workflows, SRE teams move from reactive firefighting to proactive reliability engineering.

To ensure that AIOps insights are not just informative but truly useful, they must be designed around four essential dimensions. *Table 3.9* details these critical dimensions, outlining the design requirements and the direct impact on the SRE workflow and incident resolution:

Dimension	Description	Impact
Contextualization	Combine telemetry with topology, business impact, and historical patterns	Eliminates guesswork and accelerates RCA
Prioritization	Rank incidents by severity, user impact, and SLA risk	Focuses attention where it matters most
Prescriptive guidance	Suggest remediation steps or trigger automated runbooks	Reduces MTTR and operational toil
Explainability	Show evidence behind recommendations (logs, metrics, traces)	Build trust and foster adoption

Table 3.9: Dimensions of actionable AIOps insights

Key capabilities for insight delivery

The AIOps engine must execute several sophisticated functions to transform raw data into the high-value, actionable insights required by SRE teams. These capabilities move the platform beyond basic alerting and into the realm of intelligent diagnostics and predictive operations. The following five key capabilities define the functional requirements for a robust AIOps knowledgebase to deliver maximum value:

- **Correlated alerts**:
    - Aggregate related events into a single, enriched incident.
    - For example, *Instead of 50 alerts for downstream services, surface one root cause alert with dependency context.*
- **Root cause analysis (RCA)**:
    - Use machine learning and topology awareness to identify probable cause.
    - For example, *Deployment X caused CPU saturation on Node Y, impacting Service Z.*
- **Impact analysis**:
    - Quantify business and user impact for prioritization.
    - For example, *Incident affects checkout service; estimated revenue impact: $5,000/hour.*

- **Predictive insights**:
  - o Forecast potential failures based on historical trends.
  - o For example, *Storage capacity will breach the threshold in 48 hours; recommended scaling action.*
- **Prescriptive actions**:
  - o Suggest or automate remediation steps.
  - o For example, *Recommended action: Restart Service A with increased memory allocation.*

Workflow integration

Actionable insights must live where work happens:

- **Incident management systems**: Push enriched incidents to PagerDuty or Opsgenie.
- **ITSM platforms**: Auto-create tickets in ServiceNow or Jira with RCA and recommended actions.
- **Collaboration tools**: Share summaries in Slack or Teams for rapid coordination.
- **Automation engines**: Trigger runbooks in Ansible or StackStorm for self-healing.

The following figure visually represents the flow from telemetry sources (logs, metrics, traces) to actionable insights (correlated alerts, RCA, impact analysis, prescriptive actions), and finally to integration and remediation via incident management, collaboration tools, and automation:

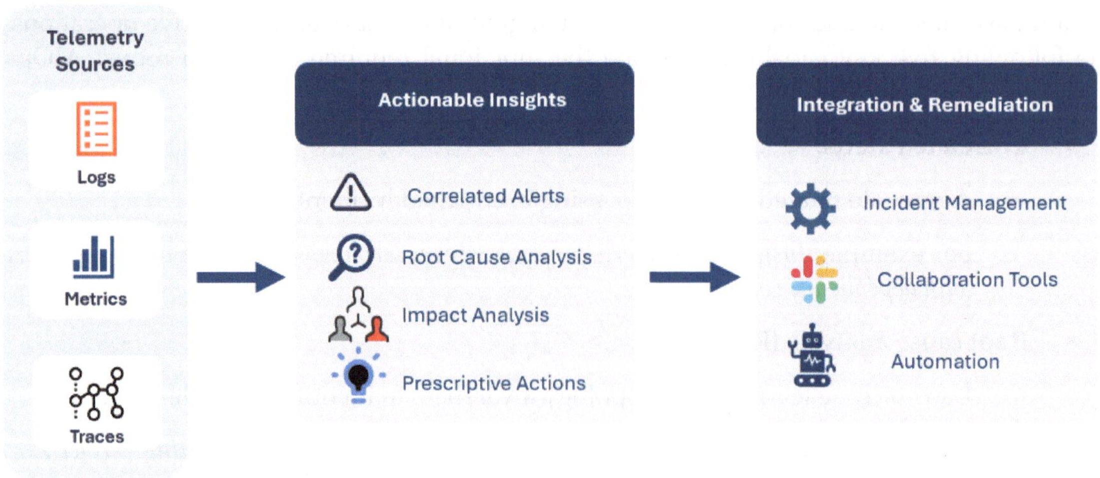

***Figure 3.5**: Actionable insights delivery framework*

Common misconceptions

As SRE teams adopt sophisticated AIOps capabilities, it is critical to manage expectations regarding what these insights can achieve. Misunderstandings can lead to unrealistic goals and misuse of the platform. *Table 3.10* clarifies common misconceptions about AIOps insights, ensuring a realistic foundation for operationalizing the knowledgebase:

Misconception	Reality
Insights is equal to more alerts	Actionable insights reduce noise by correlating and prioritizing events
Automation replaces judgment	Automation augments human decision-making, not eliminates it
Predictive models are perfect	Forecasting is probabilistic; it combines predictions with human oversight

***Table 3.10**: Common misconceptions in actionable insights*

Real-world example

A global e-commerce platform integrated AIOps insights into its incident workflow:

- Correlated alerts reduced noise by 90%.
- RCA surfaced probable causes within two minutes of detection.
- Automated remediation handled 40% of recurring incidents without human intervention.

Impact

MTTR dropped from 45 minutes to 12 minutes, helping preserve error budgets and significantly improving customer experience during peak traffic.

Practical workflows and real-world examples

Theory without practice is incomplete. This section demonstrates how the concepts covered in this chapter, such as unified data models, telemetry ingestion, service discovery, single pane dashboards, and actionable insights, translate into real-world workflows. These examples showcase how leading organizations operationalize AIOps to deliver reliability at scale.

Workflow 1: Unified observability and correlated incident management

The primary goal here is to cut through the noise: to drastically reduce alert fatigue and accelerate RCA. *Table 3.11* outlines a representative workflow for unified observability and correlated incident management:

Stage	Action	Description
Telemetry ingestion	Collect and normalize	Logs, metrics, and traces are collected via Open Telemetry and instantly normalized into a unified, coherent schema
Topology mapping	Contextualize	The service mesh or CMDB provides real-time service dependency maps, giving the AI crucial context on flow and impact
Correlation engine	Group and enrich	The AIOps platform applies machine learning to group hundreds of related alerts into a single, high-fidelity, enriched incident
Single pane of glass	Visualize	The central dashboard displays the impacted services, the probable root cause, and the recommended remediation action
Actionable integration	Handoff	The enriched incident is pushed to the SRE's system (PagerDuty, etc.) with the AI-generated RCA hypothesis and a direct runbook link

***Table 3.11**: End-to-end workflow for unified observability and correlated incident management*

The following are the impacts:

- Alert volume dropped by 90%, effectively eliminating alert fatigue and improving focus during incidents.
- MTTR improved by 50%, enabling faster recovery and protecting critical error budgets.

Workflow 2: Predictive capacity management

This workflow shifts from reactive monitoring to proactive prevention, using data to forecast and mitigate outages caused by resource exhaustion. It not only forecasts potential breaches but also prescribes and automates corrective actions, ensuring service-level objectives remain intact. *Table 3.12* presents the sequential stages of this workflow, illustrating how organizations can operationalize predictive analytics to prevent outages caused by resource exhaustion:

Stage	Action	Description
Historical data analysis	Ingest	Service-level metrics (e.g., disk I/O, storage utilization) are ingested into a time series database (like Prometheus)

Stage	Action	Description
Predictive modeling	Forecast	The AIOps engine applies ML algorithms (e.g., ARIMA or Prophet) to forecast when a critical resource, like storage capacity, will breach its threshold
Prescriptive action	Recommend	The system generates a high-confidence recommendation: *Scale storage cluster capacity within the next 48 hours to avoid an SLO breach*
Automation trigger	Execute	An automated provisioning runbook (Ansible, Terraform, etc.) is triggered to provision and integrate the additional capacity

***Table 3.12**: Workflow for predictive capacity management using AIOps*

The following are the impacts:

- Eliminating resource-exhaustion outages prevented SLA breaches and improved service reliability.
- Preserving error budgets provided engineering teams with greater flexibility for feature delivery.

Workflow 3: Automated remediation for known failure modes

The objective here is to eliminate toil for SREs by fully automating the recovery process for common, recurring incidents. By leveraging historical incident patterns and predefined remediation sequences, this workflow ensures that recurring issues are resolved without human intervention, while maintaining transparency and accountability through automated documentation. *Table 3.13* outlines the sequential stages of this process, demonstrating how organizations can achieve near-instant recovery for predictable failure scenarios:

Stage	Action	Description
Incident detection	Identify	AIOps detects a critical, recurring event, such as a repeating memory leak pattern in a specific microservice instance
Root cause identification	Confirm	The correlation engine confirms the pattern matches a known failure mode stored in the incident knowledge base
Automated response	Resolve	A workflow automation engine (StackStorm, etc.) is triggered to execute a trusted remediation sequence: container restart, cache flush, and queue clearing
Post-incident ticketing	Log	A Jira or similar ticket is automatically created, flagging the underlying issue for a developer to implement a permanent code fix

***Table 3.13**: Workflow for automated remediation of known failure modes*

The following are the impacts:

- MTTR decreased from 30 minutes to under 2 minutes for automated incidents.
- SRE teams were relieved of repetitive, hightoil tasks.

Workflow 4: Proactive security anomaly detection

The SRE mandate extends to system resilience, which includes security posture. This workflow details how AIOps turns massive security log data into early, actionable threat warnings, preventing security events from becoming operational outages. Through advanced behavioral modeling and zero-threshold anomaly detection, AIOps provides proactive defense mechanisms that integrate seamlessly with operational data for context-aware decision-making. *Table 3.14* illustrates the sequential stages of proactive security anomaly detection, demonstrating how organizations can operationalize intelligent threat prevention at scale:

Stage	Action	Description
Log and flow aggregation	Consolidate	Logs from application firewalls, intrusion detection systems, and network flow data are aggregated into the **security information and event management** (**SIEM**) system
Baseline behavioral modeling	Learn	AIOps builds a baseline of *normal* system behavior, including common user access patterns, typical traffic volume by region, and standard configuration changes
Zero-threshold anomaly detection	Flag	ML models flag subtle deviations from the baseline, e.g., an unusual login attempt from a country never before seen, or a sudden, small spike in outbound data to an external address
Security correlation	Contextualize	The AIOps platform correlates the network anomaly with operational data (e.g., a recent deployment, a container restart) to rule out false positives and determine if the event is a genuine, coordinated threat
Automated isolation	Quarantine	A high-confidence threat triggers an immediate, automated response (e.g., Kubernetes Network Policy update to isolate the affected pod, or suspension of the compromised user account)

***Table 3.14**: Workflow for proactive security anomaly detection using AIOps*

The following are the impacts:

- Security incidents were detected 75% faster compared to manual review.
- **Mean time to containment** (**MTTC**) was significantly reduced, limiting overall breach exposure.

Real-world operational examples

The power of AIOps is best illustrated through its impact across diverse industries:

- **Financial services**: A major banking institution implemented predictive modeling not just for capacity, but for transaction latency. By anticipating when load balancers would begin seeing minor slowdowns, they were able to preemptively reroute traffic. This effort reduced critical outages by 40% in their core payment processing services, saving millions annually in lost revenue and regulatory fines.
- **E-commerce**: During their peak holiday season (Black Friday/Cyber Monday), a leading retailer used AIOps to correlate the massive surge of traffic-related alerts. By grouping symptoms, the platform reduced alert noise by 98%, ensuring the on-call SREs only saw actual service-breaking incidents, allowing the company to maintain perfect uptime during the critical surge.
- **Telecommunications**: A global telecom achieved massive efficiency gains by applying automation to its vast network infrastructure. They focused on automated remediation for recurring network switch and routing failures. Through this initiative, they have achieved 90% automation for their most common Level 1 and Level 2 recurring incidents.
- **Healthcare**: A major hospital network used AIOps to tackle *phantom latency* in their core **electronic health record** (**EHR**) system, where minutes of delay could jeopardize patient safety. The correlation engine cross-referenced previously siloed storage logs, database metrics, and application traces, discovering that intermittent slowdowns were caused by a subtle, periodic storage synchronization delay. By isolating and rescheduling the problematic job, the SRE team eliminated daily latency spikes and reduced the MTTR for P0 incidents from 90 minutes to 15 minutes, ensuring clinicians maintained reliable, fast access to critical patient data.

Note: **These practical workflows demonstrate that AIOps is not a theoretical concept; it is a transformative operational discipline. By embedding intelligence directly into operational pipelines, organizations transition from a reactive firefighting stance to a model of proactive reliability. This focus on efficiency through automation leads directly to business resilience by ensuring the alignment of system reliability with the ultimate customer experience.**

Conclusion

This chapter established that the AIOps knowledgebase serves as the central, intelligent fabric of a successful reliability engineering program, enabling SRE teams to transition from reactive troubleshooting to proactive operational excellence. We explored the essential pillars that form this foundation: the unified data model, which emphasizes the importance of standardizing and enriching logs, metrics, and traces to create a coherent and contextual structure where quality matters more than sheer volume; the dynamic service topology, which replaces outdated manual CMDBs with automated service discovery and dependency mapping to provide real-time context for accurate root cause analysis and impact assessment in ephemeral cloud environments; and actionable intelligence delivery, which integrates these components into a single pane of glass designed as a decision-support system that offers correlated alerts, predictive warnings, and prescriptive guidance to reduce MTTR and cognitive load. Together, these elements transform raw telemetry into a nervous system of reliability, embedding intelligence into every operational workflow. By mastering data unification, dynamic mapping, and contextual delivery, SRE teams create a robust platform capable of handling modern complexity.

The next chapter will build on this foundational context by exploring the specific AIOps functions that leverage this knowledgebase to dramatically accelerate the incident lifecycle, from intelligent alerting and event correlation to automated diagnosis and streamlined resolution.

CHAPTER 4
Intelligent Incident Management for SREs

Introduction

Incident response is the ultimate test of any SRE practice. In the age of distributed systems, manual triage and noise management are no longer tenable; they lead to burnout, delayed resolutions, and eroded SLOs. This chapter explores how AIOps fundamentally re-engineers the incident lifecycle. By leveraging the unified knowledgebase built in *Chapter 3, AIOps Knowledgebase*, SRE teams can move beyond mere reaction, employing intelligence to cut through alert fatigue, automate complex diagnostics, and achieve true predictive prevention. We will detail the advanced AIOps functions that reduce cognitive load, accelerate MTTR, and transform every failure into a structured, long-term learning opportunity.

Structure

In this chapter, we will cover the following topics:

- Advanced alert correlation and noise reduction
- Proactive incident prevention through predictive analysis
- Automating triage and initial response
- Accelerating resolution with predictive models
- Streamlining postmortems with data insights
- Practical workflows and real-world examples

Objectives

By the end of this chapter, readers will master the core AIOps techniques required to establish an intelligent incident management pipeline. This includes learning how to deploy advanced correlation to eliminate alert noise, architect predictive models for preemptive incident prevention, automate the initial triage process to speed up response, and leverage data-driven insights to create efficient, objective, and effective postmortems.

Advanced alert correlation and noise reduction

The largest obstacle to effective incident response is alert fatigue, the volume of low-context, duplicate, or symptomatic alerts that drown out critical signals. AIOps solves this by moving beyond simple rule-based grouping to employ sophisticated machine learning models that correlate related events across time, service topology, and semantic content. This process consolidates dozens of raw alerts into a single, high-fidelity, and contextualized **incident root cause alert** (**IRCA**).

Alert correlation as AIOps foundation

In a distributed, microservices environment, a single failure (e.g., a database connection slowdown) can trigger a chain reaction of symptoms: load balancer alerts, web server latency metrics, HTTP 500 errors in logs, and timeouts in several downstream services. Without correlation, an SRE might receive 100 alerts for one incident, causing a critical loss of time spent manually grouping signals instead of diagnosing the cause. The primary goal of AIOps is to achieve a 100:1 signal-to-noise ratio, turning 100 alerts into one clear, enriched incident. This immediate noise reduction is the fastest way to reduce the SRE's cognitive load and, consequently, the **mean time to engagement** (**MTTE**), elapsed time between when an incident is first detected or alert is generated and when a qualified engineer or SRE actively begins investigating and responding to it.

Core techniques for alert correlation

The journey from raw alerts to a high-fidelity incident begins with the correlation engine, which employs several machine learning and topology-aware techniques. *Table 4.1* details the primary techniques used to correlate related events and drastically reduce the overall alert volume:

Technique	Description	Role in noise reduction
Topology-based grouping	Uses the real-time service map (from *Chapter 3, AIOps Knowledgebase*) to group alerts that originate from dependent services or components	Eliminate symptomatic alerts by linking them to the root service
Time series clustering	Groups alert that occur within a specific, small-time window, indicating they are likely symptoms of the same singular fault event	Reduces noise from concurrent, related alarms firing across metrics and logs
Semantic similarity (NLP)	Analyzes the natural language of log messages and alert descriptions to group events with similar meanings, even if the source is different	Unify alerts from legacy systems or unstructured log sources

Technique	Description	Role in noise reduction
Historical pattern analysis	Identifies recurring alert sequences that lead to known incident types based on past incidents and alerts, grouping them immediately when the pattern emerges	Accelerates diagnosis and prevents the creation of duplicate, repetitive tickets

***Table 4.1**: Core techniques for intelligent alert correlation*

The following lists the correlation techniques:

- **Topology-based correlation**: This technique is the most effective in modern cloud environments, relying heavily on the dynamic dependency map created in *Chapter 3, AIOps Knowledgebase*. When an alert fires on Service A (e.g., a latency spike), the correlation engine immediately checks the topology. If it observes subsequent alerts on Services B, C, and D, which are known downstream dependencies of A, it automatically designates Service A's original alert as the primary IRCA. The alerts from B, C, and D are suppressed or attached as supporting evidence, ensuring the SRE is alerted only to the point of origin, not the points of impact. This method effectively filters out cascading failure noise.
- **Time series clustering**: This model specializes in grouping simultaneous events that may not have an explicit dependency link but are statistically co-occurring. For instance, a sudden power event in a data center might cause a simultaneous drop in network throughput (metric) and a flood of hardware error messages (log). By analyzing the high-resolution timestamps of all incoming telemetry, the clustering algorithm identifies the micro-burst of activity, confirming a single external event is the likely trigger. This is particularly valuable for detecting infrastructure-level faults.
- **Semantic correlation (NLP)**: Traditional correlation fails when dealing with unstructured data, such as legacy system logs or proprietary error messages that lack standardized tags. Semantic correlation uses **natural language processing** (**NLP**) techniques to understand the meaning of the alert text. For example, if Alert 1 says, **DB connection pool exhausted**, and Alert 2 says, **Failed to acquire database lock, shutting down**, the NLP model recognizes that these messages share the same fundamental cause (database resource shortage) and groups them, even if they originated from different applications written in different languages.

Probabilistic alert scoring and signal fidelity

A critical advanced feature of the correlation engine is the use of probabilistic scoring. Once alerts are correlated into an IRCA, the system assigns a confidence score to the grouping. This score is based on:

- **Frequency of pattern**: How often this exact sequence of correlated alerts has led to a confirmed incident in the past?

- **Time deviation**: How closely did the alerts match the expected timing pattern defined by the historical model?
- **Severity weight**: The initial severity of the correlated alerts (e.g., P0 metrics contribute more weight than P3 logs).

This scoring ensures that SREs trust the system. A high-confidence IRCA (e.g., 95%) can immediately trigger an automated response, while a low-confidence grouping might simply be logged for human review, preventing unnecessary paging. *Figure 4.1* illustrates the journey of raw telemetry through the correlation pipeline to produce a single, high-fidelity IRCA:

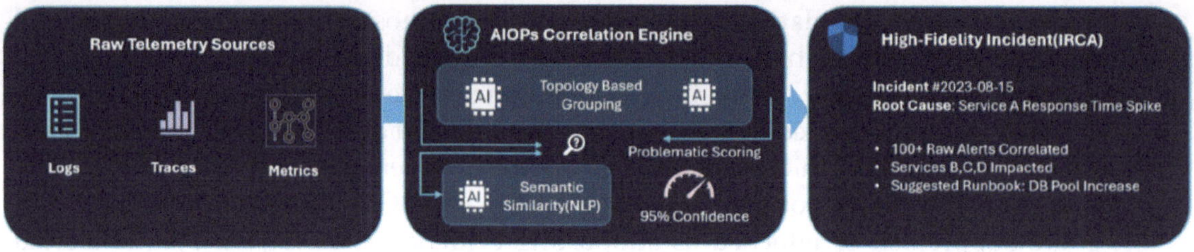

***Figure 4.1**: Intelligent alert correlation pipeline*

Proactive incident prevention through predictive analysis

The goal of intelligent incident management is not faster response, but effective prevention. AIOps achieves this by moving beyond real-time response to actively forecasting potential issues before they become user-impacting incidents. This capability, known as predictive analysis, relies on applying machine learning to the unified knowledgebase to identify subtle trends and anomalies that signal latent problems.

Proactive baselines for incident prevention

Traditional monitoring relies on static thresholds (e.g., *Alert if CPU > 85%*). While simple, this approach is inherently reactive and prone to failure, as legitimate spikes cause false alarms, while slow, chronic degradation is missed.

AIOps introduces the concept of dynamic baselining. Instead of rigid numbers, the system learns the normal behavior of every metric and service over time, accounting for daily, weekly, and seasonal cycles (e.g., *Normal CPU usage is 30% during the day, but 5% at 3 AM; alert if it deviates from this pattern*). This shift allows the platform to detect subtle anomalies much earlier than any human-defined threshold ever could.

Essential predictive signals and indicators

Moving beyond real-time response, AIOps provides the capability to forecast potential issues before they become incidents. This predictive ability relies on analyzing historical data to identify early warning signs or anomalies in trend data. The following predictive signals and indicators are essential for establishing a proactive incident prevention program:

- **Capacity saturation trends**: Forecasting when resources (CPU, memory, disk I/O) will breach critical thresholds based on growth trends, allowing for pre-emptive scaling actions to be executed automatically.
- **Service degradation indicators (SDIs)**: Metrics derived from learned service baselines that indicate gradual degradation in performance or reliability. They capture subtle, sustained deviations (e.g., a 10% increase in 95th-percentile latency over 72 hours) that signal latent issues before official SLOs are breached.
- **Change impact prediction**: Correlating recent deployment activities (from the CI/CD pipeline) with post-deployment performance telemetry, enabling the system to predict high-risk rollouts and trigger automated rollbacks or safeguards.
- **Statistical anomaly detection**: Applying machine learning to detect deviations from established seasonal or cyclical patterns, flagging non-obvious issues like sudden drops in traffic or slow, cumulative memory leaks that would be missed by traditional static thresholds.

Advanced modeling for capacity forecasting

Capacity planning, traditionally a manual effort, is automated using sophisticated time series modeling. Techniques like **Autoregressive Integrated Moving Average** (**ARIMA**) or Facebook's Prophet algorithm are applied to resource consumption metrics (e.g., database storage size, queue depth, connection pool utilization). These models decompose the time series into trend, seasonality, and residual components to provide a clear forecast.

The goal is to calculate the **time-to-saturation** (**TTS**), the estimated time until the metric reaches a critical threshold. For example, the model may predict: *Based on the 90-day growth trend, the primary database disk will reach 90% capacity in 14 days*. This insight allows the SRE team to trigger a new capacity request or an archival job well in advance, transforming a potential P0 incident into a planned operational task.

Statistical anomaly detection and novelty identification

While capacity forecasting looks at linear trends, anomaly detection targets non-linear, unpredictable deviations. Machine learning algorithms such as isolation forest or **one-class**

support vector machine (**OC-SVM**) are used to identify *novelty*, data points that do not fit the established pattern of *normal* behavior:

- **Isolation forest**: This is effective for finding rare, isolated events. It works by randomly partitioning the data until anomalies are separated from normal observations, identifying outliers with fewer partitions.
- **Clustering**: Algorithms like DBSCAN can group similar deviations. This is used to find *slow burns*, subtle, persistent performance degradation across a fleet of instances that may individually appear normal but collectively signal a severe underlying issue (e.g., resource contention).

CI/CD integration and predictive change impact

The vast majority of P0 incidents are caused by recent deployments or configuration changes. A critical predictive function of AIOps is to integrate directly with the CI/CD pipeline to assess the risk of every change before or immediately after it hits production. This is known as the change impact prediction.

The model correlates deployment metadata (who, when, what service, what commit) with the immediate post-deployment performance metrics. If a new deployment shows a statistically significant deviation in error rates or resource usage compared to the learned baseline of the previous version, the system can automatically flag the change as *High Risk* and trigger an *Automated Rollback* or hold the rollout to the next stage. This preemptive intervention stops most human-induced errors from reaching a broad user base.

Figure 4.2 illustrates the temporal difference between traditional static thresholds, dynamic anomaly detection, and true predictive forecasting, highlighting the increased lead time gained by SRE teams using AIOps:

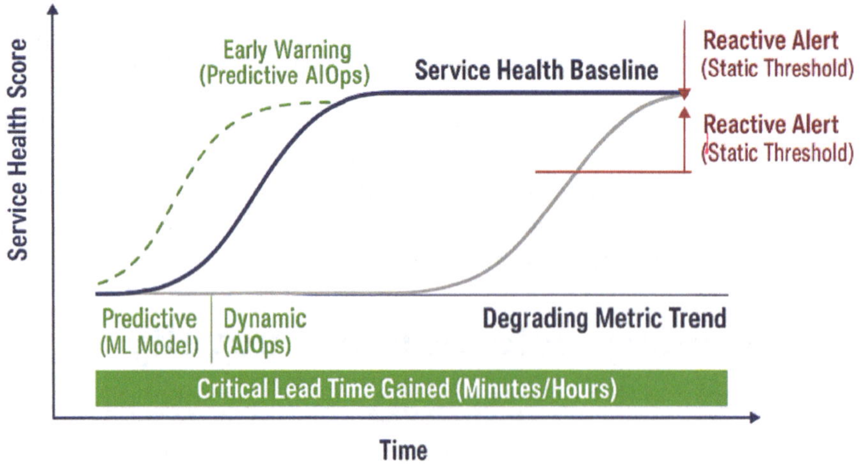

***Figure 4.2**: Predictive vs. reactive detection timeline*

Automating triage and initial response

Once the correlation engine has successfully consolidated noisy, disparate signals into a single, high-fidelity **incident root cause alert** (**IRCA**), the next critical step is automated triage. Triage is traditionally the most time-consuming phase of incident response, requiring human operators to manually assess severity, assign ownership, gather initial diagnostics, and engage with necessary teams. AIOps fundamentally changes this, ensuring that the first five minutes of any incident are handled by automated systems, delivering a fully contextualized incident ticket complete with probable root cause and initial diagnostic data. This automated function reduces the critical TTE metric, freeing SRE teams to focus immediately on strategic resolution rather than administrative overhead.

Automated triage pipeline

Automated triage is more than just ticketing; it is a sophisticated pipeline that converts a raw alert into a prioritized, actionable event in the hands of the correct on-call engineer. It must be built upon the unified knowledgebase, drawing on real-time topology and historical incident data to make intelligent decisions. *Table 4.2* details the essential components of a robust automated triage pipeline, emphasizing the shift from manual assessment to intelligent, data-driven prioritization:

Component	Description	Operational benefit
Alert to IRCA conversion	**Input**: High-volume raw alerts. **Output**: A single, correlated incident (IRCA) with noise reduction applied	Eliminates alert fatigue; ensures the SRE sees only the true incident
Context enrichment	Automatically attaches relevant data: deployment history, affected customer segments, owning team, and affected CI/CD commit	Provides the SRE with all necessary diagnostic context without manual searching
Intelligent severity assignment	Uses ML models to determine P0, P1, and P2 status based on real-time business impact (e.g., SLO breach of velocity, revenue impact)	Ensures prioritization aligns with business value and service criticality, not just technical metrics
Automated ticketing and handoff	Creates the incident ticket in the ITSM system (Jira, ServiceNow) and auto-pages the correct on-call rotation based on the owning service tag	Reduces TTE to near zero and ensures proper audit trail

Table 4.2: *Automated triage workflow components*

Intelligent severity and prioritization

Assigning the correct severity level is paramount. A misclassified incident can lead to either an unnecessarily disruptive PagerDuty escalation (P0 fatigue) or a delayed response to a critical, but under-labeled, failure. AIOps utilizes the following data points, beyond simple metric thresholds, to assign severity:

- **SLO impact**: The system checks whether the alert directly translates to a breach of a service's configured SLO (e.g., latency, availability). The velocity of the breach (how quickly the SLO is falling) can influence priority.
- **Business criticality**: By referencing the knowledgebase, the system understands the financial, legal, or customer-facing function of the affected service (e.g., the payment gateway is P0; the internal logging tool is P2).
- **Blast radius**: Using dependency mapping (*Chapter 3, AIOps Knowledgebase*), the system calculates the potential scope of failure, how many downstream services or critical user flows are currently or are likely to be impacted.

Initial automated actions and containment

A crucial step in automated triage is the execution of initial diagnostic or containment of runbooks. These are pre-approved, non-destructive actions triggered by the IRCA to gather data or halt the spread of the failure, buying the SRE precious time. The following list highlights common initial automated actions that accelerate resolution and contain damage:

- **Automated log and trace extraction**: Automatically pulls the last 60 seconds of verbose logs and the full trace of the failed requests from the affected service and attaches them directly to the incident ticket.
- **Snapshot and diagnostic dump**: Triggers a memory dump or thread dump from the affected process and moves the data to a secure storage location for later analysis, ensuring ephemeral evidence is captured before the system restarts.
- **Temporary resource scaling**: For simple capacity-related alerts, the system executes a minimal, temporary scale-out (e.g., add two instances) as a first-aid step to reduce load and prevent immediate cascading failure while the SRE investigates.
- **Isolation and fencing**: For failures in non-critical components, the system may isolate the failing instance or temporarily disable the feature flag associated with a recent deployment, effectively fencing the problem.

The combination of intelligent prioritization and automated containment radically reduces the incident lifecycle's diagnostic phase. *Figure 4.3* illustrates how this automated flow minimizes human intervention until the final resolution phase:

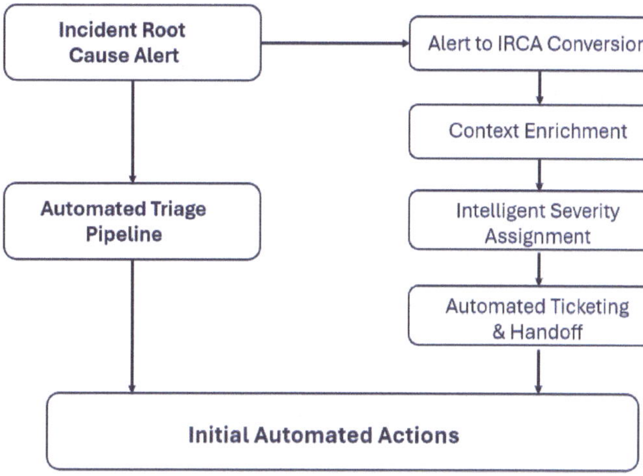

Figure 4.3: *Automated triage and containment flow*

Accelerating resolution with predictive models

While automated triage focuses on the immediate engagement and containment of an incident, the resolution phase, diagnosis, remediation planning, and execution remain the largest bottleneck to improving MTTR. This is where AIOps leverages predictive models and historical insight not just to flag a problem, but to tell the SRE how to fix it. This capability moves the SRE from hypothesis-driven investigation to evidence-based action.

Power of automated diagnostic hypotheses

The primary accelerator in the resolution phase is the AIOps engine's ability to generate an **automated diagnostic hypothesis** (ADH). This is a ranked list of the most probable root causes, complete with supporting evidence. Instead of the SRE spending 30 minutes sifting through dashboards, the ADH is presented instantly within the incident ticket.

Key models for diagnosis acceleration

The AIOps platform uses a combination of pattern matching and statistical modeling against the rich knowledge base to rapidly narrow down the cause of failure. *Table 4.4* outlines the advanced analytical models that power the ADH and provide the SRE with immediate, contextualized resolution guidance:

Model type	Input data	Diagnostic output
Change impact analysis	Deployment logs, configuration changes, topology data	Identifies recent changes that correlate exactly with the incident's start time (e.g., *Configuration file X was updated 3 minutes before the failure*)

Model type	Input data	Diagnostic output
Similarity-based matching	Current IRCA attributes, historical incident database	Matches the current failure pattern (telemetry spikes, error codes) to the most similar past incident and retrieves the successful remediation steps
Probabilistic graphical models (PGMs)	Service dependency graph, Telemetry flow data	Calculates the probability of failure propagation, highlighting the single component most likely to be the true origin based on causal dependencies
Log anomaly clustering	Unstructured log content	Groups rare or never-before-seen log messages that appeared immediately preceding the failure, flagging unique error signatures

Table 4.4*: Advanced models for ADH*

Prescriptive guidance and automated remediation

The highest level of resolution acceleration is achieved when the AIOps platform can move beyond diagnosis to prescriptive guidance, suggesting the exact fix, or even automated remediation, executing the fix itself.

Prescriptive guidance

When the ADH successfully matches the current incident to a historical one, the system can recommend the exact runbook or command that fixed the issue previously. *Figure 4.4* illustrates how this recommendation loop closes the incident faster by providing verified, historical solutions. This eliminates the second-guessing phase of incident management, moving immediately to a known, successful resolution path.

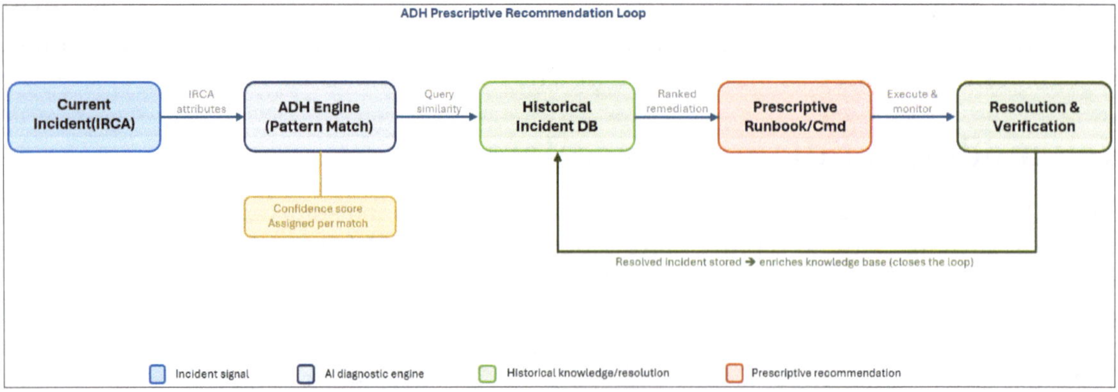

Figure 4.4*: ADH prescriptive recommendation loop*

Autonomous remediation

Autonomous remediation (self-healing) is reserved for known, low-risk, and high-frequency incident types (operational toil). It is the final, most advanced state of intelligent incident management, where the system itself acts to resolve the problem. The following list details categories of incidents suitable for safe, autonomous remediation:

- **Simple resource exhaustion**: Automatically restarting a process with a higher memory limit or scaling out a **Horizontal Pod Autoscaler** (**HPA**) when predictable capacity breaches are detected.
- **Transient network errors**: Automatically draining traffic from an unhealthy load balancer target and cycling the problematic instance (i.e., *rebooting* the container or VM).
- **Authentication or token expiration**: Automatically refreshing expired credentials or tokens for internal service-to-service communication.
- **Database connection leaks**: Executing a scheduled, rolling restart of the application tier to clear connection pools when the ADH flags a pool exhaustion warning.

Control and safety: **Autonomous remediation must always be built with robust guardrails, including: a strict rollback mechanism that reverts the action if the incident persists; rate limiting to prevent rapid-fire failure loops; and a human approval gate for any action touching customer data or critical infrastructure.**

Streamlining postmortems with data insights

The post-incident review, or postmortem, is arguably the most crucial step in the SRE lifecycle, as it transforms failure into durable knowledge and operational improvements. However, traditional postmortems are often delayed, subjective, and labor-intensive, requiring SREs to manually stitch together disparate logs, metrics, and communications timelines. AIOps fundamentally changes this by automating the creation of the postmortem draft, ensuring objectivity, accuracy, and efficiency. This process shifts the SRE's focus from data *gathering* to root cause *analysis* and action item *creation*.

Automated postmortem generation

The AIOps platform leverages the complete set of incident data, the initial IRCA, diagnostic snapshots, automated runbook executions, and the SRE's chat and ticket history to generate a comprehensive, structured draft. This automation relies on several key components:

- **Timeline reconstruction**: The system accurately reconstructs the full timeline of events, including detection time, triage start, initial containment action, resolution time, and verification. It uses the timestamps of all correlated telemetry and automated system actions, providing an objective record of the MTTR and associated metrics.

- **Narrative synthesis (NLP)**: Using NLP, the system processes the incident chat transcripts (Slack, Teams) and the ticket notes to synthesize a narrative description of *What happened*, *What the SRE thought*, and *What the SRE did*. This captures the human decision-making process alongside machine events.
- **Root cause identification evidence**: The ADH that led to resolution (from the previous section) is formally documented, along with the specific metrics, logs, or traces that validated the hypothesis. This provides the technical evidence required for a non-blaming, systems-based analysis.

Data-driven analysis of incident effectiveness

Beyond mere documentation, AIOps enable a deeper, data-driven analysis of the entire incident management process. This allows teams to identify systemic weaknesses in their own response procedures. *Table 4.5* outlines key metrics derived automatically by the AIOps platform for process improvement:

Metric	Calculation	Insight provided
Time to hypothesis (TTH)	Time from IRCA creation to the first use of the ADH/ runbook recommendation	Measures the efficiency of the diagnostic phase and the effectiveness of prescriptive guidance
Alert or incident recurrence rate	Multiple times, a specific IRCA signature has recurred within the last 90 days (about 3 months)	Highlights chronic toil and justifies investment in automated remediation or architectural fix projects
Containment effectiveness	Percentage of incidents where an initial automated action reduced severity or stopped the spread	Validates the effectiveness of automated runbooks and containment strategies
False positive ratio (FPR)	Ratio of correlated alerts that were eventually dismissed as non-incidents vs. confirmed incidents	Measures the maturity and accuracy of the alert correlation and probabilistic scoring models

Table 4.5: Key metrics for postmortem process improvement

Integrating learning into the knowledgebase

The final, and most crucial, step is closing the loop by ensuring the postmortem findings are fed back into the AIOps knowledgebase. This transforms the isolated failure into institutional intelligence, preventing future recurrences. The following actions are essential for integrating postmortem findings into the AIOps knowledgebase:

- **Model retraining and refinement**: If a new incident signature was observed, the correlation models (*Table 4.1*) are retrained with this new failure pattern. If a prediction fails, the predictive models (*Figure 4.2*) are updated.

- **Runbook automation**: If the SRE team performed a successful manual remediation, that sequence of steps is codified into a new automated runbook and flagged for potential autonomous remediation in the future.
- **Automatic remediation item tracking**: All future action items (e.g., *Increase capacity buffer, Refactor database query*) are automatically created and linked to the incident record, ensuring they become traceable work (error budget spend) rather than disappearing into a document.

Systemic pattern identification

While individual postmortems are valuable, the true power of AIOps lies in identifying patterns across hundreds of incidents over time. By applying clustering and topic modeling algorithms to the entire database of postmortems, AIOps can reveal systemic weaknesses that are invisible when looking at single events. The following highlights systemic patterns identified across multiple incidents:

- **Common failure modes**: Identifying that 40% of all P1 incidents in the last quarter stemmed from a specific shared library or a particular legacy database cluster, justifying a major architectural refactor.
- **Process bottlenecks**: Revealing that incidents involving Team X always have a 30% longer TTE due to unclear on-call handover procedures, prompting a process review.

Blameless learning culture

AIOps supports a blameless postmortem culture by providing objective data. When the timeline and root cause are derived from immutable telemetry and logs, discussions naturally shift away from *Who made the mistake?* to *How did the system allow this to happen?* This data-driven objectivity is essential for building the psychological safety required for high-performing SRE teams.

The automation of postmortem creation ensures that the process is not a burden but an immediate, objective exercise in continuous improvement. The resulting document is a starting point for discussion, not a compilation of evidence, enabling the team to focus entirely on why the incident occurred, rather than what happened. *Figure 4.5* visually represents how the postmortem process transforms incident data back into system knowledge, closing the AIOps feedback loop:

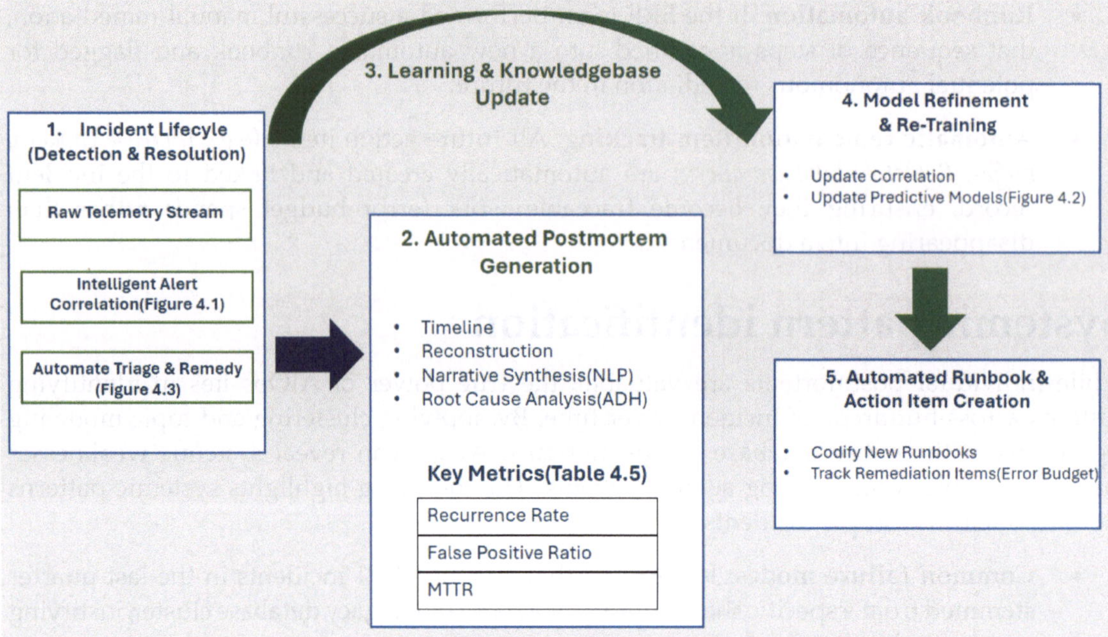

Figure 4.5: AIOps incident feedback loop

Practical workflows and real-world examples

The integration of intelligent incident management transforms abstract AIOps capabilities into tangible operational workflows that deliver massive value. This section details how these advanced concepts, alert correlation, predictive analysis, automated triage, and data-driven postmortems function together in real-world scenarios across different industries.

Workflow 1: Noise-free Network Operations Center

In many traditional enterprise organizations, the **Network Operations Center** (**NOC**) is the first line of defense, often overwhelmed by thousands of daily alerts, leading to high turnover and missed critical events. This workflow demonstrates how AIOps virtually eliminates this noise, allowing the NOC (or on-call SRE) to focus solely on actionable incidents. Key steps in achieving noise-free network operations include:

1. **Ingestion and intelligent suppression**: The AIOps platform ingests 50,000+ daily raw alerts from all monitoring tools (infrastructure, APM, logs, security). Initial filtering suppresses 95% of events: alerts below a P3 threshold, known as *flapping* metrics, and informational logs. This drastically cuts the input volume for complex correlation.
2. **Multi-dimensional correlation**: The remaining 2,500 alerts are processed by the multi-stage engine. *Topology-based grouping* links 500 downstream symptoms to 10 root-cause

services. *Time series clustering* identifies concurrent spikes. This results in 50 high-fidelity IRCAs.

3. **Probabilistic scoring and triage**: Each of the 50 IRCAs is scored for probabilistic severity (confidence score). 30 are deemed low-priority/low-confidence (<80%) and are automatically logged to Jira for day-shift review. 20 are deemed critical (P0/P1) with >95% confidence.

4. **Human engagement and context**: The on-call SRE receives exactly 20 pages per day, instead of thousands. Each page links to a confirmed IRCA, which automatically contains the ADH and relevant log/trace snippets.

Impact:

Alert fatigue is effectively eliminated. MTTE drops from an average of 30 minutes (spent shifting through noise) to <1 minute (immediate notification of a qualified, contextualized incident).

Workflow 2: Predictive auto-scaling for e-commerce

During high-traffic events (e.g., Black Friday flash sales), standard reactive auto-scaling often kicks in too late, leading to temporary 5xx errors, high latency, and lost revenue while new capacity spins up. This workflow utilizes predictive capacity modeling to preemptively manage load:

- **Forecast generation**: The AIOps predictive model, often utilizing the **Prophet** algorithm, analyzes historical traffic patterns, current user session velocity, and external factors (marketing spend, weather) to decompose the time series and build a highly accurate, short-term demand forecast.

- **Time-to-saturation (TTS) calculation**: The model tracks two critical saturation metrics: checkout-service CPU utilization and the global *database connection pool utilization*. It calculates that based on the current acceleration of traffic, the connection pool will hit 95% utilization in exactly 15 minutes, a hard failure threshold.

- **Preemptive action**: Instead of waiting for a reactive threshold to trigger, the AIOps platform initiates a pre-approved, automated runbook: scale-out for preemptive capacity. This action adds 50 new application nodes and increases the database connection pool limit *now*, 15 minutes before the failure occurs.

- **Verification and rollback guardrail**: The system monitors health, verifying that CPU utilization and pool utilization remain below the safe operating buffer (e.g., 60%). If the deployment of new nodes had failed or introduced a regression, a *rollback mechanism* would be triggered automatically.

Impact:

Zero customer-facing latency or errors during the peak traffic event. The potential incident was entirely prevented through foresight, resulting in 100% successful checkout completion during the critical surge.

Workflow 3: Automated remediation of recurring phantom failures

Transient, hard-to-reproduce failures (often called *phantom* or *ghost* bugs) plague distributed systems and consume vast amounts of SRE operational time (toil) in fruitless investigations. This workflow uses autonomous remediation to handle them efficiently while long-term fixes are built. The following workflow demonstrates automated remediation for recurring phantom failures:

- **Pattern detection (CBR)**: The AIOps engine uses **case-based reasoning** (**CBR**) to identify a recurring pattern: Service X throws HTTP 500 errors (10% rate) for exactly two minutes every day at 3:15 AM UTC, then mysteriously recovers. The system matches this signature to a known historical pattern involving a concurrent database batch job (ID 412).
- **ADH**: The ADH confirms with 92% confidence that the root cause is a brief, shared table lock contention caused by Batch Job 412 and recommends the established remediation: rate-limiting the job.
- **Autonomous fix implementation**: Since this is a proven, low-risk fix, the AIOps platform executes a temporary autonomous remediation policy: *If this specific error pattern occurs at 3:15 AM, immediately throttle Batch Job 412's query rate by 50% for 5 minutes.*
- **Guardrail and rollback**: The system executes the throttle. The error rate drops to <1% within seconds. The guardrail ensures that if the error rate had *increased* after throttling, the system would immediately halt the automated action and page a human (fail-safe).

Impact:

A recurring daily P3 incident is permanently resolved without requiring any human intervention or waking up an on-call engineer, eliminating 100% of the associated toil and freeing up SRE time for the necessary long-term refactor.

Workflow 4: Data-driven postmortem acceleration

Traditionally, generating a postmortem timeline is a manual, multi-hour effort. This workflow demonstrates how AIOps creates a complete, objective draft instantly upon incident closure, shifting the SRE's focus from data gathering to root cause analysis. The postmortem acceleration workflow consists of these critical steps:

1. **Incident closure and trigger**: When the SRE resolves and closes the P0 incident ticket, the AIOps platform automatically triggers the postmortem generation workflow.
2. **Objective timeline reconstruction**: The system queries the unified telemetry (logs, metrics, traces) and system action logs (HPA scale-outs, runbook executions). It generates a millisecond-accurate timeline, including Detection (10:00:00), IRCA Created (10:00:01), Automated Containment Action (10:00:15), Human Engaged (10:05:00), and Resolution Verified (10:45:00).
3. **Narrative and decision synthesis (NLP)**: The platform utilizes NLP to analyze the internal incident chat room transcripts (Slack/Teams). It extracts key human decisions (*We decided to roll back the config change based on the ADH*) and synthesizes the narrative section of the draft, adding crucial human context.
4. **Automatic action item creation**: The platform reviews the final root cause and the suggested permanent fix from the resolution phase. It automatically creates a structured, high-priority work item in Jira (or the engineering backlog) titled *Permanent Fix: Refactor Cache Invalidation for Service X* and links it to the postmortem document.

Impact:

Postmortem draft time is reduced from 4 to 6 hours to <5 minutes. The resulting document is objective, comprehensive, and immediately actionable, accelerating the crucial learning loop and ensuring remediation is tracked.

Real-world industry examples

Real-world industry applications of intelligent incident management include:

- **FinTech**: A global bank used AIOps to correlate alerts across its legacy mainframe and modern cloud environments. By using semantic correlation (NLP) to link obscure mainframe error codes (e.g., ABEND=U1002) with modern APM alerts (e.g., Payment Processor Service Timeout), they reduced the average MTTR for hybrid-cloud payment processing failures from 4 hours to just 20 minutes, saving millions in potential SLA penalties and regulatory fines. The NLP model successfully generalized the errors despite massive differences in underlying system technology.
- **Media Streaming**: A major video streaming provider utilizes Multivariate Anomaly Detection across its global **content delivery network** (**CDN**) and streaming microservices. The model was trained to identify the combination of *high CPU* on the regional caching layer, coupled with a *drop in outbound network I/O*, which signaled a silent internal processing stall. By detecting this subtle anomaly *before* it triggered a customer-facing threshold, the system automatically rerouted user traffic to healthy CDN nodes, preventing buffering issues for millions of concurrent viewers during major live events.

- **Logistics**: A global shipping company suffered from alert fatigue related to its 500+ microservices. The original triage process took 15 minutes just to identify which service owned the failure. With topology-based correlation, the root failing service is identified instantly by tracing the alert cascade back to the upstream component in the dependency graph. This accelerated the initial diagnosis and ensured the correct product team was paged automatically, reducing the initial **time-to-diagnose** (**TTD**) phase by over 90% and drastically improving on-call morale.

Conclusion

This chapter demonstrated that the future of SRE is not about being faster at firefighting but about eliminating the fire altogether. By applying AIOps techniques to the incident management lifecycle, SRE teams achieve a radical operational transformation. The journey begins with the correlation engine, which leverages topology, time series clustering, and semantic analysis to transform thousands of noisy, symptomatic alerts into a handful of high-fidelity, actionable IRCAs. This shift instantly reduces cognitive load and cuts the MTTE to near zero.

Moving beyond reaction, we explored predictive analysis, showing how dynamic baselining, capacity forecasting, and multivariate anomaly detection provide SREs with critical lead time, allowing them to transform potential P0 outages into planned, low-stress operational tasks. Once an incident is confirmed, automated triage and prescriptive guidance, powered by ADH, accelerate resolution, moving the SRE immediately from diagnosis to remediation execution.

Finally, we established that the postmortem is the cornerstone of the AIOps feedback loop. By automating the timeline reconstruction and narrative synthesis and systematically tracking key metrics like TTH and recurrence rate, we ensure that every failure generates durable system knowledge, driving continuous improvement and reducing future toil.

The goal of intelligent incident management is to achieve a state of operational flow where the system self-heals the known and flags the novel. However, the vast majority of severe incidents are still triggered by human error. Therefore, the ultimate barrier to reliability is the management of code deployments, configuration updates, and infrastructure shifts.

The next chapter will bridge the gap between incident response and proactive engineering by focusing on the management of change and problem lifecycle. We will explore how to apply AIOps models to the CI/CD pipeline, turning the most dangerous operational activity into the most controlled. This includes techniques for assessing change risk with AIOps models and predicting the impact of a change on SLOs, thereby making every deployment safer, predictable, and fully traceable.

CHAPTER 5
Streamlining Change and Problem Management

Introduction

Change is the single greatest cause of service instability in modern distributed systems. While SRE's strive for rapid feature delivery, they must simultaneously be the ultimate safeguard against regression. The classic dilemma is choosing between velocity and stability. This chapter argues that with AIOps, this is a false dichotomy. By embedding ML models directly into the **continuous integration/continuous deployment** (**CI/CD**) pipeline, SRE teams can transform the change process from a high-risk activity into a continuous, verified, and safe operation. We will move beyond simply detecting incidents to proactively predicting and preventing them at the source: the moment code or configuration is deployed. This involves assessing the risk of every change, mathematically predicting its impact on customer-facing SLOs, and accelerating the problem management lifecycle by automating root cause identification. Readers will learn how to leverage the unified knowledgebase (discussed in *Chapter 3, AIOps Knowledgebase*) to make change an accelerant for growth, not a source of fear.

Structure

In this chapter, we will cover the following topics:

- Assessing change risk with AIOps models
- Change impact prediction with SLOs analysis
- Rapid problem resolution with automation
- Making change safer and predictable
- Integrating AIOps in CI/CD

Objectives

By the end of this chapter, readers will master the techniques required to integrate AIOps into their deployment and problem management pipelines. This includes learning how to quantify the risk of any code or configuration change, forecast its downstream effects on service reliability, implement automated **continuous verification** (**CV**) to prevent failed changes from reaching customers, and utilize ML-driven insights to drastically reduce the time spent on formal problem investigation.

Assessing change risk with AIOps models

The goal of modern SRE is CV; the practice of mathematically evaluating the health and quality of every deployment in real-time. This is fundamentally different from traditional post-deployment checks (like basic smoke tests), which are often insufficient in complex, interdependent environments. The primary tool for CV is the **change risk score** (**CRS**), an AI-generated metric that quantifies the probability that a specific change will lead to a service degradation or incident.

Change risk score

The CRS is a composite score, typically a numerical value between 0 and 100, calculated by a supervised machine learning model (e.g., a random forest or gradient boosting machine) trained on historical deployment data. A score of 95, for instance, means the current change carries a 95% probability of causing a P1 or P0 incident. The model inputs a diverse set of deployment metadata and compares it against past successful and failed deployments.

Key input features for the CRS model

The accuracy of the CRS relies on feeding the model a rich, contextual dataset that goes far beyond simple pass or fail tests. The following categories represent the most critical features used to train a robust **change risk model** (**CRM**):

- **Change metrics (The What):**
    - **Size of change:** The number of files modified, lines of code added, and **lines of code deleted** (**LOCD**). Historically, larger changes have a higher correlation with failure.
    - **Complexity:** The cyclomatic complexity of the modified code sections, indicating the number of independent paths through the code.
    - **Test coverage:** The percentage of code paths covered by unit, integration, and end-to-end tests associated with the commit.
    - **Service tier:** The criticality of the service being deployed (Tier 1 customer-facing vs. Tier 3 internal tool).
    - **Configuration vs. code**: A categorical feature distinguishing between **infrastructure as code** (**IaC**) changes and application code changes, as they often correlate with different failure modes.

- **Author and team metrics (The Who):**
  - **Author experience:** A composite metric based on the change author's history (e.g., success rate of their last ten deployments; number of incidents they have triggered). This must be handled carefully to avoid *blame* metrics and focus solely on statistical contribution to risk.
  - **Team history:** The historical MTTR and incident recurrence rate for the owning team's service.
  - **Review depth:** The number of reviewers and the average time spent reviewing the **pull request** (**PR**). Reviews are a key human signal that can be weighted by the seniority of the reviewer.
- **Environment and topology metrics (The Where and When):**
  - **Blast radius:** The number of downstream services and customer segments relying on the component being changed (derived from the topology map). A change to a core utility service that affects 50 downstream services automatically receives a higher risk weighting.
  - **Deployment timing:** Deployments made outside of normal business hours or during known peak traffic periods (e.g., Fridays at 4:30 PM) are often penalized with a higher risk score.
  - **Pre-deployment health:** The real-time health score of the target cluster *prior* to deployment. Deploying into an environment that is already showing minor signs of instability (high memory usage, elevated disk I/O) significantly increases risk.

Training and evaluation of the CRS model

The CRS model is a binary classification problem: *Will the deployment succeed (0) or fail (1)?*

These four steps form the core training and validation pipeline, ensuring the CRS is grounded in observable deployment outcomes and continually improved through real-world feedback:

1. **Labeling data**: The training data must be accurately labeled. A deployment is labeled *failed* if a P1 or P0 incident or an SLO violation was triggered within a defined window (e.g., 60 minutes) of the deployment event.
2. **Feature engineering**: This is the most critical step. SRE teams must collaborate with data science to create meaningful features, such as change concentration (ratio of code changes to total lines in the file) or recent failure proximity (number of failed deployments in the last 24 hours in the affected service cluster).
3. **Model selection:** Gradient boosting machines (like XGBoost or LightGBM) are often preferred for their ability to handle diverse feature types (numerical, categorical) and their interpretability. The model's output, a probability, becomes the CRS.

4. **Evaluation:** The model is evaluated on its precision (avoiding false positives, unnecessarily blocking a good change) and recall (avoiding false negatives, missing a bad change). SREs must set the operational threshold (e.g., CRS > 75 requires a manual review) based on the business's tolerance for false positives versus catastrophic failure.

5. **Training data:** Ingest postdeployment outcomes and human reviews (P1 / P0 incidents, SLO violations, rollbacks, overrides) as labeled examples, store them with deployment metadata and computed features, and trigger periodic or driftdriven retraining so the CRS adapts to new failure modes.

The overall architecture of the CRS model, including its diverse inputs and probabilistic output, is illustrated in the following figure:

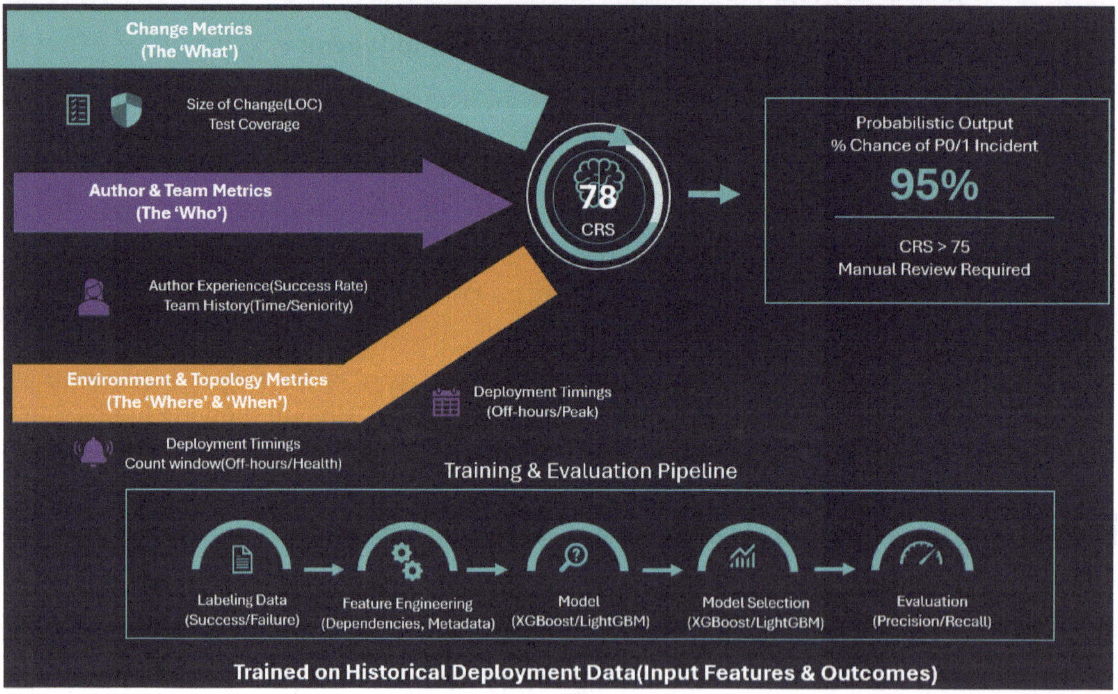

Figure 5.1: The CRS architecture

Change impact prediction with SLO analysis

The goal of change management is to ensure that a new deployment does not violate a customer-facing SLO. AIOps achieves this through predictive SLO modeling, forecasting the service's reliability metrics (latency, error rate, availability) *after* the change is applied.

Predictive service level objective model

This specialized model uses historical metric data and the calculated CRS to predict the outcome. It answers the question: *If we deploy this change, what is the expected error rate for the next 60 minutes?*

The predictive SLO model operates through the following key steps:

1. **Baseline definition:** The model first establishes the normal operating bounds of the SLO metric (e.g., 99th percentile latency must be below 200ms). This includes dynamic baselining that accounts for time-of-day and day-of-week seasonality (discussed in *Chapter 4, Intelligent Incident Management for SREs*).
2. **Impact simulation:** When a new change is introduced, the model correlates the change's feature set with similar historical changes that resulted in an SLO violation. If a change involves a new database query (a high-risk feature), the model finds historical examples where new database queries increased latency.
3. **Future state projection:** Using techniques like time series forecasting (e.g., Exponential Smoothing or Prophet), the model projects the metric forward, incorporating the predicted impact of the change. The output is a probability distribution: *There is an 80% chance the 99th percentile latency will spike above 300ms in the first 15 minutes.*

This projection is then used as a Go/No-Go signal. If the projected SLO violation exceeds a predetermined threshold, the deployment is automatically paused or rejected before any user is impacted.

Role of canary analysis and continuous verification

Canary analysis, which involves rolling out a new version to a small subset of users or infrastructure, serves as the fundamental safety mechanism in modern deployment strategies. This approach allows organizations to limit exposure by carefully monitoring the effects of a change on a controlled segment before broadening its reach.

AIOps elevates the traditional canary process by converting it from a straightforward A/B test into a system of continuous, intelligent verification. This enhancement enables real-time assessment and validation of changes, ensuring that any adverse impacts are detected and addressed promptly, thereby safeguarding overall service reliability.

Smart canary analysis

Traditional canary analysis relies on simple threshold checks (e.g., *If error rate > 0.5%, fail*). AIOps introduces multi-dimensional, statistical verification:

- **Statistical significance:** Instead of just comparing raw error rates, AIOps uses statistical hypothesis testing (like the t-test or Mann-Whitney U test) to determine if the difference in error rates between the old version (baseline) and the new version (canary) is *statistically significant* and not just random noise. A small but statistically significant increase in latency is often a better signal of an issue than a large, brief, non-significant spike.

- **Multivariate comparison:** The model simultaneously monitors dozens of metrics across the two groups (CPU usage, database connection volume, specific business-level metrics like checkout conversion rate), looking for a subtle degradation across a complex feature set. This prevents issues like a slow memory leak that might not trip a single-metric threshold but appears as a significant, albeit small, increase across CPU, memory, and GC activity.
- **Automated verification:** The system continuously compares the canary against the baseline. If the canary's performance deviates from the baseline's dynamic operating range by more than a statistically significant margin (e.g., a two-sigma deviation from the norm) for more than a defined duration, it immediately triggers an automated failure and rollback.

The resulting workflow is entirely self-regulating. The change is deployed to the canary, monitored intelligently, scored for risk, and either promoted or rolled back, all without human intervention. The smart canary analysis process is visualized in the following figure:

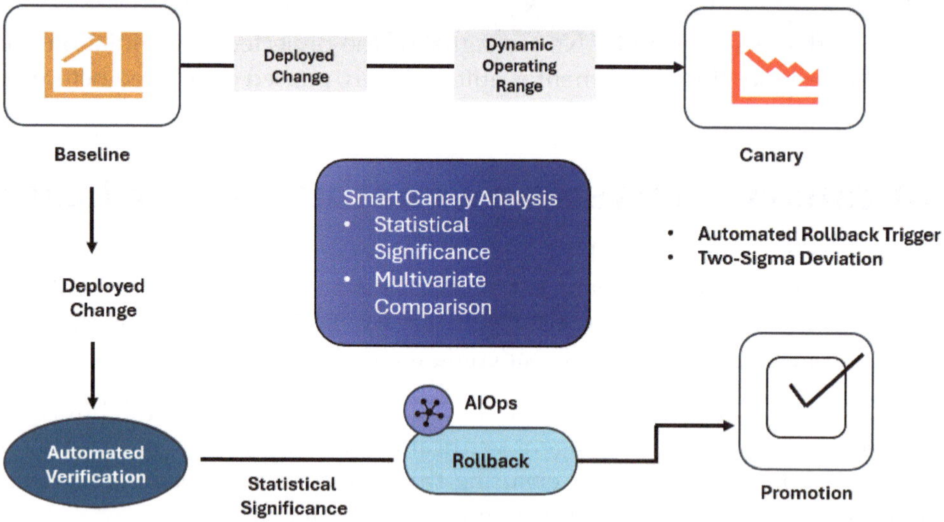

Figure 5.2: Role of canary analysis and CV

Predicting the impact of a change in SLOs

To move beyond reactive monitoring, SRE teams must anticipate system degradation caused by changes. Predicting the impact of a change on SLOs requires linking deployment events to service behavior in a mathematically rigorous way.

Causal inference for change management

Causal inference is a branch of statistics and machine learning that aims to establish cause-and-effect relationships, rather than just correlations. This is crucial for change management. While two events (Deployment X and Incident Y) may correlate in time, causal inference aims to prove that Deployment X caused Incident Y.

Causal inference for change management involves the following key approaches:

- **Intervention analysis:** The deployment itself is treated as an intervention in the time series data. By analyzing the time series of the SLO metric (e.g., latency) immediately before and after the intervention, statistical models can quantify the effect of the change, distinguishing it from general system noise or cyclical trends. The causal impact method (based on Bayesian structural time series models - decompose a series into interpretable components (trend, seasonality, regressors) and use Bayesian inference to produce probabilistic forecasts and causalimpact estimates) is a powerful tool here, allowing the system to estimate the counterfactual: what the metric would have been without the intervention.
- **Synthetic controls:** For highly critical services where even canary tests are risky, a *synthetic control group* can be established. This involves creating a control metric (a synthetic time series) composed of a weighted average of other unaffected service metrics. This synthetic control provides the model with a perfect counterfactual: *What would the metric have looked like if we had not deployed?* Comparing the actual post-deployment metric to the synthetic control provides a clean measure of the change's true impact.

Capacity forecasting

A specific, high-risk type of change is one that impacts resource efficiency, such as deploying a new, less efficient algorithm or a configuration change that increases logging verbosity. AIOps models can predict the future capacity needs resulting from such a change. The capacity forecasting model addresses resource efficiency through the following key steps:

- **Efficiency degradation detection:** During the canary phase, the model compares the resource consumption per unit of work (e.g., CPU-seconds per transaction, memory per session) between the baseline and the canary. If the canary requires 15% more CPU for the same workload, the model immediately flags an efficiency degradation.
- **Forecast adjustment:** This 15% degradation factor is then fed into the long-term capacity forecast (discussed in *Chapter 4, Intelligent Incident Management for SREs*). The model recalculates the TTS. What was previously predicted to be a 90-day buffer is now revised to a 60-day buffer.
- **Proactive problem ticket:** An automated problem ticket is created. *New deployment v5.1 introduced a 15% efficiency penalty, requiring a planned scale-up in 60 days unless a*

refactor is deployed. This preempts a future capacity incident and drives engineering action to either optimize the code or plan for infrastructure growth.

Rapid problem resolution with automation

In SRE, problem management is the process of finding the ultimate root cause of recurring incidents, documenting it, and ensuring a permanent fix is engineered. AIOps accelerates this process by automating the most labor-intensive phases: clustering similar incidents and automating the collection of deep diagnostic evidence.

Automated root cause discovery

The first step in problem management is recognizing that multiple, seemingly disparate incidents are symptoms of a single underlying flaw. This is the shift from reactive incident response to proactive problem management. The incident clustering process identifies underlying problems through the following key steps:

1. **Clustering by attributes and content:** The AIOps platform uses unsupervised machine learning (e.g., k-means clustering or **Density-Based Spatial Clustering of Applications with Noise** (**DBSCAN**)) to group all historical incidents (IRCAs) based on shared attributes (service, failure type). Crucially, it leverages the semantic similarity of the log and trace data. Logs that share common stack traces or error messages are clustered together, even if they happened on different days or affected different service instances. For log content, advanced NLP techniques, such as word embeddings or transformer models, convert noisy, variable log messages into dense, numeric vectors. Clustering algorithms then operate on these vectors, grouping messages with similar underlying meaning (e.g., grouping different variations of a *database connection failed* error).

2. **Recurrence rate and toil quantification:** The system calculates the recurrence rate for each cluster (e.g., *Cluster X, related to AuthService database lock contention, has occurred 15 times in the last 60 days*). AIOps goes further than just tracking frequency by measuring the overall toil of the cluster, which includes total resolution time and the amount of human effort involved. This allows SRE teams to focus on issues that consume most of their time. Any cluster that exceeds a high-frequency or toil threshold is automatically promoted from a recurring incident cluster to a formal problem candidate.

3. **Automatic problem ticket creation:** A centralized problem management ticket (in Jira or ServiceNow) is automatically generated for the problem candidate. This ticket automatically links all underlying incident tickets and contains a synthesized summary of the common failure signature and the potential toil cost associated with the cluster. This formally moves the issue from *firefighting* to an *engineering project*.

Problem root cause signatures and automated RCA

Problem root cause signatures (PRCS) is a set of machine-learned features that uniquely identify the underlying weakness responsible for a cluster of incidents. The PRCS is automatically stored in the AIOps knowledgebase (discussed in *Chapter 3, AIOps Knowledgebase*). The role of the problem manager shifts from being a detective to an auditor and prioritizer. The extraction of PRCS is accomplished through the following key steps:

1. **Signature extraction:** The ML model extracts the most predictive log lines, metric thresholds, and configuration states common to all incidents in the cluster. This is often achieved through feature importance analysis on the cluster data. For example: *[Log Signature: 'connection pool timeout: max connections reached'] + [Metric Threshold: 'DB_Connections > 95%'] + [Config State: 'max_pool_size = 50']*

2. **Knowledgebase update and preemptive check:** The PRCS is stored as a canonical problem record. When a new deployment occurs, the CRS model now checks against the PRCS knowledgebase; if the proposed configuration change reintroduces a known PRCS, the CRS score is heavily penalized, creating a direct feedback loop from problem management to change prevention.

3. **Prescriptive problem investigation and automated hypothesis:** If a match is found, the system provides prescriptive guidance to the problem manager. This includes a fully synthesized, structured RCA hypothesis. The system automatically performs a *counterfactual analysis*, often yielding a hypothesis like:

    a. **Hypothesis**: The underlying cause is a resource leak (memory/connection) due to an incorrect disposal pattern in module X.

    b. **Supporting evidence**: Average memory utilization for this service instance increased 15% faster during incident windows, and the fix in the last IRCA was the *restart process 4 times* (a temporary relief measure).

    For instance, the most common fix was *restart process 4 times*, suggesting a memory leak or connection leak as the underlying problem. The recommended diagnostic action is to deploy an instrumented version of the code to capture thread dumps upon failure and compare the GC_Pause_Time metric against the PRCS threshold. This eliminates guesswork and speeds up the final RCA delivery, reducing **mean time to problem identification** (**MTTPI**) from weeks to minutes.

    The relationship between automated incident clustering, PRCS generation, and the final problem ticket creation is illustrated in the workflow is shown in the following figure:

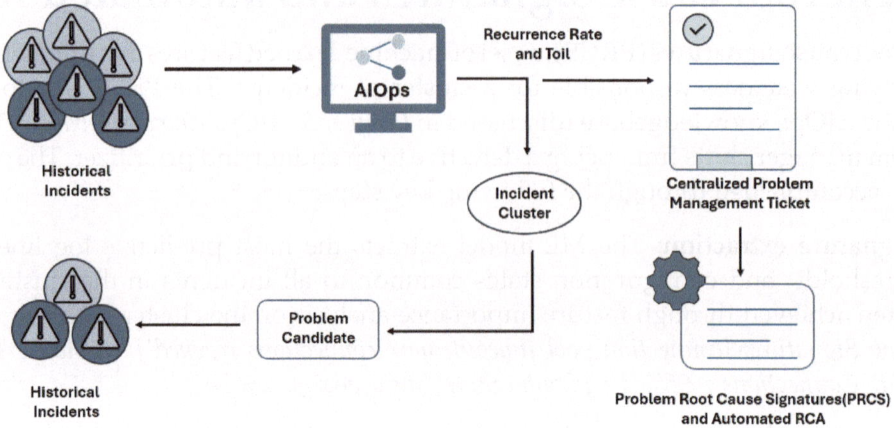

Figure 5.3: Automated incident clustering for problem identification

Making change safer and predictable

The integration of AIOps models into the software delivery pipeline creates a safety net that enforces engineering reliability standards, making change safer, predictable, and fully automated. This is achieved through advanced control mechanisms, not just monitoring.

Progressive deployment strategies

While canary analysis is essential, modern AIOps integrates with advanced deployment strategies, collectively known as progressive delivery, to manage risk at a granular level. The goal is to maximize the time spent validating a change while minimizing the exposure to failure. Modern AIOps enhances deployment safety and efficiency through the following progressive delivery techniques:

- **Intelligent traffic shaping and ramp rate:** AIOps determines the ideal sample size for the canary rollout based on the CRS and the service's traffic patterns. A high-risk change might start with a 0.1% rollout and a 30-minute verification window, whereas a low-risk change might jump straight to 5% with a 15-minute window. AIOps continuously monitors the verification metrics and dynamically adjusts the *ramp rate,* the speed at which traffic is shifted, if initial performance indicators are stable.

- **Shadowing (Dark canary deployments):** For the highest criticality services, AIOps enables shadowing. This technique duplicates a fraction of live production traffic and routes it to the new (shadow) version, while the results from the shadow environment are discarded and never returned to the customer. AIOps monitors the shadow environment's behavior against the production baseline (e.g., latency, error rate, resource consumption). If the shadow version shows significantly degraded performance, the deployment is blocked *before* any live traffic is committed, providing a risk-free, real-world stress test.

- **Feature flag integration:** A major source of risk is deploying unreleased code. Integrating the AIOps platform with feature flag systems allows for the deployment of code that is *off* by default. The AIOps system can then control the gradual *flag enablement*, not just the deployment, using the CV checks. If performance degrades when a flag is enabled, the system automatically disables the flag (a flag rollback), which is often faster and less disruptive than a full code rollback.

Configuration management challenge

Configuration changes (modifying environment variables, database connection pools, cloud resource definitions via IaC) are often more hazardous than code changes because they bypass traditional unit tests and directly impact the runtime environment. AIOps addresses this with specialized validation:

- **Configuration risk score (CRSC):** A subset of the CRS model is trained specifically on configuration changes. The CRSC penalizes changes that violate known operational constraints, such as setting low connection pool limits or configuring an aggressive garbage collection schedule that historically caused high CPU churn.
- **Drift detection and remediation:** Systems are prone to configuration drift, where the actual running state deviates from the declared desired state (the Git repository). AIOps continuously compares the real-time configuration of running instances against the source of truth (e.g., Git). When drift is detected, the system automatically opens a problem ticket for the SRE team and can optionally trigger an automated reconciliation (re-applying the desired state) if the deviation is non-compliant with security or reliability standards.

Continuous verification and automated rollbacks

The ultimate safety mechanism is the automated rollback. If the CV process detects a statistically significant degradation in the canary environment, the deployment process must halt immediately and revert the change.

To ensure this automated safety trigger is effective and aligned with business goals, the AIOps platform defines a robust set of explicit, measurable, and objective rollback criteria based on the CRS and the predictive SLO model. These criteria fall into four main categories:

- **Rollback criteria:** The AIOps platform defines explicit, measurable, and objective rollback criteria based on the CRS and the predictive SLO model. Examples are:
    - **Hard failure:** Any new deployment that generates a P0/P1 IRCA.

- **SLO violation:** The canary environment's 99th percentile latency deviates by more than 2-sigma(denotes a deviation of two standard deviations from the baseline dynamic mean) from the baseline's dynamic mean for five consecutive minutes.
- **Efficiency degradation:** The resource consumption per transaction increases by more than 10% during the first 15 minutes of the canary, threatening TTS.
- **Log signature match:** New logs generated by the canary match a known PRCS, indicating a known, recurring flaw has been reintroduced.

- **State verification prior to rollback:** Before initiating a rollback, the AIOps system executes a *pre-rollback state verification*. This is a final check to ensure the target's previous version, the **last known good state** (**LKGS**), is still healthy, confirming that the rollback itself will not revert to a previously broken state or into an environment that has since been modified by an independent infrastructure change.
- **Automated execution:** Upon meeting any defined failure criterion, the AIOps platform triggers an immediate, unprompted rollback command to the orchestrator (Kubernetes, AWS CodeDeploy, etc.), reverting the service to the last known good state. For flag-based verification, a feature flag disablement is the primary remediation.
- **Automated validation:** Post rollback, perform automated health checks and synthetic transactions to confirm critical user flows and API behavior. Ensure key SLOs and metrics, latency percentiles, error rates, and throughput, have returned to baseline within the defined verification window. Emit a definitive pass/fail signal only after all validations succeed, and persist logs, traces, and metric snapshots for audit.
- **Human notification:** The SRE is notified of the *successful rollback*, including the reason for failure (e.g., *Rollback executed: P99 latency failed 2-sigma check on CartService*). This informs them that the automated system prevented the incident and provides them with immediate context for the fix.

By automating the rollback, SRE teams ensure that the impact of failure is minimized to the short duration of the canary test, preventing the fault from ever reaching the general user population. This transforms deployment failure from a massive incident into a small, contained engineering setback.

Integrating AIOps in CI/CD

The technical models and statistical checks discussed are only effective if they are seamlessly integrated into the existing CI/CD pipeline. This requires treating the AIOps platform as a mandatory gating service.

Pipeline gates for change verification

In a typical CI/CD pipeline (e.g., Jenkins, GitLab CI, GitHub Actions), AIOps verification is implemented as distinct, mandatory stages:

1. **Pre-commit (CRS Gate):** Before the merge to the main branch or before deployment to staging, the AIOps service is called with the metadata of the change.
   - **Action**: `AIOPS_Service.check_risk(change_metadata)`
   - **Result**: Returns the CRS. If *CRS > 75* (High risk threshold), the pipeline is halted, and a manual review by an SRE is required. If *CRS < 40* (Low risk threshold), the change proceeds directly.
2. **Post-canary (SLO Gate):** Immediately after the deployment to the canary cluster, the AIOps service initiates the CV loop.
   - **Action**: `AIOPS_Service.verify_canary(deployment_id, baseline_metrics)`
   - **Result**: The service monitors the metrics for 15 to 60 minutes. If the statistical verification fails (e.g., statistically significant SLO degradation), the AIOps system calls the orchestrator **application programming interface** (**API**) to initiate a rollback and fails the pipeline step. If successful, it returns a *Go* signal to the pipeline orchestrator, which then promotes the change to the next ring (e.g., 20% rollout).

Architectural integration via webhooks and APIs

The AIOps platform rarely runs inside the CI/CD runner itself. Instead, it operates as an external, highly scalable microservice that the CI/CD pipeline calls synchronously. This architectural separation ensures that the complex ML computation and large data queries do not slow down the core deployment process. Integration between the AIOps platform and the CI/CD pipeline is achieved through the following key mechanisms:

- **RESTful API calls:** The core integration is handled by simple POST requests from the CI/CD tool to the AIOps API endpoint. For the *CRS Gate*, the payload includes the unique Commit ID, Service ID, Author ID, and the change manifest (e.g., number of changed files). The AIOps service immediately returns a JSON response containing the calculated CRS_Score and the mandatory action (e.g., PASS, HALT, or MANUAL_REVIEW).
- **Asynchronous verification (SLO Gate):** The *SLO Gate* is asynchronous. When the canary is deployed, the pipeline sends a request to the AIOps service to start monitoring. The CI/CD job then enters a waiting state, polling the AIOps service every minute. The AIOps service (which is independently querying the observability platform) updates the deployment status. If the verification fails and a rollback is executed, the AIOps

service sets the status to FAILED_AND_ROLLED_BACK, causing the pipeline to fail gracefully.

- **Kubernetes and orchestrator integration:** For automated rollback, the AIOps service must hold API credentials for the target orchestration system (e.g., Kubernetes, Spinnaker, ArgoCD). Upon verification failure, the AIOps service acts as the orchestrator itself, executing the necessary rollout undo or equivalent command against the cluster, ensuring the fastest possible reversal without waiting for the CI/CD pipeline to complete its polling cycle.

Governance and compliance enforcement

A major benefit of AIOps gating is that it enforces consistency and compliance across hundreds of disparate development teams, turning subjective risk assessment into a quantified policy:

- **Policy-as-code (PaC) enforcement:** The CRS and SLO threshold values are defined in a central policy repository, often managed as code (YAML or JSON). This ensures that rules like *No change with CRS > 80 can deploy to Production between 23:00 and 07:00* and are automatically enforced by the AIOps service, eliminating human error or willful deviation from SRE best practices.

- **Mandatory auditing and record keeping:** Every deployment event, including the calculated CRS, the SLO verification result, the human override flag, and the eventual success/failure label, is logged to an immutable audit trail. This is critical for regulatory compliance (e.g., HIPAA, SOC 2), as it provides an indisputable record that every change went through an automated, intelligent verification process that mitigated risk.

- **Security scanning integration:** The AIOps change management system can integrate with security tools (SAST/DAST) during the pre-commit phase. If the CRS detects high-risk features in the code (e.g., file system access, high-privilege configuration changes), it can automatically trigger an advanced security scan, adding a layer of intelligent defense only when the risk profile warrants it, thus avoiding scanning all low-risk changes and speeding up the pipeline.

Human-in-the-loop strategy

While AIOps enforces safety, it does not remove human oversight. The goal is to maximize the time engineers spend on novel, strategic work, not routine verification. **Human-in-the-loop (HIL)** is deployed strategically only when the automated system requires higher-level decision-making or when a high-risk change warrants explicit liability transfer. The HIL strategy manifests in three core modes of operation:

- **Zero-touch deployments:** For changes with a low CRS and successful SLO verification, the deployment should be fully automated end-to-end, requiring zero human interaction. This is where SREs derive massive toil reduction.

- **Human reviewer override:** The high-CRS changes (*CRS > 75*) are flagged for mandatory SRE review. This ensures that a human expert assesses the novel complexity of the change, perhaps overriding the AI's concern if the change is known to be structurally necessary (e.g., a critical database schema migration). The SRE is accountable for the override decision, maintaining the necessary cultural focus on reliability. The system records the SRE's name, timestamp, and justification for the override, creating a clear line of accountability for future IRCA analysis.

- **Decision support:** For medium-risk changes (CRS 40 to 75), the AIOps system does not halt the deployment, but instead provides *decision support*. It might surface a non-blocking warning: *Warning: This change has a CRS of 62 due to high LOCD. Proceeding, but the verification window increased to 45 minutes, and the rollout percentage was capped at 10%*. This informs the engineer without impeding velocity.

AIOps feedback loop and governance

The effectiveness of an AIOps system hinges on its ability to learn and adapt through a continuous feedback mechanism. This process transforms deployment outcomes into refined intelligence, making future operations safer and more efficient. The following points detail the essential components of the AIOps feedback loop and governance that ensure the CRS model and its supporting knowledge bases remain accurate and powerful:

- **Labeling automation:** After every deployment finishes (whether promoted successfully or rolled back), the AIOps platform automatically checks the incident management system. If a P0/P1 incident or SLO Burnout (from *Chapter 4, Intelligent Incident Management for SREs*) occurred within the subsequent hour, the deployment is automatically labeled as *Failure*. If no such incident occurred, it is labeled as *Success*.

- **Model retraining trigger:** The collected stream of labeled data (change metadata + success/failure label) is the fuel for the CRS model. The model is retrained on a defined cadence (e.g., weekly or after 5,000 new labels) to incorporate the latest changes in code structure, author behavior, and failure signatures. This ensures the CRS model remains accurate and relevant as the services evolve.

- **PRCS enrichment:** When a new failure is labeled, the associated log and metric data are fed into the problem management module to look for PRCS. If a new signature is extracted, it is immediately added to the PRCS knowledgebase, ensuring the next deployment that contains that same flaw will be blocked by the CRS gate.

This continuous, intelligent feedback loop is the distinction between a simple automation system and a true AIOps platform; it gets smarter with every deployment, constantly learning the subtle ways in which code breaks production, and proactively enforcing that learning in the delivery pipeline.

Conclusion

This chapter demonstrates how AIOps transforms the core challenges of change management and problem management from human-intensive, reactive processes into automated, preventative disciplines. By introducing concepts like the CRS, predictive SLO modeling, and automated PRCS, we established a closed-loop system where every deployment is mathematically verified, every failure is automatically diagnosed, and the system intelligence grows with every operational event. The CI/CD pipeline is no longer just a delivery mechanism; it is the gatekeeper of reliability, enforcing policy-as-code through intelligent gates that automate the decision to proceed, halt, or rollback.

We have successfully resolved the false dichotomy between speed and stability. By embedding intelligence, teams can now deploy faster, more frequently, and with greater confidence than ever before. Change has been demoted from the greatest source of risk to the most predictable event in the operational lifecycle.

However, the question remains: what is the ultimate, measurable return on this intellectual and architectural investment? The promise of AIOps is to eliminate toil and boost service quality, but how do we quantify that in terms of dollars and engineering hours?

In the next chapter, we will shift focus from implementation to quantification. We will use the metrics and automated data streams developed in the preceding chapters to build a concrete business case for AIOps. The chapter is dedicated to showing tangible outcomes, providing the data-backed argument necessary to secure further investment and prove the strategic value of SRE. We will explore the hard metrics that define success: quantifying toil reduction with metrics, calculating ROI of intelligent operations, and ultimately measuring the massive gain in freed-up engineering time and improved availability that an AIOps-enabled SRE practice delivers.

CHAPTER 6
Path to Productivity and Reliability

Introduction

In the domain of intelligent operations, the implementation of AIOps is not an end in itself; it is a means to a critical business outcome: value realization. While previous chapters focused on the architectural mechanics, building the knowledgebase, unifying data models, and automating discovery, this chapter pivots to the measurable impact of those efforts.

The transition from traditional IT Operations to AIOps-enabled SRE is defined by the shift from reactive toil to proactive engineering. This chapter examines how organizations can quantify this shift. By rigorously measuring toil reduction, calculating the **return on investment** (**ROI**) of intelligent automation, and assessing improvements in system availability, leaders can build a data-backed argument for the continued investment in operational intelligence.

Structure

In this chapter, we will cover the following topics:

- Quantifying toil reduction with metrics
- Calculating the ROI of intelligent operations
- Engineering productivity improvement
- Maximizing service reliability
- Real-world examples of AIOps-enabled SRE success

Objectives

By the end of this chapter, readers will possess the analytical framework necessary to measure the success of their AIOps initiatives. This includes mastering the calculation of toil reduction, understanding the direct correlation between AIOps and preserved error budgets, and learning how to articulate the business value of invisible reliability work through concrete financial and operational metrics.

Quantifying toil reduction with metrics

Toil is the primary challenge for SRE. It is defined as work that is manual, repetitive, tactical, devoid of enduring value, and scales linearly with service growth. AIOps serves as the primary engine for toil elimination, but anecdotal evidence of perceived workload reduction is insufficient for an engineering organization.

SRE teams need a rigorous metrics framework to track the migration of effort from low-value maintenance to high-value engineering. This section explores how to instrument the AIOps platform to emit meta-metrics, data about the operations process itself.

Defining toil and opportunity cost

Before measuring, the organization must standardize its definition of toil. It must be made clear that toil is not merely *busy work*, but an expensive opportunity cost. Every hour an SRE spends manually triaging alerts, restarting failed services, or chasing false positives is an hour *not* spent on critical architecture reviews, security enhancements, or the development of new features that drive business growth. The quantification of toil is, therefore, the quantification of reclaimed engineering capacity. This reclamation allows for two strategic outcomes:

- **Decoupling scaling from hiring**: The organization can absorb more service growth and complexity without a corresponding linear increase in operational headcount.
- **Recovering cognitive capacity**: Engineers move from spending their mental energy on rote, reactive tasks to focusing on complex, non-obvious systemic problems.

Core toil metrics

To effectively manage and reduce toil, SRE teams must adopt a specific set of operational metrics. The following table details the essential metrics required to quantify toil reduction:

Metric	Description	SRE impact
Alert compression ratio (ACR)	The ratio of raw telemetry events (logs, traces, metrics) to actionable, unique incidents (e.g., 10,000 events consolidated into five incidents)	Directly reduces alert fatigue and cognitive overload by filtering noise into signal
Human-free recovery rate (HFRR)	The percentage of incidents that are automatically detected, diagnosed, and resolved by the AIOps platform without any human intervention	Validates the effectiveness of automated runbooks and directly lowers MTTR

Metric	Description	SRE impact
Toil percentage (TP)	The proportion of total engineering time spent on reactive, operational work versus proactive, strategic project work (SRE target: below 50%)	Ensure the team has sufficient capacity for long-term reliability engineering
Tickets per engineer (TPE)	The average volume of manually created or triaged operational tickets handled per engineer per week	An inverse indicator of successful automation implementation

***Table 6.1**: Essential metrics to quantify toil reduction*

Toil reduction funnel

A visual way to understand the work of AIOps is through the **toil reduction funnel**. This concept models the progression of raw operational data from its initial generation to its final, consolidated action. The efficiency of the AIOps engine is measured by the magnitude of reduction at each stage.

The funnel stages are:

1. **Raw telemetry (The wide mouth)**: Millions of data points (logs, metrics, traces) generated across the infrastructure.
2. **Event filtering (Initial sieve)**: Suppression of known harmless or redundant events (e.g., standard startup messages).
3. **Event correlation (Grouping)**: AI/ML algorithms group related events into a single, comprehensive incident, often across multiple components.
4. **Automated diagnosis (Labeling)**: The system identifies the likely root cause and impact of the correlated incident.
5. **Automated remediation (Action)**: The system triggers a corresponding runbook to resolve the incident instantly.
6. **Actionable incidents (The narrow tip)**: The handful of critical issues that remain and require human oversight or strategic intervention.

The success of the funnel is defined by a high **alert compression ratio** (ACR), minimizing the human touchpoints required.

Operationalizing toil measurement

Toil measurement must be embedded into the daily workflow. The most effective method is through mandatory ticket tagging within the **issue tracking system** (ITS). Every operational ticket must be tagged with a category (toil: manual triage, toil: manual restart, project: feature X, project: automation build). This data is then aggregated and analyzed automatically. The data collected from the ITS, when combined with time-tracking data, provides the raw inputs for calculating the toil percentage and generating reports on reclaimed engineering hours, the crucial first step in calculating ROI.

Refer to the following figure:

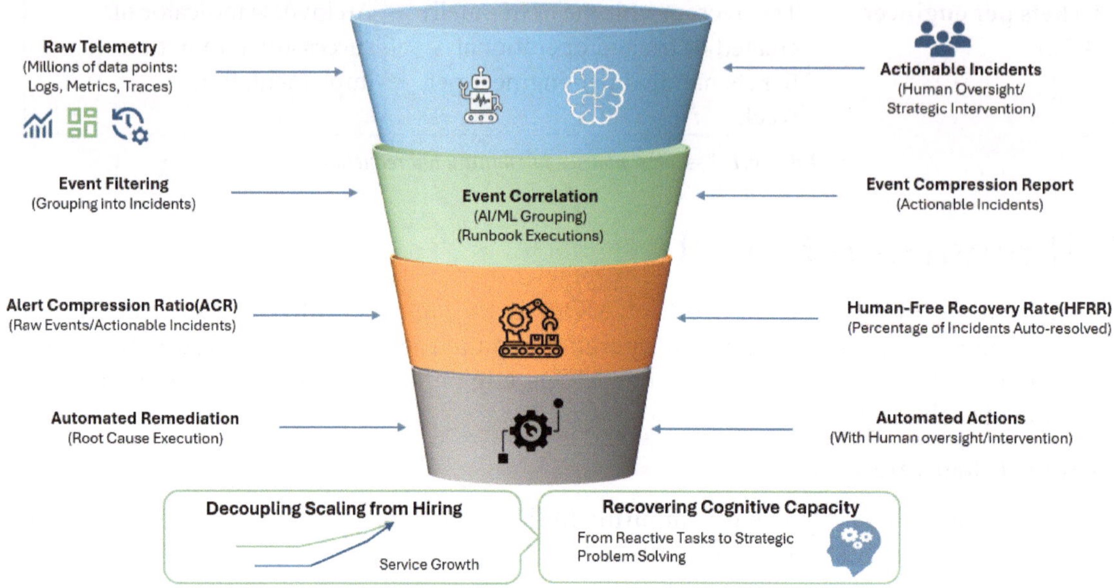

Metric	Description	Description	SRE Impact
Toil Percentage(TP) **Tickets per Engineer(TPE)**	% Time on Manual, Repetitive Work(<50% Target)	Avg Manual Operation Tickets Inverse of Automation Success	< 50%
Alert Compression Ratio(ACR) **Human-Free Recovery Rate(HFRR)**	Inverse of Automation Access(ACR)	% of Issues Resolved without Human Intervention, MeanTimeToRecover(MTTR)	Lowers Toil

Toil is Opportunity Cost: Manual Work=Lost Innovation, Quantify Toil to Reclaim Engineering Capacity

Figure 6.1*: SRE toil reduction and AIOps funnel; reclaiming engineering capacity*

Calculating the ROI of intelligent operations

Implementing an AIOps platform represents a significant capital expenditure, encompassing licensing, infrastructure, and training. To secure continued investment and organizational buy-in, SRE leadership must transcend technical jargon and articulate the ROI in financial terms that directly align with the C-suite's objectives. AIOps ROI is a complex calculation that must account for both tangible cost savings and intangible value creation.

Components of the AIOps ROI equation

The ROI calculation for an AIOps solution must be comprehensive, incorporating all factors that contribute to profitability and resilience. The core framework is as follows:

```
ROI = ({Cost of Downtime Avoided} + {Engineering Hours Saved} + {Reduced Infra
Spend}) - {Total Cost of Ownership (TCO)}\{Total Cost of Ownership (TCO)} X 100
```

The primary value drivers are:

- **Cost of downtime avoided**: The financial impact of preventing or shortening service outages.
- **Engineering hours saved**: The monetary value of time reclaimed from toil and reinvested into value-added projects.
- **Reduced infrastructure spend**: Savings from improved capacity planning and optimization (e.g., avoiding over-provisioning).

Quantifying the cost of downtime

The most immediate and high-impact component of the ROI formula is the cost of downtime. This cost is rarely simple revenue loss; it involves multiple layers of financial and reputational damage as described in *Figure 6.2*:

- **Direct revenue loss**: Revenue stream interruption during the outage.
- **SLA penalties**: Contractual payments due to customers for violating Service Level Agreements.
- **Recovery costs**: Overtime pay for engineers, consultant costs, and infrastructure scaling to cope with backlogs.
- **Reputation damage (Shadow cost)**: Loss of future business, brand erosion, and negative press coverage.

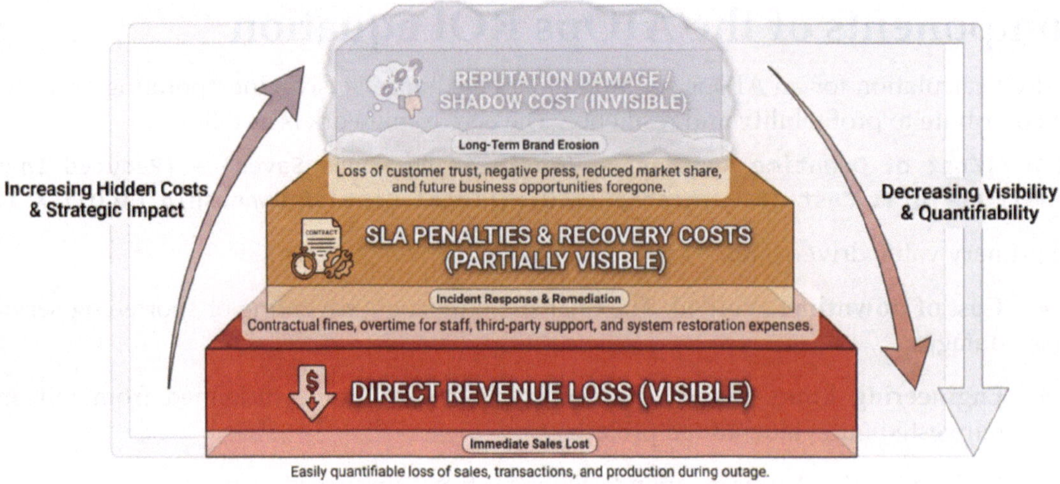

Figure 6.2: Cost of downtime

A crucial first step is to establish a credible, documented **cost per minute of downtime** (**CPMD**) figure *before* AIOps implementation. This baseline allows the team to later claim the value of the reduction in MTTR and the overall reduction in outage frequency.

Monetizing engineering time

The time saved through AIOps must be converted into a monetary figure. This requires calculating the **fully loaded cost of an engineering hour** (**FLCEH**). This calculation goes beyond salary, including benefits, overhead, office space, and tooling.

Calculating the true cost: FLCEH:

The cost of a manual intervention is not merely the engineer's hourly wage; it is a fraction of the total investment the company makes in that resource. The formula for FLCEH is:

```
$$ FLCEH = \frac{S + B + O + T}{H_{effective}} $$
```

Where:

- S = **Base annual salary**: The gross compensation paid to the engineer.
- B = **Benefits and taxes**: Employer-paid payroll taxes, health/dental/vision insurance, 401(k) matching, and equity/stock options. (Typically, 25 to 30% of base salary).
- O = **Overhead**: Allocated costs for office space (or remote work stipends), HR support, legal, electricity, and internet infrastructure.
- T = **Tooling and licensing**: The per-seat cost of the technical stack, including **integrated development environments** (**IDEs**) (e.g., IntelliJ), **software as a service** (**SaaS**) subscriptions (Jira, Slack, PagerDuty), and cloud development environments.

- **$H_{effective}$ = Annual effective hours**: Total potential hours (2,080) minus PTO, holidays, sick leave, and non-billable administrative time (all-hands meetings, mandatory training).

Example calculation:

Consider a senior SRE with a base salary of $160,000:

- **Total annual cost ($S+B+O+T$)**: *$160k (Salary) + $48k (Benefits) + $25k (Overhead) + $7k (Tooling) = $240,000.*
- **Effective hours ($H_{effective}$)**: 1,750 hours (after deducting 6 weeks of leave and 5 hours/week of admin time).
- **FLCEH**: $240,000 / 1,750 ~$137.14 per hour.

Its impact is:

Every 30-minute manual restart performed by this engineer effectively costs the business $68.57 in direct sunk costs, ignoring the opportunity cost of lost innovation.

If an AIOps solution, via the human-free recovery rate, automates 100 incident resolutions per month, and each resolution previously took a Senior SRE 45 minutes, the total time saved is 75 hours. Multiplying the 75 hours by the FLCEH provides a direct, measurable financial saving that is sustained month over month, demonstrating cumulative ROI. This metric transitions AIOps from a simple cost-saving tool to a profitability accelerator by increasing the production capacity of the existing talent pool.

Compounding ROI of automation

While the FLCEH establishes the cost of the *status quo*, the implementation of AIOps automation introduces a financial dynamic known as *compounding ROI*. Unlike manual remediation, where the cost scales linearly with the number of incidents, automation breaks this correlation, delivering non-linear returns.

Write once, resolve forever dynamic

Building an automation runbook requires an upfront **Capital Expenditure** (**CapEx**) of time, such as designing, scripting, and testing the remediation logic. However, once deployed, the runbook becomes a permanent asset that pays *dividends* every time it executes:

- **Cumulative savings**: If an automated script takes 10 hours to build (costing $1,370) but autonomously resolves an issue that usually takes 30 minutes, the break-even point is reached after just 20 incidents. Every subsequent execution is essentially *free* (pure profit) relative to the manual baseline.
- **Zero marginal cost**: As traffic scales and incident volume grows, the cost to handle those incidents via automation remains flat. Manual teams would require headcount

expansion (linear cost growth) to handle the same surge, whereas the AIOps platform absorbs the load with near-zero marginal cost.

Here is a *cost of toil* calculator table comparing the 1-year and 3-year costs of manual operations against an automated AIOps approach, based on the FLCEH derived previously.

This analysis uses the FLCEH of $137.14. It assumes a base of 10,000 incidents per year that would otherwise require manual intervention, with each incident typically requiring {0.5} hours (30 minutes) of SRE time.

Phase 1: Manual operations

The following table summarizes the costs and operational challenges associated with manual incident management in phase 1:

Metric	Calculation	Annual cost (1 year)	Cumulative cost (3 years)
Total annual toil hours	10,000 incidents × 0.5 hours/incident	5,000 hours	15,000 hours
Total labor cost (FLCEH)	5,000 hours × $137.14/hour	$685,700	$2,057,100
Opportunity cost (Lost innovation)	5,000 hours diverted from feature work	High	Very high
Fatigue and turnover risk	High operational burden on SREs	Significant	Extreme

Table 6.2: Manual cost of operations

Manual summary: Without AIOps, the company pays over $2 million in direct labor costs over three years simply to keep systems operational, with zero return on innovation from that time investment.

Phase 2: AIOps automated operations

This calculation assumes an upfront 1-time CapEx of 500 hours of SRE time costing $68,570 to design, build, and deploy the automation runbooks, achieving a 90% automation rate on the initial 10,000 incident type. The following table outlines the cost savings and operational improvements achieved through AIOps-driven automation in incident management:

Metric	Calculation	Annual cost (1 year)	Cumulative cost (3 years)
Upfront automation CapEx	500 hours × $137.14/hr	$68,570	Initial investment($68,570)

Metric	Calculation	Annual cost (1 year)	Cumulative cost (3 years)
Automated incidents	90% of 10,000 Incidents	9,000 Incidents	27,000 incidents
Manual escalations remaining	10% of 10,000 × 0.5 hr	500 hours	1,500 hours
Total 3-year AIOps labor cost	CapEx + (3 × manual escalation cost)	N/A	$274,280

***Table 6.3**: AIOps automated cost of operations*

Financial comparison

The following table shows the ROI comparison between the manual vs. the AIOps automated approach:

Metric	Manual (3 years)	AIOps (3 years)	3-year net savings
Total labor cost	$2,057,100	$274,280	$1,782,820
Time reinvested (SRE hours saved)	0 hours	13,500 hours	13,500 hours
ROI	N/A	≈ 650%	Financial savings only

***Table 6.4**: ROI comparison; manual vs automated*

The initial investment in automation pays for itself rapidly, yielding an ROI of over 650% in direct labor savings alone over three years. More importantly, it unlocks 13,500 SRE hours to be reinvested into developing new, revenue-generating products and features, embodying the compounding ROI of automation.

Total cost of ownership and depreciation

For a responsible ROI calculation, the **total cost of ownership** (**TCO**) of the AIOps platform must be accurately captured. TCO includes:

- Initial software licensing and subscription costs.
- Infrastructure costs (compute, storage) are required for data ingestion and machine learning pipelines.
- Personnel costs (onboarding, training, and internal maintenance of the platform).

The ROI calculation must be tracked over a defined period (e.g., 3 to 5 years) to account for the depreciation of the platform and the compounding effect of sustained operational improvements. The goal is to demonstrate that the net benefit significantly exceeds the TCO, ideally showing a rapid payback period often achievable within 12 to 18 months for mature implementations.

Engineering productivity improvement

The true power of an AIOps knowledgebase is realized in the operational shifts it creates. One of the two primary dimensions of impact is the liberation of engineering talent, moving them from a state of constant reaction to one of proactive contribution. This section examines how to measure and maximize the value of this reclaimed time.

Shift in site reliability engineering workload

When AIOps absorb the burdens of event correlation and routine remediation, it does more than just save time; it fundamentally changes the nature of the work performed by the SRE team. The workload shifts from toil-heavy (reactive, unpredictable, manual) to engineering-centric (proactive, planned, strategic).

The qualitative shift is defined by the following changes in activity:

- **Incident response**: Shifts from reactive firefighting to proactive observation and intervention only on verified, critical issues.
- **Root cause analysis (RCA)**: Shifts from manual log hunting and multi-hour *war rooms* to AI-assisted context and topology mapping, reducing diagnosis time from hours to minutes.
- **Security posture**: Shifts from delayed patching due to *lack of time* to scheduled, proactive vulnerability remediation and infrastructure hardening.

Value of contiguous time

In a highly reactive environment, SRE time is fragmented. An engineer might only have 15 to 30-minute blocks between pages, which is insufficient for deep cognitive work like writing code or designing a new architecture. AIOps creates contiguous blocks of uninterrupted time by suppressing alert noise. This is a critical, often-overlooked value proposition. Reclaimed time that is fragmented is nearly worthless for engineering; reclaimed time that is consolidated is invaluable.

The best measure of this qualitative improvement is the *Deep Work Index*, a metric that tracks the average duration of time an SRE can spend on a single, strategic task without being interrupted by a PagerDuty alert. A rising Deep Work Index correlates directly with higher quality code, better architectural decisions, and reduced technical debt.

Measuring cultural impact

The impact of freed-up time extends beyond pure productivity to the cultural health of the SRE team. A manually intensive operations environment fosters a *hero culture*, where individuals are celebrated for working long, stressful hours to fix outages. This culture is toxic, unsustainable, and leads to high rates of burnout and turnover among senior staff.

AIOps facilitates a shift to an *engineering culture*, where the system, not the person, is the hero. This impact can be measured quantitatively:

- **Reduced pager duty hours**: Tracking the total hours SREs are actively paged outside of business hours.
- **Lower team churn**: Monitoring the retention rate of SREs, especially senior staff, has a direct cost-saving benefit (recruiting a new SRE can cost hundreds of thousands of dollars).
- **Improved employee net promoter score (eNPS)**: Gauging team morale and satisfaction with the work environment.

Reinvesting the time dividend

The ultimate strategic goal is to ensure the time saved by AIOps is systematically reinvested into high-value engineering. If the saved time is simply absorbed into other operational tasks, the ROI is diluted. The SRE leadership must actively track how the *time dividend* is spent, as shown in the following:

- **70% engineering**: Writing new platform code, building advanced automation, and contributing to the product roadmap.
- **20% reliability work**: Reducing technical debt, improving monitoring, and writing new SLOs.
- **10% toil**: Routine platform maintenance that cannot be automated.

The following figure illustrates how AIOps strategically reallocates time saved for the SRE team, maximizing the impact of reclaimed engineering hours:

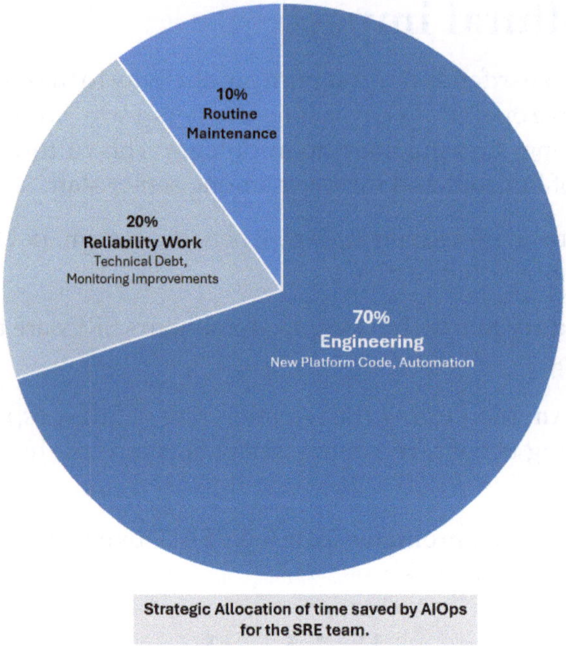

***Figure 6.3**: Time dividend reinvestment model*

This explicit budgeting of time ensures that the AIOps investment is continually self-funding by producing strategic outcomes.

Maximizing service reliability

Reliability is the ultimate product of the SRE team, and it is the direct currency of trust with the customer base. AIOps is indispensable in the pursuit of higher availability, as it delivers performance improvements beyond human capability. This section details how AIOps directly influences availability metrics by shrinking the duration and frequency of service outages.

Accelerating the incident lifecycle

The lifecycle of an incident, from the first sign of a problem to full resolution, is a race against the clock. AIOps reduces the total duration by automating the initial detection and diagnosis phases, which are the most time-consuming and cognitively demanding for human engineers.

The key metric accelerations are:

- **Detection phase (MTTD)**: AIOps uses *anomaly detection* to spot deviations in system behavior *before* a static threshold is breached. This moves the detection point from a reactive state (e.g., CPU is 95%) to a proactive state (e.g., CPU behavior is statistically abnormal for this time of day).

- **Diagnosis phase**: The AIOps *dynamic service topology* (as detailed in *Chapter 3, AIOps Knowledgebase*) instantly correlates the impacted component to the likely root cause, eliminating manual investigation time.
- **Resolution phase (MTTR)**: The human-free recovery rate executes the resolution workflow the moment the diagnosis is confirmed, removing human latency from the response loop.

The following figure depicts how AIOps streamlines incident response, reducing resolution times and enhancing overall system availability:

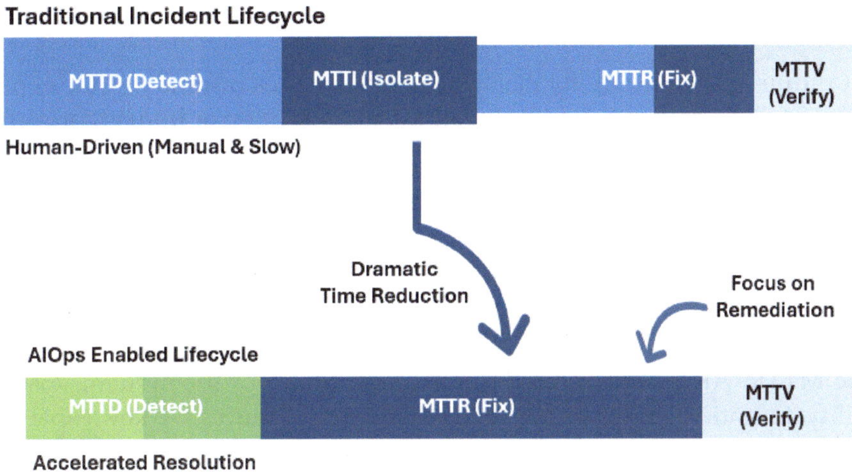

***Figure 6.4**: The MTTR acceleration curve*

Reducing mean time to detect and resolve

The correlation between AIOps and system availability is mathematically precise, centered on the reduction of MTTD and MTTR:

$$Availability=(Total\ time - Total\ downtime)\ /Total\ time$$

Since total downtime is the sum of all incidents multiplied by their respective MTTRs, any reduction in MTTR (which includes MTTD) has a direct, compounding effect on overall availability. For mission-critical systems, moving from 99.9% (Three Nines) to 99.99% (Four Nines) reduces permissible downtime from approximately 8.7 hours per year to 52 minutes per year. Achieving this leap requires machine-speed automation, making AIOps non-optional. The goal is to transition the MTTR equation from:

$$MTTR = MTTD + MTTI\ (Isolate) + MTTF\ (Fix) + MTTV\ (Verify)$$

To one where the initial two stages (*detect and isolate*) are near-instantaneous and fully automated by the platform.

Error budget protector

AIOps is a crucial enabler for organizations operating under the SLO or error budget framework. The error budget is the maximum allowable downtime (unreliability) over a period, and its preservation is paramount to maintaining development velocity.

AIOps acts as the error budget protector in two ways:

- **Predictive alerting**: The platform analyzes the current error rate and predicts if the team is on track to exhaust the budget. It can issue a warning: *error budget will be consumed in 48 hours unless the current deployment is rolled back*. This allows for proactive intervention before a policy violation occurs.
- **Blast radius containment**: By isolating faulty services instantly, AIOps ensures that a localized failure only consumes a small fraction of the error budget, preventing a total stoppage of feature releases.

A well-implemented AIOps platform allows the business to maintain both high reliability *and* high feature velocity, often seen as competing goals.

Resilience and blast radius reduction

Beyond basic MTTR, AIOps enhances the overall resilience of the system. Resilience is the system's ability to anticipate, absorb, and recover from failures. A key capability is blast radius reduction, the ability to limit the scope of impact from a failure. The AIOps topology map identifies dependent services in real-time. When an anomaly is detected in a non-critical microservice, the platform can automatically apply a circuit breaker or throttle traffic to that component, isolating the failure and preventing it from cascading across the entire application stack. This turns a potential **service-level 1 (Sev-1)** catastrophic outage into a minor Sev-3 degradation, dramatically limiting the cost, reputational damage, and error budget burn.

The AIOps engine employs three primary mechanisms to achieve this containment: intelligent circuit breakers, dynamic rate limiting, and automated quarantining:

- **Intelligent circuit breakers**: The circuit breaker pattern is a standard resilience mechanism that prevents an application from repeatedly trying to execute an operation that is likely to fail. However, traditional circuit breakers rely on static, lagging indicators (e.g., trip after five consecutive 500 errors). AIOps evolves this into an *intelligent circuit breaker* by using predictive anomalies rather than just failure counts:
    - **Predictive tripping**: Instead of waiting for hard failures, the AIOps engine monitors leading indicators, such as a deviation in microservice latency or a spike in thread pool exhaustion. If the anomaly score breaches a critical threshold, the AIOps platform can signal the service mesh (e.g., Istio or Linkerd) to open the circuit *before* the service completely collapses.

- **The half-open state**: AIOps optimizes the recovery phase. In a *half-open* state, where the system allows a limited number of test requests to pass through to check if the underlying issue is resolved, AIOps can analyze the success of these probes in real-time. It validates not just availability, but performance regression, ensuring the circuit only closes when the service is fully healthy.

- **Dynamic rate limiting (Adaptive throttling)**: Static rate limits (e.g., 1000 requests per second) are often too rigid: they either choke legitimate traffic during safe peaks or fail to protect the system during partial degradation. AIOps introduces *dynamic rate limiting,* which adjusts traffic flow based on real-time component health:

  - **Backpressure propagation**: When the AIOps topology map detects that a downstream database is exhibiting high write latency, it calculates the maximum sustainable throughput for that specific state. It then automatically updates the API Gateway configurations to throttle incoming requests to a matching level.

  - **Prioritized shedding**: Rather than randomly dropping requests, AIOps logic can differentiate between traffic types. During a *brownout,* it can instruct the gateway to shed low-priority traffic (e.g., background batch jobs or free-tier users) while preserving bandwidth for high-value transactions (e.g., checkout flows or premium users). This ensures that even if the blast radius cannot be zero, the *business impact* is minimized.

- **Automated quarantining (Bulkheading)**: When a specific service instance or *pod* becomes a bad actor, perhaps due to a memory leak or a corrupted cache, it can infect the rest of the pool by consuming shared resources. AIOps utilizes *automated quarantining* to surgically remove the faulty component:

  - **Identification of patient zero**: Using distributed tracing data, the AIOps platform identifies the specific instance causing error spikes.

  - **Isolation action**: It triggers an orchestration command (e.g., via Kubernetes API) to label the pod as *unhealthy* or remove it from the load balancer rotation immediately. This effectively *air gaps* the problem, preventing the failure from cascading to healthy instances. The failing service is kept alive but disconnected, allowing SREs to perform forensics on the *live* corpse without affecting customers.

Figure 6.5 shows how AIOps improves the overall resilience of the system:

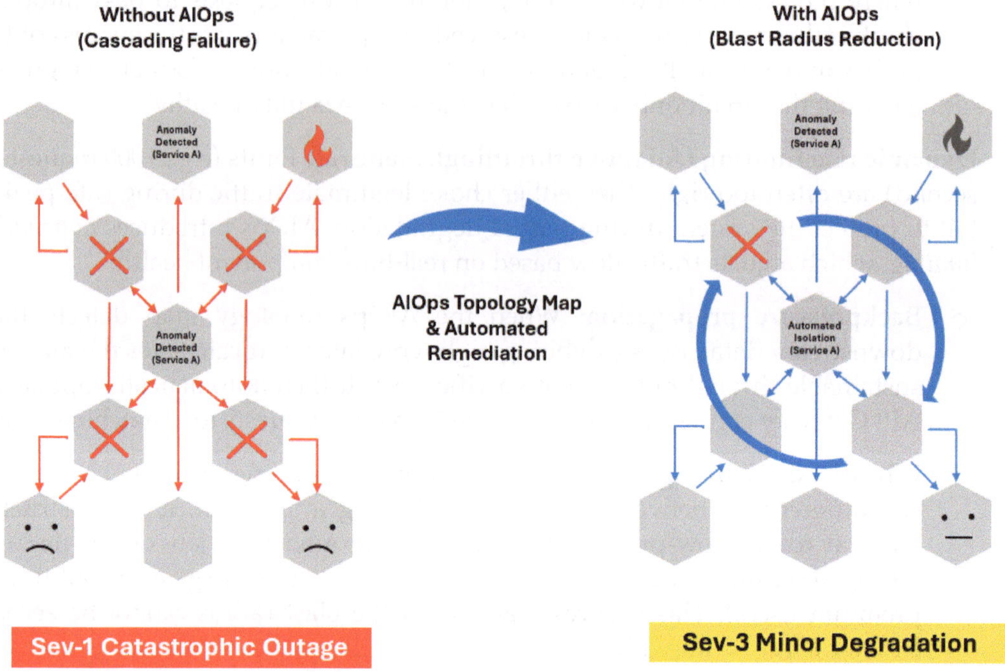

***Figure 6.5**: Resilience and blast radius reduction*

Real-world examples of AIOps-enabled SRE success

To solidify the concepts of quantified toil reduction and measurable ROI, this section provides concrete case studies from diverse industry verticals, illustrating how AIOps-enabled SRE practices drive both productivity and reliability. These examples serve as blueprints for organizations embarking on their own intelligent operations journey.

Case study 1: Financial services, zero-touch remediation

Challenge:

A large investment bank, operating 24/7 trading platforms, faced recurring issues with *stuck* order processing threads during high-volume market activity. These incidents occurred multiple times per week, each requiring a senior SRE to manually log in, diagnose the specific service, and initiate a targeted restart. This process averaged 20 minutes per incident.

AIOps solution:

- **Data unification**: Unified log data from the **order management system** (**OMS**) and JMX metrics from the **Java Virtual Machine** (**JVM**).
- **AI/ML logic**: The AIOps engine used machine learning to learn the specific *fingerprint* of a stuck thread (e.g., low CPU consumption combined with an abnormally high memory wait time).
- **Automated action**: The knowledgebase triggered an automated runbook to gracefully restart the *specific thread* via an API call, rather than the entire service, ensuring maximum service continuity.

Impact metrics:

- **Toil reduction (HFRR)**: 100% of these specific incidents were transitioned to automated resolution.
- **Engineering hours saved**: Approximately four hours of SRE time returned per week (200+ hours annually).
- **MTTR improvement**: Order processing latency during *stuck* states dropped from 20 minutes to 30 seconds, preserving order flow and revenue.

Case study 2: Retail e-commerce, predictive scaling for flash sales

Challenge:

A global fashion retailer struggled with unpredictable traffic spikes during major events like Black Friday. Their traditional cloud auto-scaling groups were reactive, spinning up new instances *after* the site had already begun slowing down, leading to lost transactions and shopping cart abandonment.

AIOps solution:

- **Predictive modeling**: The platform ingested historical traffic data, current marketing campaign schedules, email send volumes, and real-time user session metrics.
- **Forecasting**: A time series forecasting model (often a form of ARIMA or Prophet model) accurately predicted massive traffic surges 15 minutes before they occurred.
- **Proactive action**: The AIOps engine triggered a *pre-scale* event, warming up necessary infrastructure resources (database connection pools, app servers, cache layers) in anticipation of the load, avoiding reactive latency.

Impact metrics:

- **Revenue preservation (ROI)**: Estimated $2.5 million in revenue preserved by maintaining low checkout latency during peak hours.

- **Availability**: Maintained 100% application uptime during the peak shopping hour, compared to 99.5% the previous year.
- **Reduced infrastructure spend**: The intelligent pre-scaling avoided the costly *overshooting* and subsequent *throttling* of manual scaling efforts, optimizing cloud usage.

Case study 3: SaaS platform, reducing cascading failure

Challenge:

A major cloud software provider frequently experienced cascading failures where a benign bug in a minor microservice would rapidly overwhelm a shared resource (e.g., a database), resulting in a total platform-wide outage.

AIOps solution:

- **Dynamic topology and tracing**: The platform utilized distributed tracing (e.g., OpenTelemetry) and its dynamic dependency map to monitor resource contention in real-time.
- **Anomaly detection**: The AIOps engine detected abnormal queue depths and resource contention starting in the minor service.
- **Isolation action**: The system automatically identified the misbehaving service as the source of the blast and immediately applied a rate limit and circuit breaker to its database connection pool, isolating the fault while keeping the rest of the platform online.

Impact metrics:

- **Resilience**: Converted potential platform-wide Sev-1 outages into minor, localized Sev-3 degradations.
- **MTTR**: Reduced diagnosis and isolation time from an average of 45 minutes to instantaneous isolation, minimizing customer impact.
- **Customer trust**: Quantifiable reduction in customer churn rates due to a proven track record of platform stability.

Conclusion

The journey documented in this chapter is a declaration. The value of AIOps is not a philosophical argument. It is a quantifiable business reality. By transitioning from reactive operations to AIOps-enabled SRE, an organization shifts its operational model from a high-cost, high-stress cost center to a strategic, value-creation engine. We have moved beyond the subjective assertion that we feel less busy to the empirical truth. Millions of events have been compressed into minutes of focused work, freeing up hundreds of hours of senior engineering capacity.

The strategic imperative for leadership is clear. The success of intelligent operations must be rigorously measured in the language of the business, using metrics like dollars, hours, and nines. The ROI of AIOps is not merely the cost savings from avoiding an occasional outage. It is the sustained, compounding return from converting expensive, scarce toil time into profitable engineering time. This reclaimed time is the most valuable dividend of intelligent automation. Leaders must actively govern their reinvestment into future architectural work and platform resilience, creating a self-funding virtuous cycle of reliability.

AIOps is therefore the investment that preserves both system health and human capital. It is the tool that ensures your organization can afford to remain reliable while simultaneously accelerating its pace of innovation. By mastering the metrics of toil, MTTR, and error budget preservation, SRE leaders can prove that AIOps is not just a technological upgrade. It is a fundamental strategic asset that guarantees high availability and propels the business forward.

The foundation of this quantitative success rests entirely on the speed and accuracy of initial detection. For AIOps to deliver instantaneous diagnosis and automated resolution, it must first be capable of seeing problems that humans cannot. It must identify subtle anomalies far ahead of traditional, static thresholds. This capability is the true engine of proactive SRE.

In the next chapter, we will delve into the advanced machine learning techniques that power this critical capability. We will explore how specialized algorithms move beyond simple threshold monitoring to identify subtle deviations in system behavior. These techniques provide critical early warning signals that make zero-touch resolution possible. The chapter also focuses on anomaly detection and advanced techniques used to anticipate system failures and maintain continuous, autonomous operations.

Join our Discord space

Join our Discord workspace for latest updates, offers, tech happenings around the world, new releases, and sessions with the authors:

https://discord.bpbonline.com

CHAPTER 7
Advanced Anomaly Detection

Introduction

In the preceding chapters, we established the AIOps Knowledgebase and explored the mechanics of intelligent incident management. We learned how to correlate noisy alerts into high-fidelity incidents, significantly reducing the MTTE. However, reliance on reactive alerting, even when highly correlated, still operates on the premise that a failure has already occurred and impacted the system.

SRE aims to identify instability before it affects customers, rather than simply repairing failures quickly. This chapter explores the computational engine that powers proactive reliability. In modern, ephemeral, and distributed environments, defining normal via static thresholds is an obsolete practice. A fixed threshold cannot account for the elasticity of cloud infrastructure, the complexity of microservices interactions, or the cyclical nature of user traffic.

AIOps solves this by utilizing a spectrum of intelligence, ranging from robust statistical methods like **interquartile range** (**IQR**) to advanced unsupervised machine learning algorithms such as autoencoders and isolation forests. By mastering these techniques, SRE teams can move beyond simple threshold breaching to identify unknown unknowns(e.g., a sudden spike in CPU without a matching rise in traffic is flagged by an autoencoder as a latent defect, while an isolation forest detects a novel error pattern in logs unseen in prior deployments), identifying subtle deviations in behavior that signal latent defects. This chapter will guide you through the architecture of these models and, critically, how to integrate their output into your error budget strategies to prevent alert fatigue.

Structure

In this chapter, we will cover the following topics:

- Evolution of anomaly detection
- Foundational statistical techniques
- Advanced machine learning techniques
- Forecasting and seasonality with time series modeling
- Operationalizing anomaly detection

- Model lifecycle and drift detection
- Advanced anomaly detection techniques
- Building anomaly detection into error budget strategy

Objectives

By the end of this chapter, readers will master the mathematical and architectural logic behind automated detection. This includes understanding when to apply simple statistical models versus complex machine learning. Readers will learn to deploy IQR for robust latency analysis, utilize autoencoders for multivariate reconstruction, and apply time series modeling for capacity forecasting. Finally, readers will learn to operationalize these models by mapping anomaly severity directly to SLOs consumption rates.

Evolution of anomaly detection

The journey to intelligent detection requires a fundamental shift in mindset within SRE. Historically, **IT operations (ITOps)** followed a simple, reactive model: monitor a value, wait for it to exceed a limit, and then alert. This approach is defined by its rigidity and lack of context, a model that has become untenable in the age of hyperscale, cloud-native architectures.

Generation 1: Manual and static thresholds

The first generation of monitoring relied entirely on human intuition and manual configuration. An SRE, based on experience or vendor recommendations, would define a fixed limit (e.g., *CPU > 90%*, *Latency > 500ms*).

This model suffers from two critical drawbacks that directly lead to alert fatigue and missed incidents:

- **The brittle boundary problem**: In a dynamic cloud environment, where auto-scaling groups routinely create and destroy resources, and traffic patterns shift hourly, a fixed boundary is always wrong. A legitimate traffic surge (e.g., after an email campaign) often violates the threshold, leading to a false positive, or noise. Conversely, a critical, but slow-burning issue (e.g., a gradual memory fragmentation) might stay below the high limit until the system is already nearing collapse, resulting in a false negative and a sudden, user-impacting outage.

- **The lack of context**: Static thresholds treat every point in time equally. They cannot distinguish between a high-load event during peak business hours (normal) and the identical high-load event at 3:00 AM on a Sunday (critical anomaly). This contextual blindness forces SREs to constantly tune and maintain thousands of redundant rules, leading to significant toil.

Generation 2: Statistical and dynamic baselining

The second generation introduced basic statistical awareness to overcome the rigidity of *Generation 1*. This is where concepts like dynamic baselining and simple standard deviation limits emerged. Instead of fixing the limit, the monitoring system would calculate the rolling mean and standard deviation of a metric over a recent time window (e.g., the last 7 days).

- **The approach**: The system would alert if the current metric value exceeded a statistically significant band, typically the 3-sigma rule, implying the value is a statistical rarity.
- **The improvement**: This was a massive step forward, as the thresholds automatically adjusted for high-frequency trends.
- **The limitation**: While better than static limits, this approach still makes two key mathematical assumptions that often fail in SRE data:
    - It assumes the data is normally distributed (Gaussian), which is rarely true for latency or error rates.
    - It only analyzes univariate data (one metric at a time). It fails completely when a failure is defined not by the value of a single metric, but by the impossible relationship between multiple metrics (e.g., high throughput with zero database I/O, a classic Gray Failure).

Generation 3: Multivariate and contextual AIOps detection

The third and current generation of anomaly detection, powered by AIOps, addresses the multivariate and non-Gaussian nature of modern telemetry. This is the transition from looking at individual gauges to understanding the entire operating state of a complex machine.

This generation relies on unsupervised machine learning to model the intrinsic behavior of the system, including complex feature interactions and temporal patterns:

- **Multivariate awareness**: Models like the autoencoder do not monitor CPU or I/O independently. They learn about the holistic, high-dimensional relationship between all metrics. This allows detection of failures that occur when all metrics are individually within their bands, but their combination is mathematically impossible.
- **Contextual awareness**: Models like time series forecasting (e.g., Prophet) explicitly model seasonality and trend. They remove these predictable components, focusing only on the unexplained residual noise, thereby eliminating alerts for predictable spikes and dips.

Table 7.1 summarizes the operational shift required to move through these generations:

Generation	Methodology	Mathematical Foundation	Operational outcome
1. Static	Fixed, human-defined limits	None (Rule-based)	High noise, high toil, inability to scale
2. Statistical	Rolling mean, standard deviation, or IQR	Univariate statistical distribution	Better adaptive thresholds, but blind to complex, multivariate failures
3. AIOps (Advanced)	Machine learning (autoencoders, isolation forests, time series models)	Multivariate analysis, non-parametric modeling, and deep learning	Proactive: Catches unknown unknowns, low noise, contextualized alerting

***Table 7.1**: The three generations of detection strategies*

This evolution is critical: static monitoring helps you *react* to simple failures. AIOps-driven advanced detection helps you *prevent* complex ones.

Foundational statistical techniques

While advanced machine learning is powerful, it is often overkill for simple, common metrics. Before implementing complex neural networks, it is vital to understand and utilize statistical anomaly detection. These techniques are computationally efficient, interpretable, and highly effective for monitoring single metrics.

Standard deviation and the average

The most intuitive statistical method relies on the idea of an **Average** (or mean) and the **Typical Variation** (standard deviation):

- **The logic**: Imagine you monitor the CPU utilization of a stable server. Over a week, you calculate the average CPU usage. Then, you calculate the typical amount by which the CPU moves away from that average; this is the typical variation.

  The system defines a *normal zone* that includes almost all data points; for example, a zone three times the size of the typical variation, centered on the average.

- **Problem**: This system works well if your data follows a smooth, symmetrical pattern (like a bell curve). However, many critical metrics, especially latency, do not. Latency is often fast (10ms) but has occasional massive spikes (10,000ms). When a spike occurs, it drags the overall average up and drastically increases the typical variation, effectively stretching the normal zone. This stretching hides future, less severe but still important anomalies.

Interquartile range

For the majority of IT metrics, especially latency and response time, the data is not symmetrically distributed; it is highly skewed. In these cases, the traditional variation method is unreliable because extreme outliers artificially inflate the normal zone.

To address this, SREs should utilize the IQR technique. IQR is a measure of statistical dispersion that is robust, meaning it is not heavily influenced by extreme outliers. Instead of relying on the average, IQR focuses on the data's central distribution.

Mechanics of IQR or the box method

Imagine you line up all your metric readings (e.g., thousands of latency values) from smallest to largest. IQR defines the *box* around the central 50% of the data:

- **The median**: Find the middle point of the entire line (the 50th percentile). This is a reliable center point that is not skewed by massive spikes.
- **The box boundaries (Q1 and Q3)**: Find the point that marks the 25% boundary (Q1) and the point that marks the 75% boundary (Q3). The distance between Q3 and Q1 is the IQR. This represents the stable, common zone of performance.
- Alerts are typically triggered when metric values fall outside the lower or upper fences, beyond *Q1 – 1.5×IQR* or *Q3 + 1.5×IQR*, indicating statistically significant outliers.

Figure 7.1 illustrates the box plot representation of IQR, including the central box and the outlier boundaries:

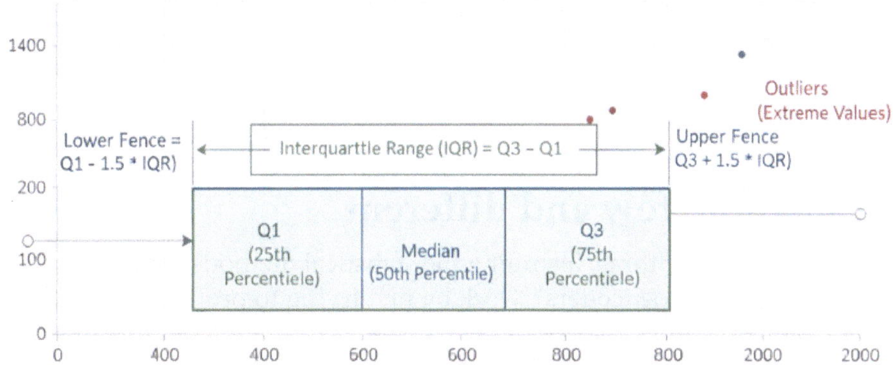

***Figure 7.1**: Box plot components showing the IQR and outlier boundaries*

Advanced machine learning techniques

While statistical methods are excellent for single metrics (Univariate), modern distributed systems often fail in complex ways that involve the relationship between metrics. For this, we turn to autoencoders, a type of unsupervised neural network.

Autoencoders

An autoencoder does not classify data as good or bad. Instead, it attempts to learn the identity function, compressing input data and then reconstructing it:

- **Encoder**: Compresses high-dimensional input data (CPU, Memory, I/O, Network, Thread Count) into a concise, lower-dimensional representation called the latent space. This forces the model to learn the most essential correlations of the *normal* state.
- **Decoder**: Attempts to reconstruct the original input from this compressed latent space.

Reconstruction error

The mechanism of detection is reconstruction error:

- **Training**: The model is trained on historical, healthy system data. It learns that, typically, when the request count rises, CPU usage rises. It reconstructs this pattern perfectly (low error).
- **Detection**: When the model encounters a *zombie process* (high CPU but zero requests), the encoder compresses it, but the decoder fails to reconstruct it because this correlation breaks the learned laws of the system.
- **Signal**: The difference between the input and the reconstructed output is the reconstruction error. A high error score signals a multivariate anomaly.

Isolation forests

While autoencoders excel at understanding complex relationships between continuous time series metrics, they can be too computationally intensive for handling massive volumes of high-cardinality, discrete data, such as application logs or distributed traces. For this data, we need an algorithm that is designed for speed and scale. Here, the isolation forest algorithm becomes the industry standard.

Logic of isolation, few and different

Most anomaly detection algorithms, including the statistical methods we discussed (like IQR) and complex models (like autoencoders), work by first trying to profile the *normal* state. They build a tight model of what the vast majority of data looks like, and anything that falls outside is flagged as an anomaly.

Isolation forests take a fundamentally different, and highly effective, approach: They ignore normal and explicitly seek to isolate the abnormal.

The entire logic rests on one simple premise that anomalies are few and different:

- This is because an anomaly is rare (few), and it does not take much effort to find it.
- This is because an anomaly is unlike the rest of the data (different), and it lies far away from the main cluster of data points.

Forest and the isolation path

The algorithm constructs an ensemble of simple, random decision trees, the forest. Imagine a vast space containing every piece of telemetry (logs, traces, metrics):

- **Random splitting**: The isolation forest starts cutting this space up randomly. It randomly selects a feature (say, an error code number) and then randomly selects a value to split the data (e.g., all codes above 500 go left, all below go right).
- **Recursive cutting**: This process of random cutting continues recursively until every single data point is isolated on its own leaf.
- **Measuring the path length**: The true signal of the anomaly is the Path Length, how many cuts (splits) it took to isolate a data point from all others.
    - **Normal points**: This is because normal data points are densely packed together, they look alike, and they are deep inside the cluster. It requires *many* random cuts to finally separate one normal point from its close neighbors. This results in a long path length.
    - **Anomalous points**: It is because anomalies are sitting far away on the edges of the data space, a random cut is likely to hit near them, separating them quickly from the dense cluster. They require *very few* random cuts to be isolated. This results in a short path length.

To visualize the efficiency of this *few and different* logic, the diagram below illustrates how the random partitioning mechanism quickly isolates outliers near the surface, resulting in a much shorter path length compared to normal data points. *Figure 7.2* visualizes how random partitioning in an isolation forest quickly isolates outliers with shorter path lengths:

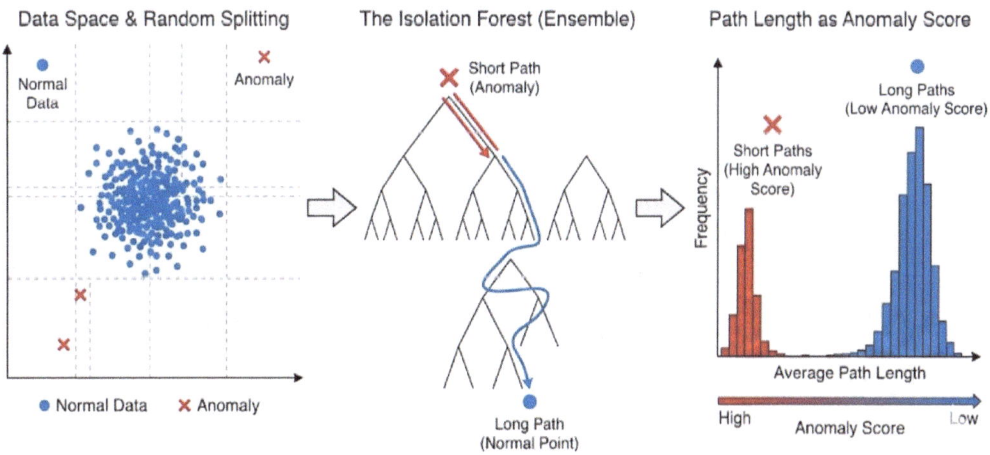

***Figure 7.2**: Isolation forest partitioning mechanism identifying outliers*

SRE use case for log anomaly detection

This simple, efficient structure makes the isolation forest the ideal tool for handling operational logs:

- **Scenario**: A new version of your microservice is deployed, and it introduces a brand new, never-before-seen error message deep in the logs.
- **Detection**: Traditional tools would have to be manually updated with a regular expression for this new error. The isolation forest, however, ingests the entire log stream. When it sees the new error message, it recognizes its unique combination of characters and attributes (the specific function name, the log severity level, etc.). Since this combination is completely different from the millions of normal log lines, the algorithm needs only a couple of random splits to isolate it. It registers a very short path length, immediately flagging it as a novelty anomaly, allowing SREs to investigate a true unknown without ever writing a manual rule.

Table 7.2 compares the key differences between the complex correlation models and the efficient isolation models:

Feature	Autoencoder	Isolation forest
Data type	Continuous time series metrics (CPU, Latency).	High-cardinality discrete data (Logs, Traces).
Complexity	High (deep learning). Captures non-linear correlations.	Low (tree ensemble). Fast and scalable.
Best for	Gray failures, partial degradation, hardware faults.	New errors, novel stack traces, security breaches.
Output	Reconstruction error score.	Anomaly score (0 to 1).

Table 7.2: Model selection guide

The isolation forest provides a powerful, scalable foundation for sifting through the massive volume of operational data that flows from a modern distributed system, ensuring that true novel events are detected quickly and cheaply.

Forecasting and seasonality with time series modeling

The statistical and machine learning methods discussed so far, like IQR and autoencoders, are brilliant at analyzing the system in the moment; they tell you if the current data point is unusual compared to others around it. However, they lack context and foresight.

To achieve true proactive reliability, SREs must answer two critical questions:

- **Context**: Is this high load acceptable because it is 9:00 AM on a Monday?
- **Foresight**: When will a system resource run out, given its current growth rate?

Time series modeling

This is the technique that treats system telemetry (metrics like CPU, latency, or disk space) not as a simple stream of numbers, but as a sequence of events with inherent memory and predictable patterns. This modeling allows the AIOps platform to move from observing the *now* to accurately predicting the *future*.

Advanced timeseries analysis decomposes every metric into three independent components, easier-to-analyze components:

- **The trend (The long-term path)**: This is the general, long-term direction in which your metric is moving. Think of it as a child's growth chart: while their weight fluctuates daily, the overall trend is steadily upward.
  - **SRE example**: A slow but consistent increase in the average memory usage of a database server over six months. This trend signals application bloat or poor garbage collection.
  - **AIOps action**: The model isolates this trend to determine the fundamental direction of the service's resource consumption.
- **Seasonality (The repeating cycles)**: This component captures the cyclical, predictable patterns of your business. These cycles can be hourly, daily, weekly, or yearly. They are crucial because they explain most of the system's normal variation:
  - **SRE example**: An e-commerce site always sees a massive, predictable spike in requests between 11:00 AM and 1:00 PM (daily cycle). It also experiences a predictable drop in traffic every weekend (weekly cycle).
  - **AIOps action**: The model learns these cycles so that a massive spike during 11:00 AM is treated as normal, while the exact same spike at 3:00 AM is flagged as an anomaly.
- **The noise or residual (The surprise)**: Once the trend and seasonality have been mathematically accounted for and removed, the only thing left is the unpredictable variation, the residual. This residual is pure, unexplained system behavior.
  - **SRE example**: An unexpected bug causes a database query to suddenly lock up, leading to a small, non-seasonal spike in latency. This spike is not explained by trend or time of day.

- **AIOps Action**: The model focuses its anomaly detection efforts almost entirely on this residual. If the residual exceeds a small, dynamic confidence buffer, it signals a true, unpredicted anomaly.

Figure 7.3 shows how a timeseries metric is decomposed into trend, seasonality, and residual components:

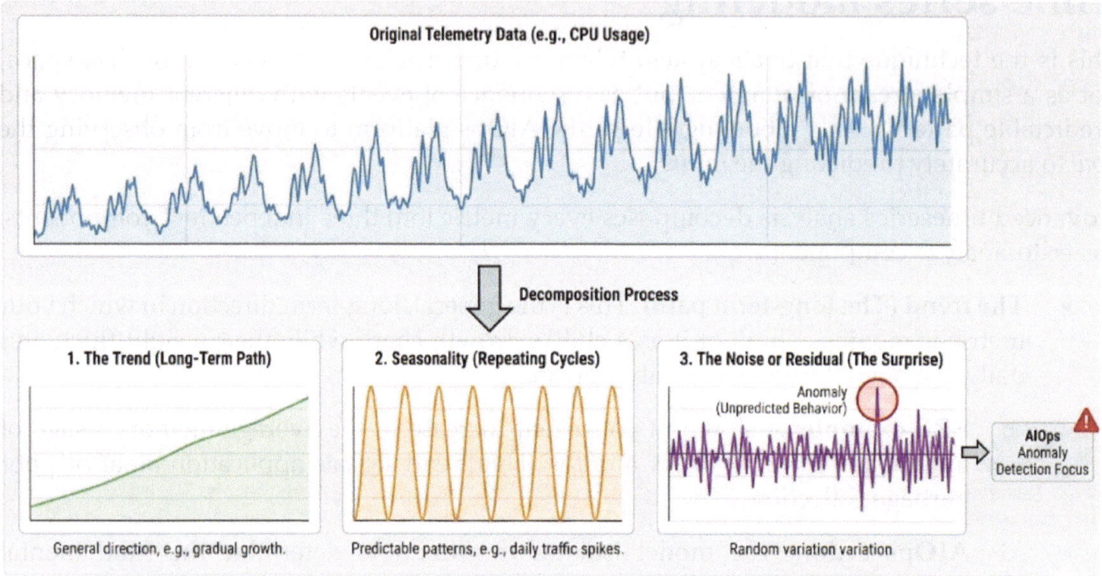

Figure 7.3: Decomposition of service telemetry into predictable and unpredictable components

Anomaly detection through contextual filtering

By using this decomposition, the AIOps platform achieves contextual anomaly detection. The model first predicts what the metric *should* be right now, based on the trend plus the seasonality. It then checks the actual value against this prediction:

- **Traditional monitoring**: An alert fires when the CPU hits 80%.
- **Time series monitoring**: If the model predicted 85% CPU because it's the annual Black Friday traffic peak, the 80% reading is ignored. The system is operating within context. If the model predicted 20% CPU because it is 4:00 AM, the 80% reading is flagged immediately as a contextual anomaly.

Predictive capacity planning in practice

Predictive capacity planning relies on extending the trend line into the future, enabling proactive scaling decisions:

- **The problem (Reactive scaling)**: Most teams reactively scale their storage or compute. They receive an alert: *Disk is 90% full!* The SRE is paged and must scramble to provision new storage, often working overtime to resolve what should have been a planning task. The team is always behind the curve.
- **The solution (TTS)**: The time series model continuously analyzes the trend of resource consumption (e.g., how much disk space is being added per day). It then mathematically calculates the exact future date when that trend line will cross the 100% capacity threshold. This is the TTS.
  - **AIOps alert**: *Based on the current data ingestion trend, Storage Volume vol-prod-db-1 will reach 95% capacity in 21 days, 4 hours.*
  - **SRE action**: This transforms a potential P0 outage into a scheduled, low-stress P3 Jira ticket. The SRE can execute the capacity upgrade during a planned maintenance window three weeks later, eliminating the last-minute fire drill entirely. This is one of the clearest examples of AIOps turning operational toil into strategic engineering work.

Operationalizing anomaly detection

The most critical challenge in deploying advanced anomaly detection is the transition from mathematical discovery to operational action. An Autoencoder may detect a statistically unusual data point, or an isolation forest may flag a novel log line. However, a mathematical anomaly is not always a business problem. If SREs are paged for every statistical outlier, two detrimental outcomes are guaranteed: rapid alert fatigue and the complete erosion of trust in the AIOps platform.

To prevent this, anomaly detection must be tightly and programmatically coupled with the error budget. The error budget acts as the indispensable filter, ensuring that SREs are only engaged when an anomaly poses a verifiable threat to the reliability promise made to the customer (SLO).

Operationalizing detection requires a structured, three-pronged framework that moves the AIOps platform beyond simple alerting and into the realm of proactive, risk-based reliability management. This framework ensures that every alert is not just an observation of variance, but a precise calculation of business impact.

Principle 1: Burn alert strategy

We must shift the alerting paradigm away from static thresholds and even raw anomaly scores toward error budget burn rate. Instead of asking, *Is the latency high? or Is the anomaly score above 0.9?* we ask: *Is this current state of performance consuming the error budget at a rate that threatens to exhaust it within a critical time window?*

The operational flow for converting anomalies into actionable alerts is as follows:

- **Raw anomaly detection**: The chosen model (e.g., IQR, autoencoder) detects a deviation and outputs an anomaly score or deviation magnitude.
- **SLI correlation**: The platform immediately maps this deviation to the relevant **service level indicator** (**SLI**) for the service. For example, a latency spike from IQR must be linked to the SLO: *99.9% of requests must complete in under 300ms*.
- **Budget consumption calculation**: The platform calculates how many bad events (latency over 300ms) are currently occurring per minute due to the detected anomaly.
- **Burn rate calculation**: The system determines the current burn rate. This is a factor representing how fast the budget is being spent relative to the budget's maximum allowable spend rate.

  For example, if the budget allows for 10 minutes of downtime per month, and the current error rate projects spending that entire budget in 5 days, the burn rate is very high.

The alert is then based on the projected TTH of the budget, not the raw metric value. *Figure 7.4* shows a visual representation of this burn alerting pipeline:

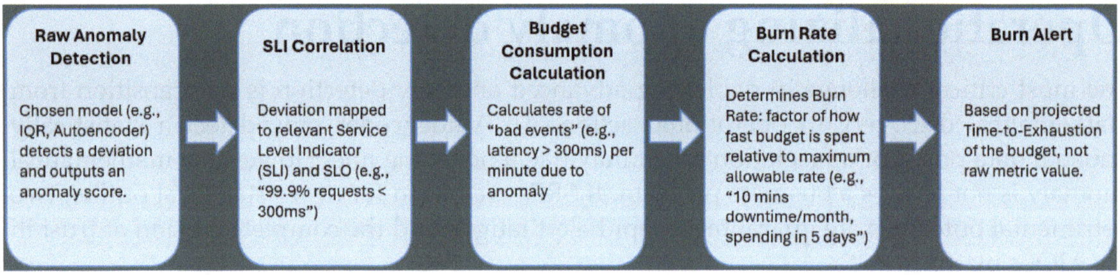

***Figure 7.4**: The burn alerting pipeline for anomaly operationalization*

Principle 2: Alert tiers and time-to-exhaustion

Effective operationalization requires defining clear tiers of action based on the calculated burn rate. Not all anomalies warrant a page. The following table summarizes the recommended alert tiers, associated burn rates, response actions, and cognitive load for effective anomaly management:

Alert tier	Burn rate factor	TTS	Recommended action	Cognitive load
P0 (Immediate Page)	12x to 30x the normal burn rate	< 1 hour (Fast Burn)	**Immediate paging**: Engage on-call SRE. Trigger automated diagnostics, failovers, or rollbacks	Highest (Requires immediate attention)

Alert tier	Burn rate factor	TTS	Recommended action	Cognitive load
P1 (Working Hours Ticket)	2x to 10x the normal burn rate	1 day to 3 days (Slow Burn)	**Jira ticket (P1/P2)**: Assign to the owning team for review during working hours. No page, but requires prompt action	Medium (Planned attention)
P3 (Telemetry Logging)	0.5x to 1x the normal burn rate	>7 days (Degradation)	**Log event**: Record the anomaly score and contributing metrics to a dashboard. No ticket, no page. Used to explore postmortems	Lowest (Informational only)

***Table 7.3**: Alert tiers, burn rates, and recommended response actions*

This framework eliminates false alarms for events that are mathematically unusual but are not critical enough to breach the SLO. For example, a latency spike that costs 1 minute of the monthly error budget, but then immediately resolves, might simply be logged as a P3 event, preserving SRE focus.

Principle 3: Automated diagnostic snapshot

Once a P0 or P1 anomaly alert is triggered via the burn alert strategy, the work of the AIOps platform is not complete. The single most frustrating part of incident response is logging in and finding no evidence.

To address this, the burn alert must automatically trigger an **automated diagnostic snapshot** (**ADS**). This process leverages the intelligence that detected the anomaly to collect and package the relevant evidence before the state changes.

ADS consists of the following core components:

- **Feature attribution (Why did the model alert?)**: The AIOps platform uses the internal workings of the detection model to identify the most significant *contributing factors*:
    - **For autoencoders**: Identify which input features (e.g., specific CPU threads, network socket counts) contributed most to the high reconstruction error. This tells the SRE exactly *where* to look.
    - **For isolation forests**: Immediately grab the top 100 log lines or trace IDs that led to the short path length, providing the exact novel error messages.
- **Contextual dump**: Capture the state of the relevant service(s) at the moment of the anomaly peak. The contextual dump must include the following diagnostic artifacts:

- Full container logs and system logs for the 5 minutes preceding the alert.
- Heap dump or thread stack traces if memory/CPU was the primary indicator.
- Configuration files (e.g., Kubernetes YAML) of the affected component to rule out configuration drift.

- **Triage narrative**: Generate a one-paragraph summary for the SRE:
  - **Anomaly type**: Multivariate degradation (Autoencoder score 0.95).
  - **Budget impact**: Projected exhaustion in 45 minutes (15x Burn rate).
  - **Suggested cause**: High correlation between database connections and memory consumption indicates pool exhaustion.

By the time the SRE acknowledges the page, they have a fully compiled, contextualized diagnostic package, accelerating the MTTD from hours to minutes. This operational maturity is the difference between a functional AIOps tool and a transformative reliability engine.

Model lifecycle and drift detection

Deploying an advanced anomaly detection model, be it an autoencoder or a time series predictor, is not a static engineering task; it is the beginning of a continuous maintenance cycle. In the dynamic, ever-changing environment of distributed systems, a model trained on healthy data from six months ago is likely wrong today. New code deployments, infrastructure shifts, marketing campaigns, and genuine growth all conspire to change the system's performance baseline.

The moment a model's performance degrades because the underlying system has changed, it is experiencing **model drift**. It is the nemesis of sustained AIOps value, leading directly to an increase in false alarms and missed incidents. Effective operationalization requires implementing a clear strategy for model governance and lifecycle management.

Understanding model drift

Model drift manifests in two distinct forms, each requiring different operational responses:

- **Concept drift (The target changes)**: This is the most challenging form of drift. It occurs when the *relationship* between the input metrics and the output performance changes.

  For example, a new feature is launched that fundamentally redesigns the database access pattern. Previously, the normal relationship was that high latency leads to low throughput. Now, due to highly efficient caching, the normal relationship is that high latency leads to high throughput. The old autoencoder, trained on the pre-release concept of normal, will flag the new, healthy behavior as an anomaly. The model is technically correct, but the underlying system behavior (the *concept*) has shifted.

- **Data drift (The input distribution changes)**: This occurs when the statistical properties of the incoming telemetry change, even if the system is still functionally healthy.

  For example, a service handles traffic mostly from Europe. A marketing push expands the user base significantly into Asia, where network round-trip times are inherently higher. The model suddenly sees a shift toward higher average latency values across the board. The model is now receiving input data it has never seen, even though the service itself is performing optimally for its new environment.

Strategies for model retraining and adaptation

To combat drift, an AIOps platform must employ a robust, automated retraining strategy that moves beyond simple time-based schedules:

- **Scheduled retraining (Baseline maintenance)**: A non-negotiable component is scheduled retraining. Typically, models are retrained weekly or monthly on a rolling window of recent, healthy data (e.g., the last 30 days). This ensures the model adapts to gradual, legitimate system growth and slow-moving trends without human intervention. The critical constraint here is that the training data must first be filtered to exclude known incidents or anomalies from the window to prevent the model from learning failure as normal.
- **Event-based retraining (Responding to change)**: The fastest way to introduce concept drift is a major software release. The AIOps system must leverage its connection to the **continuous integration/continuous delivery** (**CI/CD**) pipeline to recognize and respond to these moments.
  - **Deployment signal**: When a successful deployment to production is confirmed, the AIOps platform should mark the subsequent 24 to 48 hours. If no major incidents occur during this window, the model should be retrained immediately on the new, successful post-deployment data. This ensures the model learns the new *normal* quickly.
- **Drift detection monitoring (Early warning)**: The most sophisticated AIOps platforms actively monitor the model's performance on live data before it alerts. Instead of waiting for the model to issue false alarms, the platform monitors metrics like:
  - **Prediction stability**: How much does the model's prediction of a metric deviate from the actual input? High, sustained deviation suggests the model is losing relevance.
  - **Feature importance change**: Has the relative importance of input features (e.g., CPU vs. network I/O) suddenly flipped? This can signal a major code refactor or a database change that the model has not yet learned.

When these drift indicators exceed a threshold, the AIOps platform can trigger a proactive notification: *Anomaly Detection Model Service-A-Autoencoder is experiencing high Data Drift.*

Recommend an immediate revalidation and scheduled retraining. This transforms model maintenance from a reactive task to a controlled, predictive function, safeguarding the integrity of the entire detection pipeline.

Advanced anomaly detection techniques

In contemporary SRE, anomaly detection has evolved beyond basic statistical models to encompass sophisticated machine learning and hybrid approaches. These advanced techniques are designed to address the complexity and scale of modern distributed systems, where failures often manifest in subtle, multivariate patterns.

- **Hybrid statistical-machine learning models**: Modern anomaly detection frameworks frequently combine statistical baselining with machine learning algorithms. For example, systems may use rolling averages and IQR to establish dynamic baselines, then apply unsupervised learning models to identify deviations that escape traditional thresholds. This layered approach ensures both computational efficiency and contextual sensitivity.

- **Autoencoders for multivariate analysis**: Autoencoders, a class of neural networks, are particularly effective for detecting anomalies in high-dimensional telemetry data. By learning compressed representations of normal system behavior, autoencoders can flag instances where the reconstructed output diverges significantly from the input. This method excels at identifying *gray failures*, where individual metrics appear normal, but their combined state is anomalous.

- **Isolation forests for log and trace data**: Isolation forests offer a scalable solution for anomaly detection in large volumes of discrete data, such as application logs and distributed traces. Unlike models that profile normal behavior, Isolation forests focus on isolating rare and different data points through recursive partitioning. This technique is well-suited for identifying novel errors and security breaches, as it quickly isolates outliers with minimal computational overhead.

- **Time series forecasting and contextual filtering**: Advanced time series models, such as Prophet or ARIMA, decompose telemetry data into trend, seasonality, and residual components. By predicting expected values based on historical patterns, these models enable contextual anomaly detection, distinguishing between predictable spikes and genuine anomalies. This capability is essential for proactive reliability, allowing SRE teams to anticipate capacity issues and respond before service degradation occurs.

- **Model lifecycle management and drift detection**: Deploying advanced anomaly detection models is not a one-time effort. Continuous monitoring for model drift, whether due to changing system behavior (concept drift) or shifts in input data distribution (data drift), is critical. Automated retraining strategies, triggered by scheduled intervals or significant system changes, ensure models remain accurate and relevant. Drift detection mechanisms, such as monitoring prediction stability and feature importance, provide early warnings for necessary model updates.

In summary, practitioners can apply statistical models like IQR for single-metric baselining, Autoencoders for detecting multivariate anomalies, and isolation forests for uncovering novel patterns in logs and traces. Time series models such as Prophet or ARIMA enable forecasting and contextual filtering, while drift detection ensures models stay accurate as systems evolve. This layered approach balances precision, scalability, and operational relevance.

Building anomaly detection into error budget strategy

Integrating anomaly detection with error budget management transforms raw statistical insights into actionable reliability decisions. This coupling ensures that operational alerts are not only mathematically justified but also aligned with business objectives and customer commitments:

- **Error budget as an operational filter**: The error budget represents the allowable margin for service unreliability within a defined period, typically governed by SLOs. By mapping anomaly detection outputs directly to error budget consumption, organizations can prioritize incidents based on their impact on reliability promises. This approach filters out noise, ensuring that only anomalies threatening the error budget trigger operational responses.

- **Burn rate-based alerting**: Traditional alerting mechanisms often rely on static thresholds or anomaly scores, leading to alert fatigue and reduced trust in monitoring systems. A burn rate-based strategy shifts the focus to the rate at which the error budget is consumed. Alerts are generated when the projected time to error budget exhaustion falls within critical windows, such as less than one hour (fast burn) or several days (slow burn). This method aligns operational urgency with business risk.

- **Tiered response framework**: Effective operationalization requires a tiered response system, categorizing alerts based on burn rate and time-to-exhaustion. Immediate pages (P0) are reserved for rapid error budget depletion, while slower burns may result in tickets or informational logging. This structure ensures that SRE attention is directed where it is most needed, reducing cognitive load and preserving focus for high-impact events.

- **Automated diagnostic snapshots**: When a critical anomaly is detected, automated diagnostic snapshots capture relevant system state and contributing factors. Feature attribution identifies which metrics or log entries triggered the alert, while contextual dumps preserve logs, configuration files, and resource states for post-incident analysis. This process accelerates MTTD and supports efficient incident resolution.

- **Continuous improvement and governance**: Integrating anomaly detection with error budget Strategy is an ongoing process. Regular reviews of alerting effectiveness, coupled with feedback loops from incident postmortems, drive continuous improvement. Governance mechanisms, such as automated retraining and drift monitoring, ensure that detection models and operational policies remain aligned with evolving system behavior and business requirements.

Conclusion

In this chapter, we have successfully navigated the entire spectrum of advanced anomaly Detection, completing the critical transition from reactive monitoring to proactive intelligence. We moved beyond the brittle simplicity of static thresholds and the limitations of traditional statistics, embracing models that understand the fluid, complex nature of modern distributed systems.

We established a robust foundation by mastering statistical techniques like the IQR, demonstrating its superiority for analyzing skewed operational metrics like latency, where simple averages fail. We then scaled our capabilities into the realm of unsupervised machine learning, detailing the architecture of autoencoders to identify complex, multivariate gray failures by modeling correlations, and utilizing isolation forests for high-speed, scalable detection of novel outliers in massive log and trace streams. Furthermore, we ensured our detection was grounded in business reality by using time series modeling to account for seasonality and trend, enabling both contextual alerting and critical TTS capacity forecasting.

Most importantly, we operationalized these powerful tools. We recognized that the output of a mathematical model is meaningless without a decisive action plan, establishing the burn alert strategy. By tightly coupling anomaly scores with the error budget and the projected TTS, we ensure that every alert is not merely a signal of variance, but a precise calculation of business risk. This framework guarantees SREs are only engaged in response to events that genuinely threaten customer-facing reliability. Finally, we addressed the crucial engineering discipline of model lifecycle and drift detection, ensuring that our AIOps intelligence remains accurate and relevant as the underlying environment inevitably changes.

We have built a highly sensitive and supremely intelligent system capable of detecting the known unknowns and flagging the unknown unknowns with high fidelity. However, detection is only half the battle. When an anomaly is confirmed, and the error budget is burning rapidly, the SRE team needs to know *why* with surgical precision.

The next chapter will take the high-fidelity anomaly events generated here and connect them to their source. We will pivot from detection to diagnosis, exploring techniques like intelligent event grouping to aggregate telemetry chaos and applying probabilistic root cause identification to automatically narrow down the millions of possible causes to the single most likely culprit. This transition is the final step in reducing human cognitive load, preparing the system to move from smart diagnostics to automated runbooks and true self-healing capabilities.

CHAPTER 8
Causal Inference and Efficient Root Cause Analysis

Introduction

In modern SRE and AIOps, detecting anomalies is no longer the hardest problem. The real challenge lies in determining why the anomaly occurred and identifying the true root cause among hundreds of cascading alerts and symptoms. In distributed microservices environments, failures rarely present as isolated events. Instead, a single underlying fault propagates across interconnected systems, creating a storm of secondary symptoms that obscure the original cause.

For example, a database connection pool exhaustion in a production system may initially manifest as increased API latency, elevated error rates, and service timeouts across multiple microservices. Traditional monitoring tools generate hundreds of alerts across application, infrastructure, and network layers. However, these alerts represent symptoms rather than the true cause. Without intelligent causal analysis, engineers must manually investigate each signal, significantly increasing MTTD and prolonging service disruption.

Traditional RCA relies heavily on manual investigation, intuition, and tribal knowledge. In hyperscale, cloud-native environments, this approach is no longer viable. The volume, velocity, and complexity of telemetry data demand an automated, intelligent approach to diagnosis. Causal inference and probabilistic reasoning provide this capability by transforming RCA from a reactive forensic activity into a predictive, automated diagnostic system.

This chapter introduces causal inference, the analytical brain of the AIOps platform. We move beyond simple correlation, which merely observes that events occur together, and toward causation, which establishes definitive cause-and-effect relationships. By applying intelligent event grouping and probabilistic root cause analysis, the system collapses alert noise into a single, high-confidence diagnosis. This transformation converts fragmented telemetry signals into a precise diagnostic pathway, enabling rapid root cause identification and laying the foundation for automated remediation and self-healing infrastructure.

Structure

In this chapter, we will cover the following topics:

- Intelligent event grouping and incident aggregation
- Probabilistic root cause identification through observability data
- Transforming post-incident analysis into automated runbooks
- Reducing downtime with predictive insights

Objectives

By the end of this chapter, you will be able to build a system that automatically collapses thousands of noisy alerts into a single, actionable incident. You will understand the mathematical logic required to identify the first domino in a failure chain and learn how to map these insights to automated remediation workflows. Our goal is to reduce the MTTD from hours to seconds.

Intelligent event grouping and incident aggregation

Imagine a typical day in the life of an SRE. A single database slowdown triggers hundreds of alerts: **application programming interface** (**API**) latency spikes, error rates climb, user complaints flood in, and dashboards light up like a Christmas tree. This is the infamous alert storm: a cascade of symptoms, each one a clue, but together forming a wall of noise.

Modern systems are deeply interconnected. A single root cause can manifest as dozens or hundreds of downstream symptoms. Without intelligent grouping, every symptom generates its own alert, overwhelming on-call engineers and obscuring the true cause.

Think of a doctor faced with a patient who has a fever, cough, headache, and fatigue. Treating each symptom in isolation is inefficient and potentially dangerous. The real goal is to diagnose the underlying illness, be it the flu, COVID-19, or something else. Similarly, SREs must look beyond individual alerts to find the root cause.

Event correlation vs. event causation

To understand how AIOps moves from noise to knowledge, it is essential to distinguish between event correlation and event causation:

- **Event correlation**: Grouping alerts that occur together in time or share common attributes (e.g., same service, same host).
- **Event causation**: Understanding which events are symptoms and which are causes. Not all correlated events are causally linked.

For example:

- **Correlated**: API latency and database errors spike at the same time.
- **Causal**: Database connection pool exhaustion causes API latency.

Clustering techniques for related events

AIOps platforms typically use three main logic *engines* to group alerts:

- **Temporal grouping (Time)**: Alerts that occur within the same narrow time window (e.g., a 2-minute *sliding window*) are likely related to the same root event.
- **Topological grouping (Space)**: This leverages the *service map (topology graph of dependencies)*. If an alert fires on *Service A* and *Database B*, and the system knows Service A depends on Database B, these alerts are grouped.
- **Semantic grouping (Content)**: This uses NLP to look at the text of logs or alert descriptions. If 50 alerts mention *Connection Timeout* and *SQL Exception*, they are clustered together even if they come from different parts of the infrastructure.

Site reliability engineering perspective

Think of event grouping as a professional *triage nurse* in an ER. Instead of treating every person who walks in as a separate, unrelated event, the nurse identifies that 20 people all arrived from the same bus accident and groups them into one coordinated emergency response.

The following figure illustrates how intelligent event grouping reduces alert noise and focuses attention on the underlying incident:

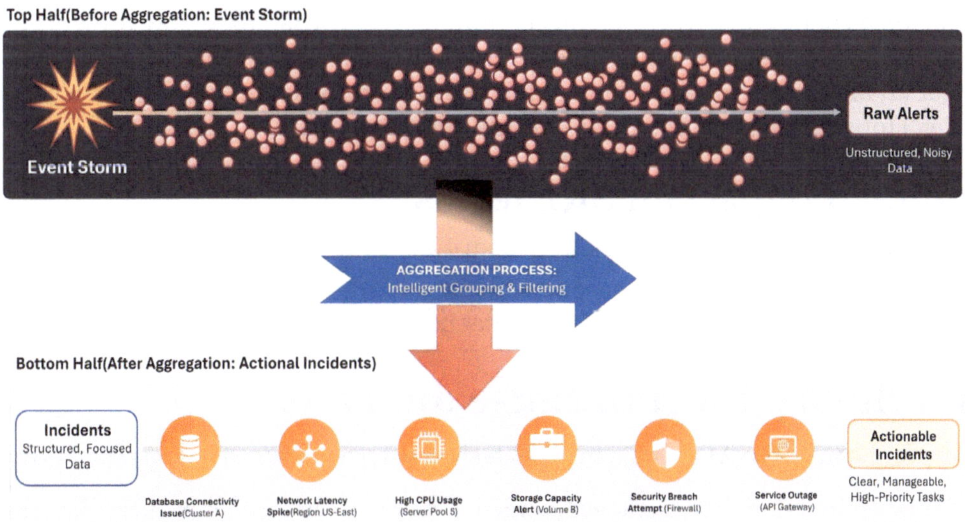

Figure 8.1: Event storm before and after aggregation

Probabilistic root cause identification through observability data

In the heat of a major system outage, the *war room* is often a place of high tension and conflicting theories. One engineer points to a spike in CPU usage on the web tier. Another points to a slow query in the database. A third mentions a recent network configuration change. In these moments, the human brain is wired to look for patterns, but it is also notoriously bad at distinguishing between things that happen at the same time (correlation) and things that actually cause each other (Causation).

To solve this, AIOps moves away from human *best guesses* and toward probabilistic root cause identification. This is the science of using math, specifically *graph theory* and *Bayesian logic,* to sift through millions of observability signals and identify the *first domino* that started the collapse.

Understanding correlation and causation

Prior to exploring the math, we must understand the fundamental problem: correlation is not causation.

Imagine a sunny day at a beach. You notice two things: sales of ice cream are at an all-time high, and the number of people getting sunburns is also at an all-time high. Therefore:

- **Correlation**: Ice cream sales and sunburns are moving up together.
- **Causation**: Did eating ice cream *cause* the sunburn? The answer is no, both were caused by a *hidden factor* (the Sun).

In information technology, this happens every minute. When a database slows down, your web server's memory usage might spike because it is holding onto thousands of open connections waiting for an answer. If you only look at the *what* (memory spike), you might try to fix the web server. However, the *why* (root cause) is the database.

Operational impact on SRE teams

If your AIOps tool only uses correlation, it will send you a *Root Cause* report saying, *Your Web Server is out of memory.* You will spend an hour adding RAM, only to realize the problem persists. Causal inference ensures you spend that hour fixing the database instead.

Graph theory for root cause analysis

To find the root cause, the AI needs a map. In technical terms, we call this graph theory.

Think of your entire IT environment, every microservice, every container, every database, and every network switch as a Node (a point on a map). The relationships between them, who talks to whom, are called Edges (the lines connecting the points).

Simple dependency chain: Consider a simple three-tier architecture:

User Service | Order Service | Database

In this structure, each component is represented as a node, and each dependency is represented as a directed edge indicating the flow of interaction. The User Service depends on the Order Service, which in turn relies on the database to process and retrieve information.

If the database experiences a failure, the Order Service is unable to complete its operations and begins generating errors. These failures propagate downstream, eventually impacting the User Service. Although alerts may first appear at the User Service, the underlying root cause originates in the database.

This dependency structure forms a **directed acyclic graph** (**DAG**), where relationships follow a defined direction without circular dependencies. By traversing the graph upstream from affected components, the AIOps system can accurately identify the originating source of failure.

Topology map

In real-world systems, these dependency chains exist at massive scale. AIOps platforms automatically construct this topology map by analyzing distributed traces, which capture how requests flow between services. This process produces a DAG representing the system's true operational structure:

- **Directed**: Dependencies follow a defined directional relationship, where downstream services depend on upstream components (for example, the web server calls the database).
- **Acyclic**: This is because we want to avoid *circular logic* where A causes B, B causes C, and C causes A.

This DAG serves as the foundational structural model that powers root cause analysis, predictive simulation, and digital twin modeling throughout the AIOps platform.

Random walk algorithm

Once we have this map, and an incident occurs, the AI performs what is known as a *random walk on a graph*. Imagine the AI is a detective walking through the streets of your infrastructure. It starts at the *alerting node* (where the fire was first spotted). It then walks upstream along the dependency chain against the direction of request flow. This traversal follows a simple decision logic as it moves upstream through the dependency graph:

- If the web server is failing, the detective walks to the load balancer and the database.
- If the load balancer looks healthy but the database is screaming with errors, the detective stays at the database.

- It continues this *walk* until it finds the node that has no *failed* neighbors further upstream. That node is your *root cause.*

Each traversal step incorporates probabilistic weighting based on observed telemetry anomalies, allowing the system to converge on the most statistically likely root cause rather than relying on deterministic rules.

Bayesian reasoning for root cause analysis

While graph theory gives us the map, **Bayesian logic** provides the brain. Named after *Thomas Bayes*, this branch of mathematics is about updating your belief in a theory as new evidence comes in.

In SRE terms, we use it to calculate the probability of the root cause.

Bayesian inference explained

Bayesian inference works in three steps:

1. **The prior (Initial belief)**: Before we look at today's data, what do we know? In this system, the payment gateway service fails about 1% of the time, but the legacy database fails 10% of the time. Our prior tells us the database is a more likely suspect.
2. **Likelihood (New evidence)**: We look at the current telemetry. The payment gateway is currently showing a 500 Error, but the legacy database shows it is 100% healthy.
3. **The posterior (The updated truth)**: We combine our prior knowledge with new evidence. Even though the database is usually the problem, the current evidence is so strong against the payment gateway that our belief shifts. We now conclude there is a 98% probability that the payment gateway is the root cause.

The following figure visualizes the Bayesian detective process of updating root cause probabilities as new evidence arrives:

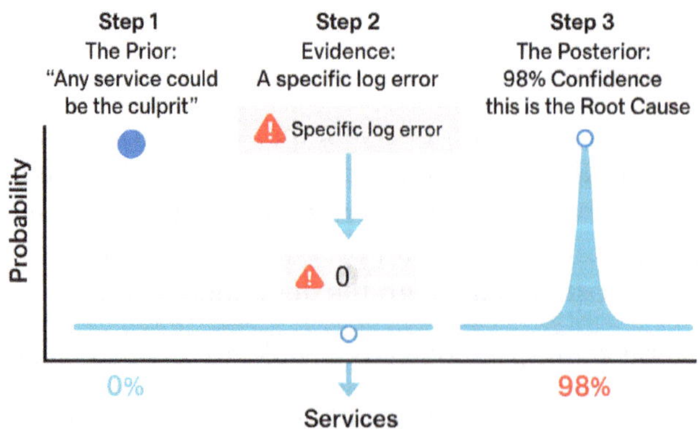

Figure 8.2: The Bayesian detective graph

Integrating the three pillars of observability

For probabilistic RCA to be expert level, it cannot rely on metrics alone. It must ingest the three pillars of observability data simultaneously:

- **Metrics (The vital signs)**: Tells the AI *when* the patient's heart rate spiked. (e.g., CPU is at 99%).
- **Logs (The diary)**: Tells the AI *what* the patient said happened. (e.g., Error: Cannot connect to host 10.0.0.5).
- **Traces (The travel map)**: Tells the AI *everywhere* the patient went before getting sick. (e.g., User | API Gateway | Auth Service | Database).

AIOps Aha! moment

The AI sees a metric spike (latency) in the Order Service. It looks at the traces and sees that 100% of those slow orders passed through the stock-check microservice. It then looks at the logs for stock-check and finds a novelty anomaly (as discussed in *Chapter 7, Advanced Anomaly Detection*), saying null pointer exception.

The graph theory shows the stock-check service is upstream. The Bayesian logic calculates that a null pointer exception in a direct dependency is a 99.9% match for the root cause.

Within seconds, before the SRE has even finished pouring their coffee, the system presents a single screen: *Root cause identified: null pointer exception in Stock-Check Service. Confidence: 99.9%.*

Probabilistic models over deterministic rules

In the old days, we used rule-based RCA. These were *If/Then* statements: *If CPU > 90% AND Latency > 2s, THEN Restart Server.*

Modern systems are too complex for rules. A rule-based system is like a doctor who only knows five diseases. If you walk in with a sixth disease, the doctor is useless.

Probabilistic RCA is different. It does not need a pre-written rule for every failure. This is because it understands the topology (the map) and the probability (the logic), allowing it to diagnose failures it has never seen before. It looks at the flow of data and says, *I've never seen this specific error, but based on the way the failure is traveling through the graph, the most likely source is node X.*

This is the transition from reactive diagnostics (looking at what happened) to intelligent inference (understanding why it happened). By mastering probabilistic RCA, we eliminate the *blame game* during incidents. We stop treating symptoms (the ice cream sales) and start fixing the source (the sun). This mathematical foundation allows the SRE team to trust the machine's diagnosis, which is the essential prerequisite for the next step: automated remediation.

The following figure contrasts reactive, rule-based diagnostics with probabilistic inference, highlighting why probabilistic approaches are essential for resilience in complex architectures:

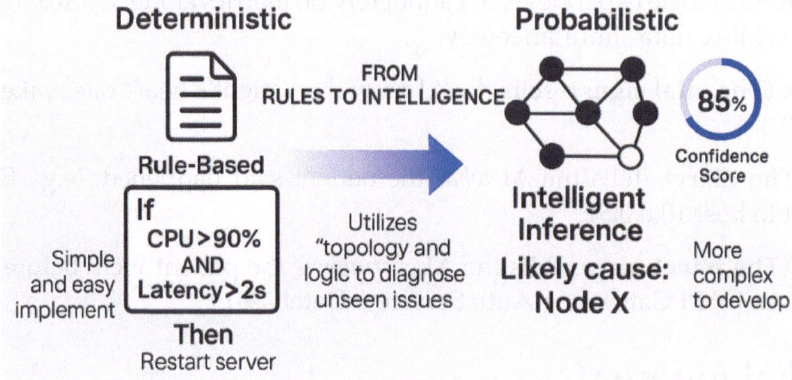

Figure 8.3: Probabilistic vs. deterministic root cause analysis

Next, we will look at how to take these probabilistic insights and map them to automated runbooks, turning a 99.9% diagnosis into a 100% automated cure.

Transforming post-incident analysis into automated runbooks

In the traditional world of IT, the end of an incident is marked by a post-mortem or a **post-incident review** (**PIR**). Engineers sit in a room, discuss what went wrong, and write a long document detailing the *Lessons Learned*.

These documents are where knowledge goes to die. They are stored in a digital folder that no one reads until the next time the same disaster strikes, at which point the on-call engineer has to frantically search through old PDFs while the system is burning. This is the **knowledge gap**.

In an AIOps-driven SRE practice, we close this gap. We do not just learn from an incident; we encode that learning into the system itself. This section explores how we move from knowing what happened to ensuring it never requires a human to fix it again.

Toil trap and the need for automation

SREs define toil as manual, repetitive, and automatable work that provides no long-term value. Manually restarting a server every time its memory hits 95% is the definition of toil.

If our probabilistic RCA (which we discussed in the previous section) can identify the root cause with 99% certainty, then asking a human to log in and type a command is a waste of time. Every second a human spends *confirming* what the AI already knows is a second of unnecessary downtime. The goal of this phase is to turn **human response** into **digital logic**.

Anatomy of an automated runbook

A runbook is essentially a *recipe* for fixing a specific problem. In the past, these were written in English. In an AIOps world, these are written in code (typically Python, Go, or YAML).

An automated runbook consists of three main parts:

- **The trigger (The If)**: This is fed directly by our causal inference engine. Example: *If the Root Cause is "Database Connection Pool Exhaustion."*
- **The action (The Then)**: The specific script to execute. Example: *Increase the connection limit by 20% and clear stagnant sessions.*
- **The verification (The Check)**: After the action is taken, the system checks the vital signs (symptom metrics) to ensure they return to normal.

Four levels of remediation maturity

You cannot go from manual work to full robot control overnight. It requires building trust. We view this as a four-step ladder:

1. **Level 0**: Manual (No automation):

   AI alerts a human. The human investigates, finds the script, and runs it manually.

2. **Level 1**: Recommended action (The GPS approach):

   The AI identifies the root cause and presents a **Fix Now** button to the SRE. The human still decides whether to click it.

3. **Level 2**: Augmented remediation (The co-pilot):

   The AI performs the initial, safe steps automatically (like gathering extra logs or clearing a cache) but waits for human approval for *heavy* actions like restarting a database.

4. **Level 3**: Autonomous self-healing (The autopilot):

   The system detects, diagnoses, and fixes the issue without waking anyone up. The SRE simply receives a report the next morning: *I found a problem at 3 AM and fixed it for you.*

Building safety circuit breakers

The biggest fear for any SRE is automated chaos, a script that goes rogue and makes a problem worse. To prevent this, we implement circuit breakers.

Think of this like the safety switch on a power tool. Even if the AI is 100% sure of the root cause, the automation is blocked if:

- **The scale is too large**: If the script tries to restart 50 servers at once, the circuit breaker trips and asks for a human.
- **The impact is unknown**: If the system is already in a *Critical* state (error budget is at 0%), we stop all automation to prevent further instability.
- **The flapping rule**: If the system has tried to fix the same problem three times in an hour and it keeps coming back, the automation stops. It clearly has not found the *real* root cause yet.

Reinforcement learning

This is where the *AI* in AIOps truly shines. Every time a runbook is executed, the system asks the SRE: *Did this fix the problem?*

- If the SRE says **Yes**, the AI increases its confidence score for that specific causal pattern.
- If the SRE says **No**, the AI analyzes the automated diagnostic snapshot (which we discussed in *Chapter 7, Advanced Anomaly Detection*) to see what it missed. It might realize that while memory was high, the actual cause was a network gateway error, but it had not weighed heavily enough.

Over time, this turns every incident into a training session, transforming your AIOps platform into an expert system that captures the team's collective intelligence. The following figure shows how post-incident analysis evolves into automated runbooks:

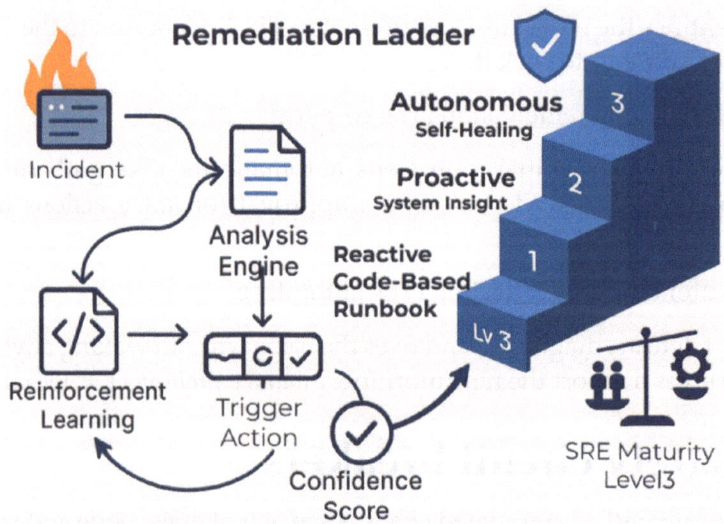

***Figure 8.4**: Post-incident analysis to automated runbooks*

By moving to automated runbooks, we are not just fixing bugs; we are buying back time for SREs to do what they do best: engineering the future.

Now that we have built a system that can detect, diagnose, and heal itself, we have one final frontier, i.e., the future. In the next section, we will explore predictive insights and how we can use all this data to stop incidents before they even start.

Reducing downtime with predictive insights

If *Chapter 7, Advanced Anomaly Detection,* taught us how to detect a fire (anomaly detection) and the previous sections of this chapter taught us how to find the source of the leak (causal RCA), then this section is about preventing the fire from ever starting. In the world of SRE, the ultimate *Holy Grail* is the transition from **reactive** (fixing things that are broken) to **predictive** (fixing things before they break). By combining our causal models with time series forecasting, we can create a system that looks into the future of our infrastructure.

Predictive timeline shift

Most monitoring systems are historical; they tell you what just happened. Even real-time monitoring is actually *Near-Past* monitoring. Predictive insights change the timeline.

Instead of asking, *Why is the Database slow right now?*, we ask, *Based on the current growth rate of data and the causal dependencies of our services, when will the Database become too slow to support our Checkout Service?*

This is the difference between a doctor's visit and a check-up. A reactive SRE is an ER doctor treating a heart attack. A predictive AIOps system is a nutritionist identifying high cholesterol months before the heart attack occurs.

Causal forecasting by predicting the domino effect

In *Chapter 7, Advanced Anomaly Detection,* we learned about TTS, calculating when a resource (like disk or memory) will hit 100%. In this chapter, we will learn about causal graphs, knowing that Service A depends on Service B.

Predictive insights are the marriage of these two concepts. We call this causal forecasting.

The causal forecasting process follows a clear reasoning sequence that links observed trends to predicted system failures:

- **Trend detection**: The AI notices that the Log Storage disk is filling up 5% faster every day.
- **Saturation prediction**: It calculates that the disk will be 100% full in **4 days.**
- **Causal impact analysis**: It looks at the dependency graph and realizes that if *Log Storage* is full, the Authentication Service will crash because it cannot write audit logs.
- **SLO impact**: It concludes that the authentication crash will cause a **100% burn rate** of the monthly error budget within two hours of the failure.

Result: The system generates a predictive incident four days in advance. The SRE team does not get paged at 3 AM on a Saturday; they get a low-priority ticket on Tuesday morning to *expand disk size.*

Digital twin

Advanced AIOps platforms use a concept called a digital twin or a shadow model. This is a mathematical simulation of your infrastructure.

For the digital twin to produce reliable predictions, it must be constructed using an accurate system topology and realistic workload characteristics. The topology defines the true dependency relationships between services, while workload models capture request rates, latency distributions, and failure behaviors. Without these inputs, simulations may produce misleading results that do not reflect actual system behavior. By grounding the digital twin in real observability data, the AIOps platform ensures that its predictions accurately represent production conditions.

Using **Monte Carlo Simulations** (a mathematical technique used to predict the probability of different outcomes in a process that cannot easily be predicted due to the intervention of random variables), the AI can run thousands of *what-if* scenarios:

- *What if traffic increases by 300% during the Super Bowl?*
- *What if the Network Latency between Region A and Region B increases by 50ms?*
- *What if the Primary Database fails and we have to failover to the Secondary?*

By running these simulations against the causal graph, the AI identifies *hidden bottleneck* services that look healthy now but are the *weakest link* under stress. This allows SREs to perform proactive hardening, reinforcing system resilience before the stress event occurs.

The outcomes of these simulations are translated into quantified risk probabilities, allowing the AIOps platform to prioritize potential failure chains before they impact production systems.

Risk scoring and the proactive dashboard

To make this data digestible for a human, we move away from alerts and toward risk scores.

An alert is binary: **ON** or **OFF**. A risk score is a spectrum: **0** to **100**.

The following examples illustrate how risk scores translate raw telemetry into clear operational priorities:

- **Risk 10**: Everything is normal.
- **Risk 40**: A trend is moving toward a threshold. Keep an eye on it.
- **Risk 80**: High probability of a failure chain starting within 24 hours. Action required.

This allows the SRE team to prioritize their morning. They do not look at a list of things that are *on fire*; they look at a list of things that *might start a fire*. They spend their time on the highest risk scores, effectively *buying* reliability for the future.

Business value

The primary business impact of predictive operations is the reduction of downtime costs and operational disruption.

The following contrast highlights the difference between reactive and predictive approaches:

- **Reactive fix**: Costs $100,000 in lost revenue, requires ten engineers to work through the night, and damages customer trust.
- **Predictive fix**: Costs $0 in lost revenue, requires one engineer to work for 20 minutes during their normal shift, and the customer never knows anything was wrong.

Predictive insights represent the highest maturity stage of AIOps-driven reliability engineering. We have moved from being fixers to being architects of stability. We have mastered the data, mapped the causes, and now, we have mastered time itself.

Conclusion

The conclusion of this chapter marks a definitive shift in the SRE paradigm from simply observing systems to understanding the deep logic of their failure. By implementing the architectural principles of causal inference, we have equipped our AIOps platform with the ability to distinguish between the noise of secondary symptoms and the signal of true root causes. This transition effectively ends the era of the war room blame game, replacing human intuition with mathematical certainty through Bayesian logic and graph theory. We have seen how aggregating events into high-fidelity incidents and mapping them to a directed acyclic graph allows us to identify the first domino in seconds, preserving the cognitive energy of our engineers for higher-order tasks.

Ultimately, the goal of these advanced diagnostic capabilities is to pave the way for a self-healing infrastructure. By moving up the remediation maturity ladder, we transform the hard-won lessons of post-incident reviews into executable, automated runbooks that protect our error budgets in real-time. The integration of predictive insights further strengthens this defense, allowing us to anticipate and mitigate risks before they ever impact the customer experience. As we master these predictive and causal models, we move closer to the ideal of the *No-Ops* future, where the system's own intelligence serves as its most vigilant guardian.

Moving forward, we shift our focus from diagnosing past and present failures to actively orchestrating future outcomes. This chapter has provided the eyes and the brain to understand system behavior and root causes. The next chapter introduces the execution layer that supplies the nervous system and hands to act on this intelligence. We move from theoretical root causes to practical, closed-loop remediation, showing how an intelligent assistant can move beyond recommendations to drive high-stakes operational workflows with minimal human friction.

Join our Discord space

Join our Discord workspace for latest updates, offers, tech happenings around the world, new releases, and sessions with the authors:

https://discord.bpbonline.com

CHAPTER 9
Intelligent SRE Assistant

Introduction

In the previous chapter, we explored the rigorous mathematics of causal inference, using Bayesian logic and graph theory to navigate the chaotic waters of an alert storm and arrive at a single, probabilistic root cause. We learned to answer the question: *Why is the system failing?*

However, diagnosis, no matter how accurate, is not a cure. Knowing that a database connection pool is exhausted does not restart the service. Identifying a rogue memory leak does not rollback the deployment. In the high-stakes world of SRE, the time between identification and action is where the SLA bleeds. Imagine a memory leak silently consuming resources on a payment gateway at peak traffic, the alert fires instantly, but the fix waits on a human to wake up, log in, and run a rollback, costing the business thousands in lost transactions per minute.

This chapter marks the transition from passive observation to active orchestration. We are moving from the brain of the AIOps platform to its hands. We introduce the concept of the Intelligent SRE Assistant, not just a chatbot or a dashboard, but a sophisticated workflow engine capable of executing closed loop remediation.

Here, automation meets action. We will explore how to build a system that does not just suggest a fix but prepares it, validates it, and, with the right level of trust, executes it. We will build the digital nervous system that connects our causal insights to the tools that manage our infrastructure, enabling concepts like one touch failovers and self-healing patching.

However, with great power comes the need for great control. We will also delve into the critical design philosophy of **human-in-the-loop** (**HITL**). We will define the boundaries where the machine stops and the human begins, ensuring that our intelligent assistant remains a tireless servant, never a rogue agent.

Structure

In this chapter, we will cover the following topics:

- Building automated closed loop remediation
- Workflow engine driving smart actions
- One-touch self-service operations

- One-touch ops for failovers and patching
- Building safety harnesses for autonomous action
- Human oversight in intelligent automation
- Turning data into prescriptive insights

Objectives

By the end of this chapter, you will be able to design an automated remediation architecture that integrates seamlessly with your observability stack. You will understand how to transform a probabilistic root cause into a deterministic set of actions. You will learn to build one-touch operational workflows that reduce the cognitive load on on-call engineers, and you will master the governance models required to deploy these powerful tools safely in production environments.

Building automated closed loop remediation

In traditional IT operations, the remediation lifecycle is an open loop. The monitoring system detects an issue and opens a ticket. A human reads the ticket, logs into a bastion host, types commands, and manually verifies the fix. The loop is closed only by human intervention. Industry data suggests that each manual handoff in this cycle adds an average of 8 to 15 minutes of delay, meaning a three-step remediation process can silently consume nearly an hour of SLA before a fix is even attempted.

Closed loop remediation is the practice of removing the manual friction from this cycle. It is the automated execution of the **observe, orient, decide, act** (**OODA**) loop.

Broken observe, orient, decide, act loop

In a manual environment, the OODA loop is fragmented:

- **Observe**: The tool does this (Alerting).
- **Orient**: The human does this (Contextualizing, reading dashboards).
- **Decide**: The human does this (Choosing a runbook).
- **Act**: The human does this (Running the script).

The friction occurs at the hand-offs. Every time the tool hands off to a human, we lose minutes. The goal of the Intelligent SRE Assistant is to digitize the *orient* and *decide* phases so that the *act* can happen instantaneously.

Anatomy of a closed loop

To build a closed loop, we must electronically bridge our insights to our infrastructure code. This requires three distinct components interacting in real-time:

- **The trigger (The signal)**: This is the output from *Chapter 8, Causal Inference and Efficient Root Cause Analysis*, the probabilistic root cause. It is not just CPU high; it is process X is stuck in a deadlock.
- **The controller (The decision)**: This is the logic layer. It evaluates the trigger against safety policies. Is this a production environment? Is it black Friday? Have we already tried this fix?
- **The effector (The action)**: This is the Kubernetes API call to your infrastructure automation tools (e.g., Ansible Tower, Terraform, **Amazon Web Services** (**AWS**) Lambda).

Site reliability engineering perspective

Think of closed loop remediation like the autopilot system in a modern aircraft. The pilot (SRE) does not manually adjust the ailerons for every gust of wind. The system detects the gust (trigger), calculates the counterforce (controller), and moves the flaps (effector). The pilot only intervenes when the turbulence exceeds the system's design parameters.

From scripting to orchestration

Many organizations fail at this stage because they rely on simple scripts. They write a bash script to restart a service and hook it up to a webhook. This is scripting, not orchestration.

- **Scripting**: Fragile, fire and forget, hard to debug, lacks state.
- **Orchestration**: Maintains state, handles retries, manages secrets, and logs every step for auditability.

True closed loop remediation requires an orchestration platform that treats operations as code. The following diagram illustrates the continuous cycle where the analytical outputs of *Chapter 8, Causal Inference and Efficient Root Cause Analysis*, directly feed the operational workflows of this chapter, creating a self-reinforcing loop of system health.

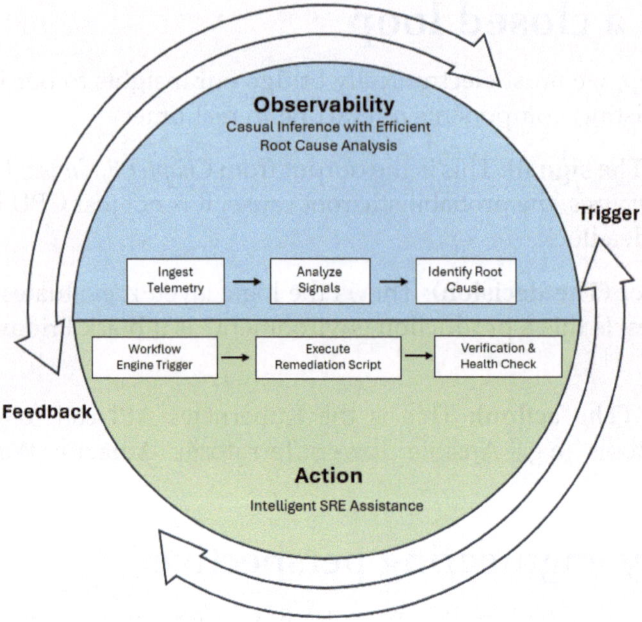

Figure 9.1: Closed-loop remediation cycle

Workflow engine driving smart actions

If causal inference is the brain, the workflow engine is the central nervous system. It is the component responsible for translating a high-level intent (fix the database latency) into low-level muscle movements (scale up the read replica fleet).

It coordinates decisions across monitoring systems, orchestration platforms, and infrastructure APIs, ensuring that every action is executed in the correct order and with the appropriate safeguards. By embedding policies, approvals, and rollback logic, the workflow engine enables automation that is not only fast but also safe and auditable.

Workflow engine as a control layer

In a distributed system, reliability is not achieved by executing isolated commands, but by managing the full lifecycle of recovery. Directly wiring alerts to restart actions creates fragile automation that can trigger cascading failures, conflict with maintenance states, and amplify outages rather than resolve them.

A workflow engine provides the necessary control layer. It acts as intelligent middleware that coordinates recovery actions, enforces safety checks, and preserves system state. By replacing brittle, linear scripts with resilient, state-aware processes, the workflow engine ensures that remediation can withstand network partitions, tool outages, and human interruptions.

Key capabilities of the intelligent engine:

- **State management and persistence**: The engine knows *where* it is in the process. If a remediation step takes ten minutes (such as a database re-indexing), the engine persists its state to a database. If the workflow service itself restarts, it picks up exactly where it left off. It does not time out or *forget* the incident context.
- **Conditional logic and dynamic branching**:
  - **Step 1**: Clear cache.
  - **Check**: Did latency improve?
  - **If yes**: Mark resolved and update Jira.
  - **If no**: Proceed to *Step 2* (Restart service).
  - **If Step 2 Fails**: Escalate to on-call via PagerDuty with the full logs of the failed attempts.
- **Context injection**: The engine pulls data from the alert (e.g., Hostname, IP, Service ID) and injects it dynamically into the remediation runbooks.
- **Idempotency and concurrency control**: This is critical. The engine ensures that if a workflow is triggered twice for the same incident, it does not create duplicate actions (e.g., launching two redundant clusters). It manages locks on infrastructure resources to ensure only one *Doctor* is operating on the system at a time.

Integration ecosystem

The Intelligent SRE Assistant is not an island. It must integrate with the *tools of the trade*. The workflow engine typically sits in the center of a star topology, acting as the bridge between the **control plane** (AIOps) and the **data plane** (infrastructure). It relies on a multi-layered integration architecture (described below) to manage the flow of data and commands across the stack:

- **Ingestion layer**: Connects to AIOps platforms (Dynatrace, Datadog, Splunk) to receive root-cause signals.
- **Governance layer**: Integrates with ITSM tools (ServiceNow, Jira). The engine automatically opens a *Change Ticket* before acting and closes it after success, ensuring compliance is automated, not manual.
- **Execution layer**: Communicates with IaC tools like Ansible, Terraform, or Kubernetes Operators to perform the actual work.
- **Notification layer**: Uses ChatOps (Slack, Microsoft Teams) to keep humans informed. It acts as the *social interface*, announcing: *I am about to restart Server A. React within 30 seconds to abort.*

Decision logic

Prior to the workflow engine pulling the lever of automation, there must be a **decision logic layer** that translates probabilistic diagnosis into a deterministic course of action. This layer acts as a policy engine, evaluating the incident through three filters:

- **Safety filter (The blast radius check)**: It calculates the potential risk of the remediation. If the action is *scale down*, but traffic is trending upward, the logic layer overrides the suggestion. It ensures that the cure is not worse than the disease.
- **Contextual filter (The operational awareness check)**: It queries external systems to see if the target infrastructure is under an existing maintenance window, a deployment freeze, or if a high-priority business event (like a product launch) is currently occurring.
- **Efficiency filter (The optimal path check)**: If multiple remediation paths exist, for example, clearing a cache versus scaling the database, the logic layer uses cost and speed metrics to select the most efficient route.

By inserting this logic between the *Brain* and the *Hands*, the Intelligent SRE Assistant ensures that every action is not just automated, but strategically sound.

The AIOps workflow engine serves as the central nervous system of automated operations, orchestrating decision-making, governance, execution, and communication across the enterprise. The following figure illustrates this architecture and the flow of logic that powers resilient, autonomous operations:

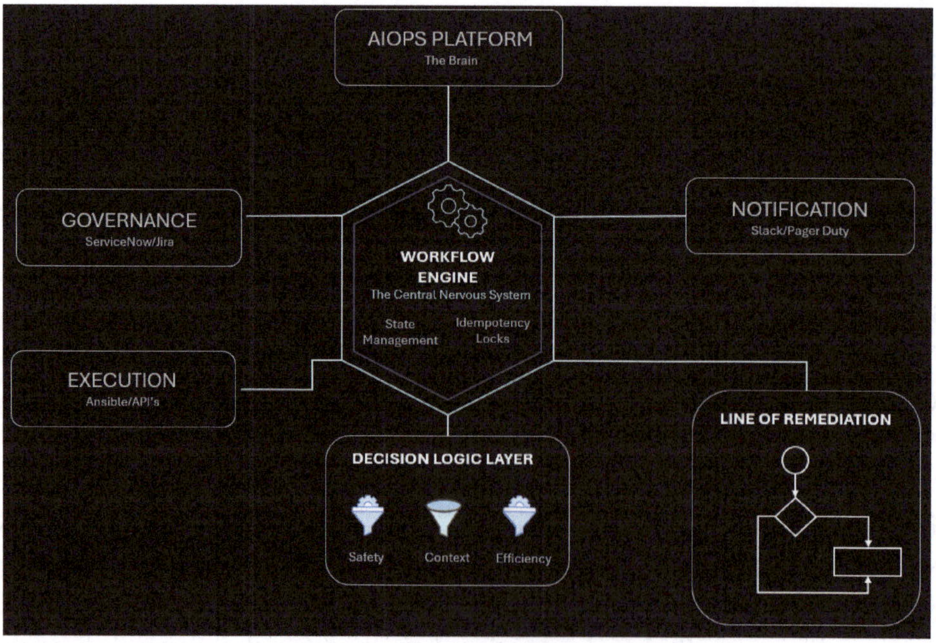

Figure 9.2: AIOps workflow architecture

Analogy

The Sous-Chef imagines a busy kitchen. The head chef (SRE) yells an order. The Sous-Chef (workflow engine) does not just throw raw food on a plate. They check if the ingredients are prepped, they assign the task to the grill cook, they time the sides to finish with the main dish, and they inspect the plate before it goes out. The workflow engine coordinates the chaos of individual scripts into a cohesive operational service.

One-touch self-service operations

While fully autonomous, zero-touch automation is the ultimate goal, it is often too risky for high-impact actions such as failing over a primary database or applying a kernel patch in production. In these situations, a human checkpoint remains essential.

One-touch operations provide a safe middle ground between manual intervention and full automation. The system performs all diagnostics, validations, and impact analysis automatically, then presents the SRE with a single, context-aware action. With one approval, the workflow engine executes a pre-validated recovery process, monitors the outcome, and rolls back if necessary.

This approach reduces response time from minutes to seconds, minimizes human error, and preserves accountability, while still ensuring that critical actions are taken with appropriate oversight.

Concept of big red button

One-touch ops provides the SRE with a pre-assembled, validated set of actions that can be triggered with a single confirmation. The AIOps platform does all the heavy lifting, gathering context, pre-flight checking, and staging the action, but it waits for a human signal to execute.

This dramatically reduces MTTR because the engineer does not have to remember *how* to execute the failover; they just have to decide *if* it is necessary. It also creates a layer of abstraction; the SRE does not need to know the specific **command line interface** (**CLI**) syntax for AWS or the obscure configuration paths for Red Hat OpenShift. They simply interact with a standardized actionable intent.

Democratizing remediation

One-touch capabilities provide SREs with a standardized toolkit to perform immediate, safe actions without relying on specialized infrastructure teams such as DBAs, network engineers, or middleware operators. By codifying expert knowledge into reusable workflows, organizations eliminate bottlenecks created by human silos.

These workflows embed best practices, validation checks, and approval policies, ensuring that less experienced engineers can execute complex remediation with confidence. Over time, this approach not only accelerates incident response but also preserves institutional knowledge and enables consistent operations across teams and environments.

One-touch ops for failovers and patching

Among the most high-stakes operations an SRE team performs, failovers and patching carry the greatest risk of human error under pressure. A missed step during a failover or an unvalidated patch window can cascade into prolonged outages or compliance violations. This section explores how one-touch operations mitigate these risks by automating the sequencing, validation, and execution of failover and patching workflows, enabling faster response with consistent, repeatable outcomes across hybrid and multi-cloud environments.

Use case 1: One-touch middleware and container restarts

In hybrid cloud environments, a *simple* service restart can be incredibly complex. One-touch ops streamlines this across various platforms are listed in the following table:

Dimension	Manual remediation	One-touch ops
Time to act	8 to 15 min (login, diagnose, execute)	Seconds (pre-validated, one click)
Knowledge required	Deep platform-specific expertise	Standardized actionable intent
Error risk	High (manual CLI, fatigue-prone)	Low (pre-flight checked, automated)
Auditability	Inconsistent, relies on human notes	Full automatic audit trail
Rollback	Manual, error-prone	Built-in, automated

Table 9.1*: Manual remediation vs. one-touch ops*

The following examples illustrate how one-touch remediation works across common platforms and failure scenarios:

- **Red Hat OpenShift or Kubernetes**:
    - **The problem**: A pod is stuck in a CrashLoopBackOff due to a corrupted local cache.
    - **The one-touch action**: The SRE Assistant identifies the specific deployment and namespace. It offers a **Graceful Rolling Restart** button.
    - **Under the hood**: The engine does not just kill the pod. It performs a rolling restart (Kubernetes rollout restart), monitors the readiness probes of the new pods, and ensures at least 50% capacity is maintained throughout the operation.

- **AWS Elastic Beanstalk or Amazon Elastic Container Service**:
    - **The problem**: An application instance is responding with 5xx errors, but the underlying EC2 instance passes health checks.
    - **The one-touch action**: Drain and replace instance.
    - **Under the hood**: The engine interacts with the AWS Auto Scaling Group to detach the instance, trigger a new one, and wait for the load balancer to register the new target before terminating the faulty one.
- **Legacy middleware (WebSphere or Tomcat)**:
    - **The problem**: A thread pool is exhausted in a legacy JVM environment.
    - **The one-touch action**: Thread dump and JVM restart.
    - **Under the hood**: The engine executes a script to capture a thread dump for later analysis (observability) and then triggers a controlled restart of the middleware service across the cluster, ensuring session persistence where possible.

Use case 2: One-touch patching with state restoration

A **critical security vulnerability** (**CVE**) has been discovered in your core OS image. The challenge is that traditional patching is destructive. It stops services, updates files, and often leaves the server in a *clean* but *empty* state where services have not restarted in the correct order, or local configuration has not been re-applied.

The intelligent assistant solution (The *safe-patch* workflow) is to provide a true One-touch experience, the Assistant performs a sophisticated state-preserving sequence:

- **Pre-patching snapshot**: The workflow engine communicates with the virtualization layer (e.g., AWS EBS, VMware vCenter) to trigger a point-in-time snapshot of the server. This provides a zero-second roll back point.
- **State capture**: The Assistant records the current operational state. It identifies all running middleware services, PID files, and open ports. It essentially takes a *DNA sample* of the running system.
- **Controlled shutdown**: It gracefully stops services in the correct dependency order (e.g., App Server before Web Server) to prevent data corruption.
- **Execution**: The patch is applied via the execution layer (Ansible or Terraform).
- **Post-patching state restoration**:
    - **Reboot and verify**: The server is rebooted, and the engine waits for the OS to become reachable.

- **Automated service restart**: The engine refers back to the *State Capture* log and restarts all services that were running prior to patching.
- **Health check**: It executes a synthetic transaction to verify that the application is not just *up*, but *functional*.

- **Final report**: If health checks fail, it offers a *one-touch roll back to Snapshot* button. If they pass, it notifies: *Patch Applied and State Restored. 5/5 Services verified healthy.*

Use case 3: Automated database failover

Your primary **structured query language** (**SQL**) database in us-east-1 is experiencing 80% packet loss. The traditional response is manual and time-consuming: the SRE is paged, logs into the AWS console, checks replication lag, promotes a read replica, updates connection strings across dozens of microservices, and flushes DNS records.

The intelligent assistant replaces this manual process with an automated, closed-loop workflow:

- **Detection**: AIOps detects the packet loss and correlates it to the database master.
- **Preparation**: The workflow engine triggers a pre-flight check. It verifies the replica in us-west-2 is healthy, and replication lag is near zero.
- **Presentation**: The assistant posts a message to the **#incidents-db** Slack channel:

  Primary DB connectivity is degraded. Replica is healthy (Lag: 2ms). Ready to initiate Failover to us-west-2.

- **Execution**: The SRE clicks the **Execute Failover** button. The workflow engine executes the Terraform plan to promote the replica and update Route53 DNS entries.
- **Verification**: The engine watches error rates drop and reports back: *Failover Complete. System healthy.*

Figure 9.3 bridges the theoretical discussion of *one-touch ops* with the practical ChatOps visualization:

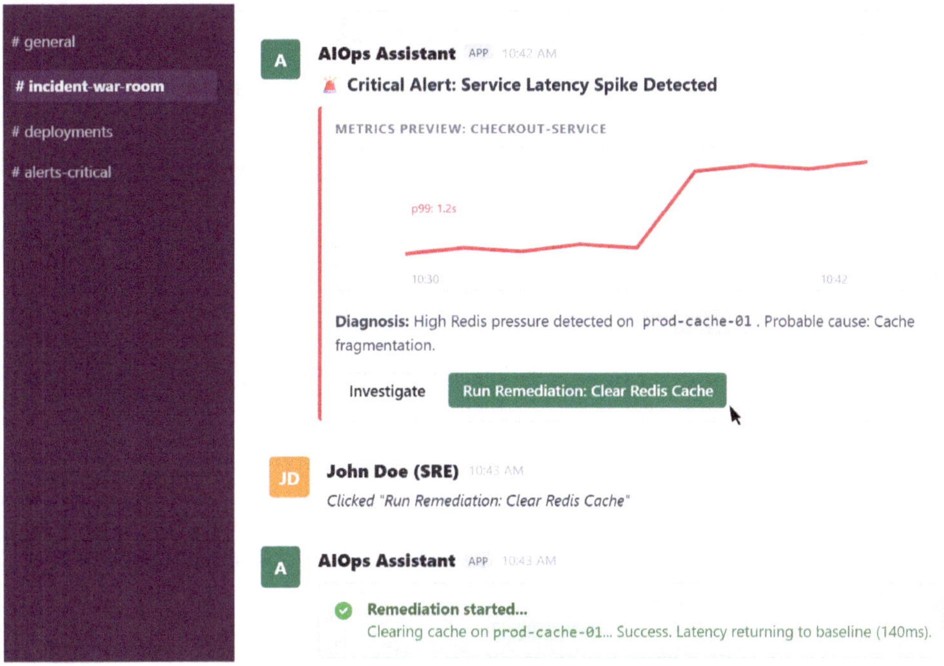

Figure 9.3: ChatOps example in action

SRE perspective is that one-touch ops shifts the SRE's role from *Mechanic* to *Pilot*. You are not turning the wrench; you are authorizing the maneuver.

Building safety harnesses for autonomous action

As organizations progress from one-touch operations, where a human provides the final approval, to fully autonomous execution, safety becomes the primary design requirement. A safety harness is a set of architectural controls that ensures automation can never amplify risk or cause irreversible damage.

These controls include execution limits, impact thresholds, roll back checkpoints, and real-time health verification. If an automated action exceeds a predefined blast radius, violates an error budget, or fails to restore service after multiple attempts, the system halts further actions and escalates to a human.

By embedding these safeguards directly into the workflow engine, autonomous remediation remains fast, predictable, and reversible. This allows teams to trust automation at scale while maintaining operational stability and accountability.

Three pillars of remediation safety

To operationalize autonomous remediation safely, engineers must implement a rigorous governance framework built on three architectural pillars:

- **Rate limiting and quotas**: Even if the AIOps brain is 100% certain that a service restart is needed, the safety harness must prevent it from restarting the entire fleet at once. We implement global token buckets for automation. The following guardrails define how rate limiting and quotas are enforced in practice:
    - **Rule 01**: *No more than 5% of the fleet can be undergoing remediation at any given time.*
    - **Rule 02**: *If remediation is triggered on more than 3 instances in 10 minutes, pause and escalate to a human.*
- **The circuit breaker pattern for actions**: Just as software circuit breakers prevent cascading failures in code, we need them for remediation. If the clear cache workflow is triggered and fails to resolve the issue three times in a row, the circuit *trips*. The system marks that specific remediation path as *ineffective* and blocks it from running again for that incident context.
- **Drift detection and post-remediation stability**: Remediation should not just fix a symptom; it must be verified. The safety harness performs *continuous drift detection*. If the assistant scales up a cluster to handle a spike, the harness monitors the cluster. If the new instances fail to join the load balancer or if the CPU remains pegged despite the scaling, the harness triggers an automatic undo or a freeze to prevent further resource wastage.

Semantic validation

Before an autonomous action is taken, the harness performs a semantic validation. It asks: Does this action make sense given the current environmental state? If the AIOps engine suggests a database restart because of slow queries, but the context layer reports that a massive data migration is currently running, the harness blocks the restart. The harness understands that the slowness is expected and transient, while a restart would be destructive.

Human oversight in intelligent automation

As we introduce automation into the remediation chain, we encounter the **trust paradox**: *We want the system to handle the work, but we are terrified it will break something.* This fear is not unfounded; an automated script with global permissions and a high-frequency trigger can cause more damage in seconds than a human engineer could in an entire day.

To solve this, we must design robust HITL architectures. This is not about slowing down the machine for the sake of bureaucracy; it is about providing the governance guardrails that allow the machine to move fast and safely.

Trust but verify framework

A resilient SRE Assistant operates under a *trust but verify* model. This means the system is granted the authority to execute actions, but every action is subject to a hierarchy of validation checks. This validation hierarchy is enforced through the following control stages:

- **Pre-flight validation**: Before a command is sent to the infrastructure API, the assistant must perform a *ready-for-action* check. For example, if the remediation is to *scale up a kubernetes cluster*, the assistant verifies that the cloud provider's quota has not been reached and that the cluster's control plane is currently healthy.
- **In-flight monitoring**: During execution, the assistant does not just *fire and forget*. It attaches a monitoring hook to the process. If a rolling restart is initiated and the first pod fails to reach a *ready* state within the timeout period, the assistant must immediately halt the workflow.
- **Post-flight confirmation**: Once the automation reports success, a separate *auditor* service queries the telemetry. If the AIOps engine cleared the cache to fix latency, the auditor verifies that P99 latency actually dropped. If the metrics do not move, the assistant flags the remediation as a *false fix* and notifies a human.

Levels of autonomy

We can categorize our automation into specific levels of trust, similar to the standards used for autonomous vehicles. Defining these levels allows organizations to promote workflows through a *trust pipeline* as they prove their reliability:

- **Level 1: Advisory (The map)**:

  The assistant suggests a root cause and points to a runbook or wiki page. It is a purely informational layer.

- **Level 2: Staged (The co-pilot)**:

  The assistant prepares the specific remediation script, populates the variables (e.g., specific IP addresses or container IDs), and stages the change in a *draft* state. It requires a human to click **Execute**.

- **Level 3: Conditional autonomy (The autopilot)**:

  The assistant can act solo, but only within *safe zones*. For example, it might have full autonomy in the development environment but remain at *Level 2* for production. Alternatively, it may act alone only during *business hours* when SREs are readily available to intervene.

- **Level 4: Full autonomy (The autonomous agent)**:

  The assistant acts alone across all environments and only notifies the human after the fact. This is reserved for low-risk, high-confidence tasks like log rotation or temporary disk cleanup.

Iron Man suit philosophy

We should view the intelligent assistant not as a replacement for the SRE (a robot soldier), but as an exoskeleton (the Iron Man suit). It amplifies the human's capability rather than automating them out of the process. This partnership is defined by a clear division of strengths between the assistant and the engineer:

- **AI provides**: Speed of correlation across millions of logs, 24/7 vigilance, instant API execution, and the ability to manage thousands of servers simultaneously.
- **Human provides**: High-level context (e.g., *We are in a code freeze for the Super Bowl*), ethical judgment, business priority, and the gut feeling intuition that comes from years of operational experience.

Designing the break-glass mechanism

Every automated system must have a physical or digital kill switch. If the workflow engine begins to exhibit *hallucinatory* behavior, such as restarting healthy servers because of a corrupted metrics stream, the SRE must be able to *break-glass*.

A robust break-glass implementation includes:

- **The global pause**: A single, high-priority flag in the database that, when toggled, immediately kills all active remediation worker threads and blocks new triggers.
- **Contextual muting**: The ability to say stop all automation on the Payments Service while leaving automation active for the Search Service.
- **Rate limiting guardrails**: A hard-coded policy that acts as a circuit breaker for humans. If the AI tries to restart more than 10 servers in 5 minutes, the system locks itself and requires a manual override code to resume.

Legal, ethical, and compliance oversight

In regulated industries (Finance, Healthcare, Government), *The AI did it* is not an acceptable legal defense. Human oversight must therefore include an **approvability trail**:

- **Electronic sign-off**: For *Levels 2 and 3* actions, the assistant must capture the identity of the approver and the timestamp.
- **Policy-as-code alignment**: The assistant should only be able to execute actions that are explicitly defined in a version-controlled *policy repo*. This ensures that the machine cannot *invent* new ways to modify the infrastructure.

Glass box model for auditability and trust

Trust is built on transparency. The intelligent assistant must *show its work* in a way that is easily digestible during a post-mortem. This transparency is achieved through the following explainability mechanisms:

- **The decision log**: Instead of just saying *Restarting*, the assistant should log: *I am restarting because [Metric A] crossed [Threshold B] and Chapter 8, Causal Inference and Efficient Root Cause Analysis, analysis indicated a [92% Probability] of a Deadlock.*
- **Visual step-tracing**: SREs should be able to view a real-time flowchart of the active workflow, seeing exactly which branch the assistant is currently executing and what the *Exit Criteria* are for each step.

By enforcing these oversight mechanisms, we convert the *black box* of AI into a *glass box*, allowing SRE teams to adopt autonomous remediation with the confidence that they remain in total control of the system's fate.

Turning data into prescriptive insights

The final evolution of the Intelligent SRE Assistant is the transition from reactivity to a proactive strategy through **prescriptive insights**. While the previous sections focused on fixing what is broken, this layer focuses on improving the system's fundamental architecture based on its operational history. It moves the conversation from *How do we recover?* to *How do we prevent the need for recovery?*

Building on the widely recognized analytics maturity model, this evolution can be understood as a progression across three levels of operational intelligence:

- **Descriptive**: The disk is full.
- **Predictive**: The disk will be full in 2 days. (Discussed in *Chapter 8, Causal Inference and Efficient Root Cause Analysis*).
- **Prescriptive**: You should resize the disk volume to 500GB or implement a log rotation policy to delete files older than seven days.

This prescriptive layer completes the closed-loop remediation cycle introduced earlier in this chapter, where the trigger detects, the controller decides, and the effector acts, except now the system is not just reacting to failures, but proactively recommending architectural improvements to prevent them from occurring in the first place.

Recommendation engine

To deliver prescriptive value, the AIOps platform must combine real-time observability data with configuration data (CMDB/IaC) and best practice knowledge bases. The assistant acts as a persistent consultant who analyzes the delta between the current state and the desired state.

The engine functions by matching telemetry patterns to a library of optimized solution templates. This involves:

- **Pattern matching**: Identifying recurring resource exhaustion or latency signatures.
- **Resource optimization**: Analyzing billing data alongside performance metrics to suggest right-sizing (e.g., *This instance is 90% idle; downgrade to a smaller instance type to save $200/month*).
- **Compliance alignment**: Checking current configurations against industry standards (e.g., *Your S3 bucket is public-facing; prescriptive action: apply the private-access policy template*).

Example of pattern-action sequence:

- **Pattern**: *High CPU + High Traffic + Static Auto-Scaling Group.*
- **Prescription**: Your auto-scaling group is capped at five nodes. Traffic trends suggest you need eight nodes to maintain P95 latency targets. Click here to update the CloudFormation template.

Context-aware alignment with business reality

A truly intelligent assistant understands that a *fix* is relative to the business context. It evaluates recommendations through the lens of the environment's criticality and the current *business phase*. This contextual awareness is reflected in how remediation strategies adapt to different environments and risk levels:

- **Environment-awareness**: If a failure occurs on a **dev server**, the prescription might be aggressive: *Auto-restarting the server to restore state and clearing all non-essential temporary logs.*
- **Risk-awareness**: If the *same* failure happens on the **production payment gateway** during a high-stakes event like Black Friday, the prescription shifts to preservation: *Rerouting 20% of traffic to the secondary region. Do not restart the primary server; preserve current memory state for deep forensic analysis after the peak window.*
- **Cost-awareness**: During low-traffic periods, the assistant might prescribe aggressive down-scaling to optimize the cloud budget, while during peak periods, it prescribes *over-provisioning* as a safety buffer.

Continuous improvement loop for anti-fragile systems

Prescriptive insights transform the operational *OODA loop* into a *continuous improvement loop* that feeds directly back into the development lifecycle. This is where SREs shift from *Day-*

2 *Operations* (Maintenance) to *Day-N Evolution* (Hardening). This continuous improvement cycle unfolds through the following operational stages:

- **Incident**: The system fails due to a configuration drift that caused a race condition.
- **Resolution**: The assistant suggests a temporary configuration fix to restore service.
- **Analysis**: The engine performs a *post-mortem analysis* on the Git history and the incident logs.
- **Hardening**: The assistant prescribes a permanent change: *Your Terraform policy allows manual overrides in the console. Prescribed Action: Enforce GitOps-only changes for the Networking module and add a PR-linter to check for CIDR collisions.*

Bridging the gap to self-architecting infrastructure

In its most mature state, prescriptive insights allow the intelligent assistant to generate **draft pull requests**. Instead of just telling an engineer what to do, it prepares the code change.

Assistant: **`I've noticed your microservice frequently runs out of memory during the Friday morning batch job. I have opened a PR to increase the JVM heap size and adjusted the HPA (Horizontal Pod Autoscaler) minimum to 3 instances for that window.`**

This reduces the *to-do* list for SRE teams and ensures that the system is constantly evolving toward a more stable state. The following figure illustrates how organizations evolve their analytical capabilities to unlock deeper intelligence and actionable outcomes:

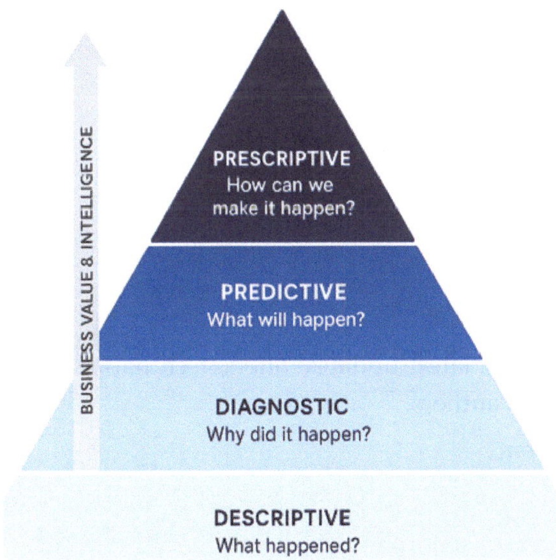

***Figure 9.4**: Hierarchy of analytics*

Conclusion

In this chapter, we have moved from conceptual understanding to practical execution. We defined the Intelligent SRE Assistant not as a speculative idea, but as a concrete architectural layer composed of workflow engines, automation libraries, and governance frameworks.

We explored the mechanics of closed-loop remediation, seeing how we can complete the OODA loop at machine speed. We discussed the pragmatic approach of one-touch ops, giving engineers superhuman capabilities to manage failovers and patches with a single click. We emphasized the necessity of human oversight, ensuring that our automation remains a trusted partner rather than an unguided missile. Finally, we looked at prescriptive insights, where the system begins to advise us on how to architect better systems.

The journey of AIOps is a journey of maturity. We started with simple monitoring, moved to anomaly detection, advanced to causal inference, and now, we have arrived at automated remediation. However, a truly resilient system does not just wait for a failure to happen so it can practice its remediation; it proactively hunts for weaknesses before they manifest as customer-facing outages.

In the next chapter, we move from reactive defense to proactive offense. We will explore how to use the very automation frameworks we built in this chapter to inject faults intentionally and measure system resilience under stress. We will learn how to orchestrate chaos with AIOps platforms to validate our SLOs and ensure our safety harnesses actually work when they are needed most.

Join our Discord space

CHAPTER 10
Chaos Engineering and Reliability Testing

Introduction

In the previous chapter, we built the hands of our intelligent assistant, the digital tools designed to detect and respond to problems with minimal human intervention. We built a high-tech ambulance. However, even the fastest ambulance in the world is not as good as preventing the accident in the first place. This chapter introduces chaos engineering. To the average person, chaos sounds like something we want to avoid. However, in the world of high-reliability systems, we intentionally invite a little bit of controlled trouble to make the system stronger.

Think of it like a vaccine. A vaccine introduces a tiny, harmless piece of a virus into your body so that your immune system learns how to fight the real thing. Chaos engineering does the same for software: we infect the system with small, controlled failures so that it learns how to stay upright when a massive, unexpected disaster strikes. This discipline emerged at scale with pioneers like *Netflix*, proving that resilience grows when systems experience controlled failure rather than quiet comfort.

Today, a rich ecosystem of frameworks, from open-source tools like Chaos Mesh and LitmusChaos to enterprise platforms like Gremlin and AWS Fault Injection Service, gives teams of every maturity level the means to practice this discipline safely and systematically.

Structure

In this chapter, we will cover the following topics:

- Principles of chaos engineering
- Safety planning for the fire drill
- Quantifying system resilience and mathematical health
- Blast radius
- AI as Chaos Master
- Scaling organizational resilience

Objectives

By the end of this chapter, you will possess the frameworks and technical confidence required to run sophisticated stress tests on your digital business. You will master the scientific method for reliability by learning to identify steady state metrics and move beyond guesswork by forming rigorous, testable hypotheses about system behavior. Beyond the technical steps, you will develop the skills to facilitate game days that combine technical testing with organizational rehearsal, ensuring your team knows how to communicate and collaborate during a crisis. You will also understand how to integrate AIOps to monitor and automatically shrink a blast radius, allowing you to test in production environments with significantly reduced risk. Finally, you will learn to manage reliability through data by using error budgets and SLO dashboards to quantify the ROI of your experiments, effectively shifting your organizational mindset toward a proactive pursuit of breaking points that turn every injected fault into a vaccine for future reliability.

Principles of chaos engineering

Imagine you own a large hotel. You have a fire alarm, a sprinkler system, and emergency exits with the hope that they work. However, if you never pull the alarm to see if the sprinklers actually turn on, you are just guessing. Chaos engineering is the discipline of experimenting on a system to build confidence in its capability to withstand turbulent conditions in production. It is the transition from hoping your systems work to proving they do.

Testing vs. experimentation

While traditional testing (like unit or integration tests) asks, *Does the code do what we intended?* chaos engineering asks, *What happens to the system when the world stops behaving?* Testing verifies known outcomes; chaos engineering explores the unknown-unknowns. In a distributed world, failures are not just *on* or *off*; they are *partial*, *grey*, and *cascading*. Chaos engineering is one of the most effective ways to find the hidden dependencies that cause these complex failures.

Scientific method of reliability

To prevent chaos engineering from becoming *chaos for the sake of chaos*, we follow a strict scientific process known as the **principles of chaos**. It includes the following steps:

1. **Define the steady state**: You must first identify the measurable output of a system that indicates normal behavior. This is rarely CPU or memory usage; it is usually a business metric like *Successful Logins per Minute* or *Orders Placed per Second*. If you do not know what *normal* looks like, you cannot identify *abnormal*.

2. **Formulate a hypothesis**: State your expectation clearly. *If we terminate one node in our primary database cluster, the standby node will take over within 30 seconds, and the checkout success rate will remain above 99.5%.*

3. **Introduce real-world variables**: Inject failures that actually happen. This includes hardware failures (server crashes), network issues (high latency or *jitter*), or resource exhaustion (memory leaks). We focus on events that have a high impact or a high likelihood of occurring.

4. **Try to disprove the hypothesis**: The goal is not to *pass* the test, but to find the point where the steady state breaks. If the checkout success rate drops to 80% during your test, you have successfully disproven your hypothesis and found a critical vulnerability that needs fixing.

The following are the four pillars of a mature chaos practice:

- **Build a hypothesis around steady state**: Focus on the user experience rather than internal system attributes.
- **Vary real-world events**: Prioritize events based on potential frequency and impact.
- **Run experiments in production**: While you start in staging, the ultimate goal is to test in the environment where your customers actually live, as that is the only environment that truly reflects real-world complexity.
- **Automate experiments to run continuously**: Resilience is not a one-time project; it is a moving target. Automating experiments ensures that a new code deployment has not accidentally created a new *dark* failure path.

The following figure depicts the lifecycle of a chaos experiment, from hypothesis definition through controlled failure injection and continuous learning:

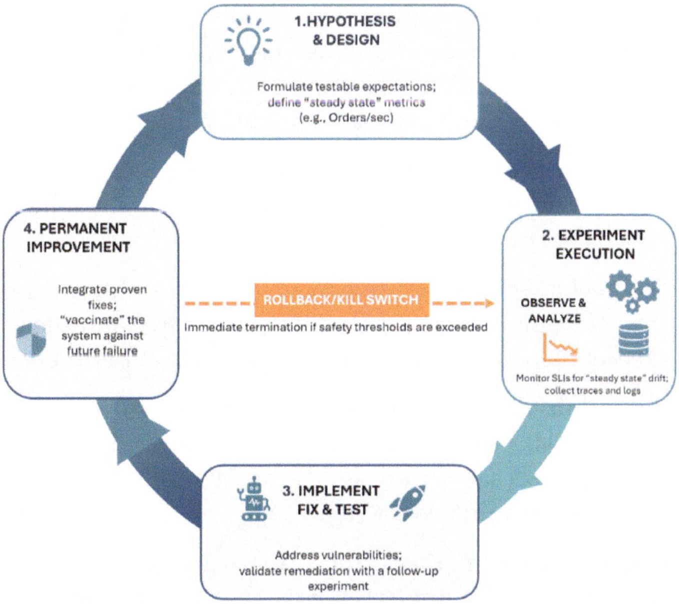

***Figure 10.1**: The chaos experiment lifecycle*

Safely planning for the fire drill

A **game day** is a dedicated, hands-on workshop where a team executes one or more chaos experiments in a controlled environment. While the tech is critical, game days are equally about the *people*. They reveal if on-call engineers know which dashboards to check, if escalation paths are clear, and if automated alerts actually reach the right person.

Specialized roles of a game day

To ensure a rigorous and safe experiment, participants assume specific operational roles:

- **The master of ceremonies (MC)**: The lead facilitator who keeps the experiment on schedule and coordinates between teams.
- **The executor**: The chaos engineer who physically triggers the fault injection (e.g., executing the CLI command to drop network packets).
- **The observers**: Team members tasked with watching specific dashboards and logs. They report on *steady state* drift in real-time.
- **The scribe**: Documenting every event, observation, and communication snippet for the final post-mortem.

Technical lifecycle for game day execution

Executing a game day requires a high degree of technical orchestration to prevent the *drill* from becoming a *disaster*. The following steps describe the technical lifecycle for game day execution:

1. **Baseline validation**: Before any fault is injected, the team must verify that the environment is currently *healthy*. Injecting chaos into an already degraded system creates *noise* that makes it impossible to validate your hypothesis.
2. **IaC readiness**: Ensure the environment can be perfectly reproduced or rolled back. If an experiment causes a *poison pill* state in a database, you must have a tested snapshot or script to restore the state immediately.
3. **Observability check**: Verify that your SLIs have a resolution fine enough to catch transient issues. If your dashboard updates every five minutes, but your failover happens in 10 seconds, you are effectively blind to the experiment's impact.
4. **Controlled execution and the kill switch**: The Executor triggers the fault at a predetermined time. All eyes are on the *Abort Conditions*. If the checkout success rate drops below the defined safety threshold, the MC calls for the kill switch, and the Executor immediately terminates the injection.
5. **Evidence collection**: Collect traces, logs, and screenshots. In distributed systems, *ghosts* (race conditions) often appear during chaos. Capturing high-cardinality data during the fault window is vital for the later fix and hardening phase.

Connecting game days to one-touch failover

In *Chapter 9, Intelligent SRE Assistant*, we introduced one-touch ops workflows, pre-baked, AI-orchestrated remediation scripts that allow a SRE to authorize a complex maneuver with a single button click. During game day, these workflows transition from reactive emergency tools to proactive experiment levers.

Executing failover via workflows

Rather than manually logging into a terminal to terminate a pod or drop a database connection, we use the Intelligent Assistant to trigger a one-touch failover. The following steps describe how one-touch workflows are used to safely execute failover during a game day:

1. **Controlled ingress shift**: In *Chapter 9, Intelligent SRE Assistant*, we saw how the Assistant could clear a cache or restart a service. On a game day, we use a traffic-shifting workflow to intentionally route users away from a healthy Cell A to a standby Cell B.
2. **Authorization as documentation**: When the executor clicks *Authorize: Regional Failover* in the ChatOps interface (as seen in *Figure 9.2*), the system automatically logs the *exact* timestamp, the authorizing user, and the current state of the SLIs. This provides the *Scribe* with perfect data for the Debrief phase.
3. **Validating the workflow itself**: A major goal of the Game Day is not just to test the system, but to test the *Remediation Workflow*. If the one-touch failover script fails because a secret key has expired or a network route has changed, the Game Day has succeeded in finding a critical bug in your *recovery* logic before an actual outage occurs.

By integrating the workflows from *Chapter 9, Intelligent SRE Assistant*, we ensure that our *Chaos* is orchestrated through the same pipelines used in production incidents, creating a seamless bridge between practice and reality.

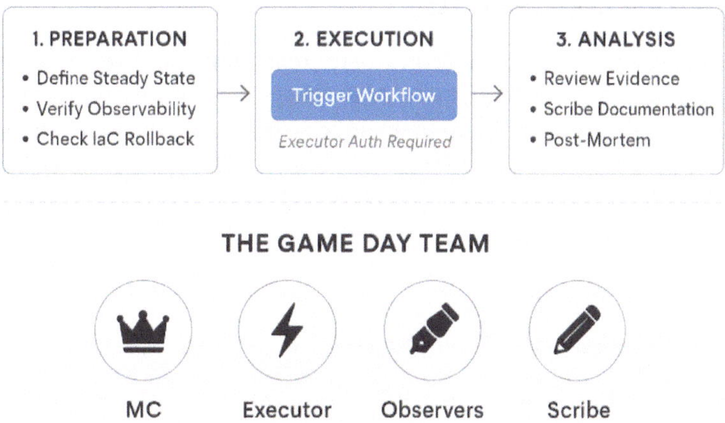

Figure 10.2: *Game Day execution workflow*

Quantifying system resilience and mathematical health

This section operationalizes how system resilience is measured under stress, translating chaos experiments into quantitative reliability signals. To determine if our chaos experiments are actually making the system stronger, we must quantify the immune system using three key SRE metrics: SLIs, SLOs, and error budgets. In a chaos context, these are not just reporting tools; they are the sensory inputs for our experimental safety logic.

SLIs and SLOs steady state definition

Your SLI is the specific metric you watch during an experiment (e.g., *availability* or *latency*). Your SLO is the target you have committed to.

In a chaos context, if your SLO is 99.9% availability, you have a total of ~43 minutes of downtime allowed per month. A chaos experiment is an intentional *spend* of that time.

Error budgets and burn rate analysis

The error budget is the *savings account* for unreliability. During a Game Day, we monitor the Burn rate, the rate at which the error budget is consumed compared to the ideal rate.

From a technical perspective, the burn rate can be calculated as follows:

If an experiment consumes 2% of the monthly error budget in ten minutes, the burn rate is $(0.02) \div (10 / 43{,}200) = 86.4$. A burn rate this high during a drill triggers an immediate AI-driven Abort signal, as it indicates the experiment is degrading the system 86.4 times faster than the acceptable baseline.

Resilience posture score

A mature intelligent assistant calculates a composite **resilience posture score** (**RPS**) to provide a *fitness grade* for your infrastructure. Instead of looking at complex math, think of RPS as the percentage of your critical risks that have been successfully survived in practice.

At its core, RPS is calculated as:

$RPS = (Coverage\ Score \times Success\ Rate) \times 100$

- $Coverage\ Score = Failure\ modes\ tested \div Total\ known\ failure\ modes$
- $Success\ Rate = Experiments\ with\ automatic\ recovery \div Total\ experiments\ run$

For example, if your team has tested 8 out of 10 known failure modes ($Coverage = 0.8$), and 7 of those 8 recovered automatically ($Success\ Rate = 0.875$), your $RPS = 0.8 \times 0.875 \times 100 = 70\%$.

The following points explain how the RPS is calculated and why it matters in practice:

- **How it is measured**: The RPS combines the **Coverage** (how many different failure modes, like *network latency* or *disk full*, have we tested?) and the **Success Rate** (how often did the system automatically recover without human intervention?).
- **Practical impact**: A high RPS tells leadership that the system is *anti-fragile*, meaning it has been vaccinated against common failures and its recovery workflows are proven to work. As you run more Game Days and fix the issues you find, your MTTR naturally drops, and your RPS rises.

Measuring the return on investment of chaos

To the C-suite, chaos engineering can look like investing in controlled resilience testing. We use the RPS to translate technical drills into business value.

Math of avoided disasters

By tracking the RPS, we can quantify the cost of an outage that *did not happen*. The following table illustrates the business impact and return on investment from chaos experiments:

Metric	Before chaos practice	After six months of chaotic practice	Business impact
MTTR	4 hours	12 minutes	95% faster recovery
RPS	35%	88%	High confidence in a system that is *anti-fragile*
Error budget spend	Reactive (Unplanned)	Proactive (Planned)	Controlled ROI on uptime

***Table 10.1**: Chaos ROI and business impact*

Note: RPS is calculated as Coverage Score × Success Rate × 100. The 'Before' value of 35% reflects a team that had tested 5 of 10 known failure modes (Coverage = 0.5) with 70% automatic recovery (Success Rate = 0.7). The 'After' value of 88% reflects testing all 10 failure modes (Coverage = 1.0) with 88% automatic recovery after six months of consistent Game Days.

By spending a few minutes of *uptime* during a Tuesday morning Game Day, we prevent an eight-hour catastrophic failure on *Black Friday*. This is the shift from insurance as a cost to chaos as an investment.

Blast radius

The biggest fear in chaos engineering is: *What if the experiment breaks the actual business?* We manage this through the **blast radius**, the maximum potential impact of a failure. Professional chaos engineering is defined by the ability to keep this radius as small as possible.

Strategies for blast radius containment

Managing the blast radius requires a multi-layered approach to infrastructure design, such as:

- **The canary group**: Instead of failing a service for all users, we apply the fault to a single *canary* instance or a small shard of users. If the canary dies, the other 99% of your users remain unaffected.
- **Regional and cell isolation**: Modern architectures use *Bulkheading*. By restricting a chaos experiment to a single **availability zone** (**AZ**) or a specific *Cell* of infrastructure, we ensure that a failure cannot cascade across the entire global platform.
- **Time-boxing**: Experiments should have a strictly defined lifespan. If the automated *Stop* command fails, the experiment should have a built-in TTL where it automatically cleans itself up after a few minutes.

AI safety officer and continuous guardrails

When we run a chaos experiment, our AIOps platform implements dynamic guardrails that act as an automated *emergency brake*:

- **The fence**: It uses service mesh logic (like Istio or Linkerd) to restrict fault injection to specific headers (e.g., only users with a test-group: chaos cookie).
- **The automated kill switch**: The AI constantly monitors the SLIs. If it detects *Collateral Damage*, such as an unrelated service starting to fail or a global latency spike, it triggers a **Halt and Rollback** in milliseconds, faster than any human could react.
- **Role-based access control (RBAC) and authorization**: Every chaos injection requires authenticated authorization via role-based access controls and audited credentials. This ensures that only authorized *Executors* can pull the trigger, and every action is audited for compliance.

To ensure chaos experiments do not unintentionally disrupt critical systems, it is essential to contain their blast radius. This involves limiting the scope of impact through layered isolation strategies, starting from the experiment itself and extending outward to partitions and the broader environment. The following figure illustrates these containment layers and associated mitigation techniques:

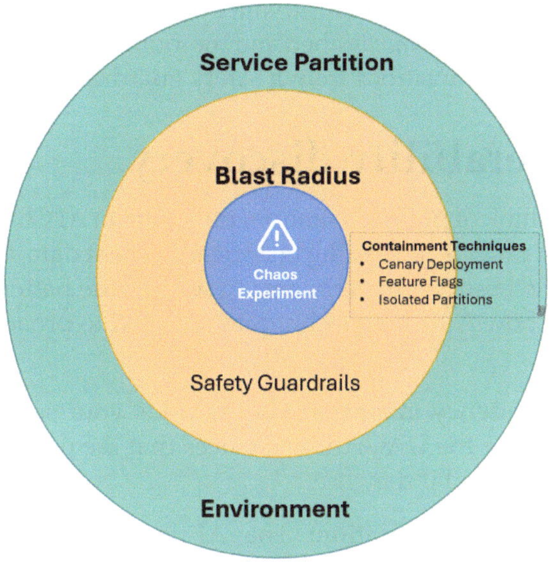

***Figure 10.3**: Blast radius containment in chaos experiment*

Advanced containment techniques

For high-stakes environments where even a canary failure is unacceptable, SRE teams utilize **traffic shadowing** (also known as dark launching). In this mode, the intelligent assistant *mirrors* production traffic to a secondary, isolated environment where the chaos experiment is actually occurring. The following points describe how advanced containment techniques are applied to safely evaluate failure scenarios without impacting real users:

- **Shadow impact analysis**: The experiment runs on the mirrored traffic. The AI compares the response of the healthy production service to the response of the *chaos-injected* shadow service. If the shadow service returns a 500 Internal Server Error, the system records the failure without the real user ever seeing an error.
- **Simulating network partitions**: One of the most difficult failure modes to test is the *Split Brain* scenario. By using tools like iptables or service mesh **mutual transport layer security** (**mTLS**) policies, we can simulate a total network partition between two data centers. The goal is to prove that the system gracefully enters a *read-only* mode rather than corrupting data, all while the AI maintains a *Virtual Fence* to ensure the partition does not leak into unrelated services.

AI as Chaos Master

This section explains how modern AIOps platforms orchestrate, govern, and continuously evolve chaos experiments at scale. In the early days of chaos engineering, experiments were manual, high-touch events planned weeks in advance by human SREs. However, as distributed systems grow in complexity, the *unknowns* become too numerous for humans to map. This is where the Intelligent assistant transitions from a safety guardrail to a proactive Chaos Master.

AI-driven vulnerability discovery

A human engineer might think of pulling a random plug, but an AI Chaos Master uses machine learning to find the *weakest* plug. By analyzing historical incident data, the AI identifies patterns in previous outages and orchestrates experiments to see if those patterns exist elsewhere. The following points describe how AI-driven techniques are used to proactively identify systemic weaknesses:

- **Graph-based dependency mapping**: The AI scans your service mesh to find *hidden dependencies* traversing the DAG; those services that are not technically required for a process but cause it to fail if they lag.
- **Heuristic weakness identification**: The AI looks for *brittle* services with low redundancy or those that have not been *vaccinated* by an experiment in over 90 days.

Orchestrating continuous chaos in CI/CD

If a Game Day is a *fire drill*, then **continuous chaos** is the automated sprinkler system. We no longer wait for a scheduled workshop to test the system's mettle. Instead, we integrate chaos experiments directly into the software development lifecycle.

Integrating fault injection into the pipeline

Modern AIOps platforms allow us to treat resilience-as-code. When a developer pushes a new microservice, the Intelligent Assistant automatically generates a Chaos Suite for that specific service based on its dependency graph. The following steps illustrate how fault injection is integrated into the delivery pipeline:

1. **The pre-flight stress test**: Before code reaches production, the assistant triggers high-latency simulations in a staging environment to ensure the new code's *Timeout* and *Retry* logic is configured correctly.
2. **The canary chaos**: As the new version is deployed to a 1% canary group, the AI Chaos Master injects small amounts of packet loss specifically to that 1%.
3. **Automatic promotion or rollback**: If the SLIs remain steady despite the chaos, the AI authorizes the promotion to 100%. If the steady state drifts, the experiment and the deployment are instantly aborted.

Scaling organizational resilience

Having established the technical *how-to* of fault injection, we must now look at how chaos engineering matures into a comprehensive strategy for business continuity. Moving beyond simple server restarts, a sophisticated practice involves identifying subtle failure patterns and learning from how global leaders protect their most critical assets. The following sections explore the nuanced failure modes that challenge even the most robust systems and the cross-industry strategies used to master them.

Advanced failure taxonomies

While traditional testing verifies if code performs its intended function, chaos engineering is designed to explore the unknown-unknowns of distributed environments. In these complex systems, failures are rarely binary; they are often grey or cascading issues that require specific experimental designs to uncover. The following points outline advanced failure patterns that chaos experiments are designed to uncover:

- **Dependency gremlins (The slow hang)**: Instead of a total crash, the Intelligent Assistant introduces specific latency to a non-critical microservice. This tests if your system's *circuit breakers* trip correctly or if the slow dependency causes a bottleneck that drags down the entire user experience.
- **Clock drift and synchronization**: In distributed systems, time is a critical variable that can lead to split brain scenarios. Chaos Masters can simulate network partitions or synchronization delays to test if the system maintains data consistency or gracefully enters a *read-only* mode.
- **Resource contention (The noisy neighbor)**: This involves simulating a sudden spike in disk I/O, memory leaks, or CPU consumption. The goal is to verify if *Bulkheading* and *Cell Isolation* strategies effectively protect other partitions from performance degradation.
- **The poison pill**: Injecting a malformed but syntactically correct request into a processing queue. This tests if the system can *Fence* the bad data or if the error will propagate and crash downstream workers.

Building a blameless Game Day culture

Game Day is a *fire drill* designed to test the people and processes as much as the technology. To move from a mindset of *blame* to *bravery*, organizations must establish a social contract that prioritizes learning over finger-pointing. The following principles define the cultural practices required to run effective, blameless Game Days:

- **The no-blame clause**: Every participant must agree that any system failure discovered is a *success* for the team, as it identifies vulnerability before it impacts a customer.

- **The scribe's narrative**: Beyond just logging technical timestamps, the scribe documents the team's internal communication and coordination. This helps identify *cognitive load* issues, such as whether on-call engineers were confused by specific dashboards or if escalation paths were unclear.
- **Psychological safety with AIOps**: The presence of an AI safety officer with an automated kill switch provides the psychological air cover needed for engineers to take bold risks.

Practical industry examples

Examining how industry leaders apply these principles helps quantify the ROI of a proactive chaos practice. The following table shows a few examples:

Industry domain	Chaos experiment scenario	Key steady state metric validated
Streaming (e.g. Netflix)	Randomly terminating production instances during peak hours to ensure stateless architecture resilience	**Stream starts per second**: Verifying users experience zero lag during server failure
Finance and payments	Simulating a *regional blackout* by triggering a *one-touch failover* between data centers	**Transaction atomicity**: Verifying that no *double-charging* occurs during a network partition
E-commerce	Using *traffic shadowing* to mirror production traffic while injecting high latency into the checkout service	**Checkout success rate**: Verifying the *error budget* can withstand transient spikes without failing the user

***Table 10.2**: Sample chaos experiment scenarios*

Tools of the trade

To orchestrate a successful Game Day, you need more than just a willing team; you need a *Chaos Toolkit* that provides safety, precision, and automation. The industry has evolved from crude scripts that randomly kill processes to sophisticated, AI-enhanced platforms that can simulate global outages with a single click.

Depending on your organization's maturity and infrastructure, the right tool can mean the difference between a productive learning session and an uncontrolled disaster. The following tools represent key platforms used to design, execute, and govern chaos experiments:

- **The progenitors**: Netflix's Simian Army and Chaos Monkey:

No discussion of chaos tools is complete without the pioneer. In 2010, Netflix changed the industry with **Chaos Monkey**, a tool originally designed to randomly terminate EC2 instances in Netflix's AWS environment, and later open-sourced for broader use.

- **Why it matters**: It shifted the industry from *preventing failure* to *surviving it.*
- **The modern evolution**: Chaos Monkey has grown into the **Simian Army**, which includes **Chaos Kong** (simulating an entire AWS region failure) and **Latency Monkey** (introducing artificial delays to test service degradation).
- **Best for**: Organizations with massive, stateless cloud architectures that want to normalize the idea of constant, random failure.

- **The enterprise standard**: Gremlin:

Gremlin was the first commercial *chaos-as-a-service* platform, founded by former Netflix and Amazon engineers. It brought much-needed **safety guardrails** to the practice.

- **Key feature, the reliability score**: Gremlin provides a standardized metric to track your system's resilience over time.
- **Game Day portal**: It includes a dedicated interface for orchestrating Game Days, allowing the *master of ceremonies* to schedule attacks, define targets, and most importantly, hit a global **Halt All** button if things go sideways.
- **Best for**: Large enterprise teams that require strict RBAC, audit logs, and a user-friendly UI to scale chaos across hundreds of teams.

- **The cloud-native leaders**: Chaos Mesh and LitmusChaos:

For those living in the world of Kubernetes and microservices, these **Cloud Native Computing Foundation** (**CNCF**) projects are the gold standard.

- **Chaos mesh**: A powerful, open-source platform that uses **Custom Resource Definitions** (**CRDs**) to inject faults directly into Kubernetes. It can simulate everything from pod kills to **Domain Name System** (**DNS**) failures and even *Time Skew.*
- **LitmusChaos**: Known for its **ChaosHub**, a community-curated library of *off-the-shelf* experiments. It focuses on *resilience-as-code*, allowing you to bake chaos directly into your **Git-based Operations** (**GitOps**) pipelines.
- **Best for**: SREs and DevOps teams working in complex, containerized environments who want deep integration with Prometheus and Grafana for observability.

- **The cloud-native leader**: AWS **Fault Injection Service (FIS)**:

If your entire stack lives on AWS, the FIS provides a unique advantage: it can inject failures at the **control plane** level.

  - **Unique capability**: Unlike other tools, FIS can simulate a database failover in Amazon RDS or throttle API requests, scenarios that are notoriously difficult to replicate with third-party agents.
  - **Safety integration**: It is natively integrated with AWS **Identity and Access Management (IAM)** and CloudWatch, ensuring that an experiment automatically stops the moment a specific alarm is triggered.
  - **Best for**: Teams heavily invested in the AWS ecosystem who want to test managed services without installing external agents.

- **The next frontier**: Harness and Steadybit (AI-driven resilience):

  The latest generation of tools is moving from manual injection to intelligent resilience.

  - **Steadybit**: Focuses on *Reliability Advice*. Instead of you guessing what to break, Steadybit scans your environment and *suggests* experiments based on your architecture's vulnerabilities.
  - **Harness chaos engineering**: Utilizes AI to automatically discover services and suggest experiments that will have the most impact on your SLIs. It specializes in integrating chaos into the *Canary Deployment* process.
  - **Best for**: Mature AIOps organizations that want to automate the entire Hypothesis | Experiment | Remediation loop.

The following table compares key chaos engineering tools and their core capabilities:

Tool	Focus area	Best use case	Killer feature
Chaos Monkey	Basic VM survival	Cloud-native/ Stateless	Randomness at scale
Gremlin	Enterprise reliability	Multi-cloud / Hybrid	Global kill switch and scorecards
Chaos Mesh	Kubernetes internal	Deep microservice testing	CRD-based chaos-as-code
AWS FIS	AWS infrastructure	Managed service failover	Control plane fault injection
Steadybit	Intelligent automation	Proactive weakness discovery	Automated reliability advice

***Table 10.3**: Pioneers in facilitating chaos engineering experiments*

Conclusion

In this chapter, we have journeyed from the foundational principles of chaos engineering to the high-stakes execution of organization-wide Game Days. We have seen how intentionally injecting failure is not an act of recklessness, but a calculated investment in *systemic immunity*, ensuring that our software learns to withstand the inevitable storms of a distributed, cloud-native world. By leveraging the *Hands* of our Intelligent Assistant and the pioneering tools of the industry, we have transformed SRE from a reactive discipline of firefighting into a proactive science of resilience.

However, the landscape of site reliability engineering is on the cusp of its most profound transformation yet. As systems grow in complexity beyond human cognitive limits, the next phase of our journey moves from intelligent assistance to autonomous operations.

In the next chapter, we examine how generative AI is extending modern site reliability engineering practices beyond reactive and assisted operations. Building on the foundations established through chaos engineering, reliability workflows increasingly incorporate automation and intelligent reasoning.

Looking ahead, hypothesis generation becomes increasingly automated as language-model-driven systems analyze source code, infrastructure configurations, and historical incident data to surface potential failure scenarios. Conversational interfaces further reduce the manual effort required to interpret logs and traces, enabling faster understanding of complex incidents. As these capabilities mature, the role of the AI SRE agent emerges, supporting portions of the reliability lifecycle while engineers focus on oversight, system design, and risk management.

The discipline of chaos engineering prepares systems for both expected and unexpected failures. With the integration of generative AI, reliability practices evolve toward systems that continuously learn from operational experience and improve resilience over time, shifting AIOps from basic automation toward adaptive operational intelligence.

Join our Discord space

CHAPTER 11
Generative AI-powered SRE Chatbot

Introduction

In *Chapter 9, Intelligent SRE Assistant*, we established the *hands* of our intelligent assistant, the automated workflows, and *one-touch ops* that execute critical remediation. In *Chapter 10, Chaos Engineering and Reliability Testing*, we built the *Immune System* through chaos engineering, learning how to vaccinate our infrastructure against the unknown. We mastered the scientific method: defining steady states, forming hypotheses, and containing the blast radius. However, even the most advanced *hands* require a sophisticated *brain* to guide them.

This progression reflects three stages of operational intelligence: descriptive intelligence, which analyzes what happened through dashboards and historical data; predictive intelligence, which forecasts what will happen by identifying patterns and burn rates; and prescriptive intelligence, which autonomously determines and executes what should be done. The generative AI-powered SRE agent represents this final stage. It is within this prescriptive tier that this chapter operates. As systems scale beyond human cognitive limits, the next phase of site reliability engineering moves from intelligent assistance to autonomous operations.

This chapter introduces the generative AI-powered SRE agent, the conversational nexus that integrates every tool we have built. We are moving toward a future where the site reliability engineer moves from a manual operator to a decision architect, interacting with an AI SRE agent that can reason, retrieve knowledge, and resolve incidents through natural language.

Structure

In this chapter, we will cover the following topics:

- Architecture of a conversational AIOps agent
- Retrieval-augmented generation in SRE
- AIOps Telemetry in the reasoning loop
- Rise of agentic AI and model context protocol
- Natural language for incident automation
- Post-incident lifecycle automation
- SRE bot implementation framework

Objectives

By the end of this chapter, you will possess the architectural blueprint to build and deploy a generative AI agent tailored for SRE. You will master the technical workflow of **retrieval-augmented generation** (**RAG**), learning how to transform static company documentation into a high-performance vector database that grounds AI responses in operational reality.

Beyond the technical setup, you will understand how to integrate real-time AIOps telemetry, including error budgets and burn rates, into a **large language model's** (**LLM**) reasoning loop. Finally, you will develop the foresight to transition from reactive chatbots to proactive agentic AI, enabling your organization to automate the entire lifecycle from incident discovery to post-mortem analysis using natural language.

Architecture of a conversational AIOps agent

A production-grade SRE chatbot extends beyond being a simple interface for an LLM; it functions as an intelligent reasoning and execution stack. For optimal performance within operational environments, its architecture must bridge unstructured natural language input with the structured operational requirements of cloud infrastructure. At a high level, it consists of three primary architectural layers as described in the following sections.

Cognitive orchestrator

The orchestrator serves as the *central nervous system*. It receives the user's natural language input and must decide how to process it. Rather than directly forwarding input to the LLM, the orchestrator applies structured **chain-of-thought** (**CoT**) reasoning to decompose the request. If an SRE says, *Check why the checkout service is slow and fix it*, the orchestrator identifies multiple sub-tasks: query the **service level indicators** (**SLIs**), identify the bottleneck, search for relevant runbooks, and finally, propose a remediation.

The orchestrator acts as the *pre-frontal cortex* of the agent. It manages the **reasoning and acting** (**ReAct**) loop, a framework where the LLM alternates between generating a *thought* (internal reasoning) and an *action* (invoking a tool).

Context engine

The context engine is what prevents the AI from *hallucinating*. It manages two distinct types of data:

- **Dynamic context (The Present)**: This involves real-time API calls to observability tools (Prometheus, Datadog). It feeds the AI the *current state*, i.e., metrics, active alerts, and recent deployment logs.
- **Static context (The Past)**: This is where RAG resides. It provides the AI with *knowledge*, historical incident reports, architectural standards, and policy documents.

Tool calling framework

This layer provides the *hands* of the assistant, enabling the LLM to interact with the physical world through **deterministic tool execution**.

- **JSON schema manifests**: Each tool (e.g., **`restart_service`**, **`check_slo`**, **`trigger_chaos_drill`**) is defined by a JSON schema. This schema tells the LLM exactly what parameters are required (e.g., **`service_name`**, **`region`**, **`grace_period`**).
- **The loop-back validation**: When a tool is executed, the output is fed back into the LLM as a new *observation*. If the command **`restart_service`** fails with a **`PermissionDenied`** error, the AI observes this failure and reasons through an alternative, such as *requesting elevation* or *checking IAM roles*, rather than simply stopping.

The following figure illustrates the SRE chatbot Architecture, a three-phase system designed to transform incident response into an intelligent, autonomous workflow. It begins with the **cognitive orchestrator (the brain)** for reasoning and task decomposition, moves to the **context engine (the memory)** for real-time and historical insights, and concludes with the **tool-calling framework (the hands)** for secure, validated execution with human oversight.

Figure 11.1 shows the architecture of the SRE agent, highlighting the orchestration, context retrieval, and tool execution layers that enable autonomous incident diagnosis and remediation:

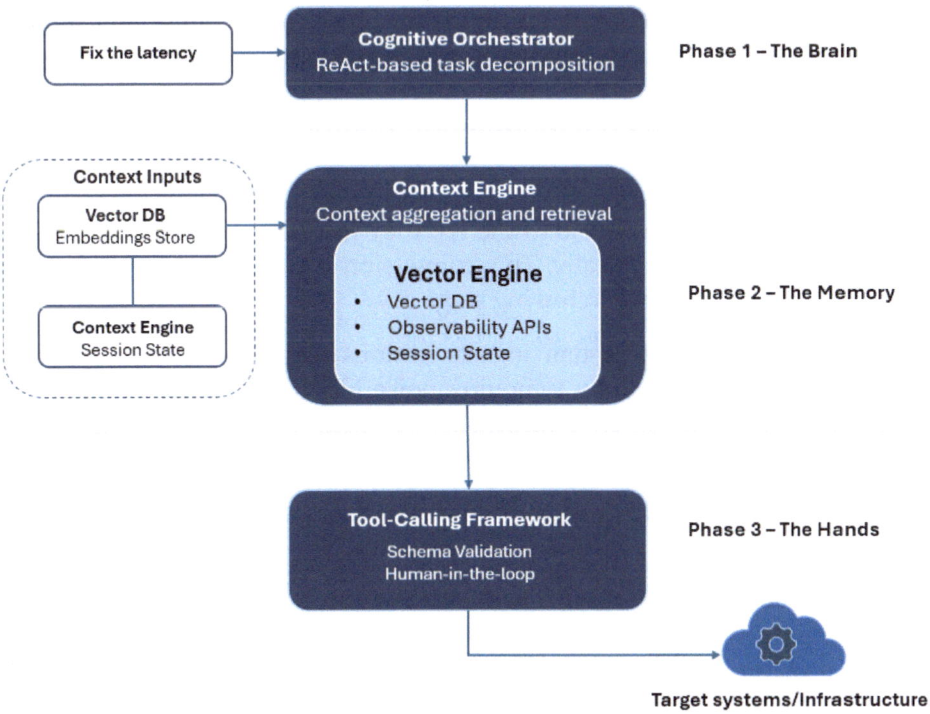

***Figure 11.1**: SRE chatbot architecture*

The safety governor

In an SRE context, giving an AI *write access* to production is a significant risk. The security layer acts as a transparent proxy between the AI's intent and the infrastructure's execution:

- **Human-in-the-loop (HITL) gateways**: For any action classified as *Destructive* (e.g., deleting an S3 bucket or scaling a database to zero), the framework requires a human operator to click an **Approve** button in Slack. The AI generates the intent, but the governance layer enforces the final authorization.
- **Role-based access control (RBAC)-aware execution**: The agent inherits the permissions of the user interacting with it. If a junior engineer asks the bot to change the **Border Gateway Protocol** (**BGP**) routing, the bot checks the user's **identity and access management** (**IAM**) context and politely declines, citing insufficient privileges.
- **Audit logging and traceability**: Every *thought* and *action* taken by the AI is logged in a centralized audit store. This allows SRE teams to conduct *post-mortems on the AI* itself if an autonomous action leads to an unintended consequence.

Retrieval-augmented generation in SRE

The most critical component of a specialized SRE chatbot is RAG. Standard LLMs are trained on public data and have a *knowledge cutoff*. They do not know about your private microservices, your specific database schemas, or your team's unique incident history. RAG allows the model to *consult* your private library before it speaks.

Ingestion pipeline

To make internal documents accessible to the AI, they must be converted into a format the machine can *understand* mathematically. This conversion is performed through a structured ingestion pipeline consisting of the following stages:

- **Document parsing**: The system ingests various formats (PDFs, Markdown, Slack threads). It cleans the data by removing noise like headers, footers, and boilerplate legal text.
- **Semantic chunking**: A 100-page *disaster recovery plan* is too large for an LLM to process at once. The system breaks the document into small *chunks* (e.g., 500 tokens). Crucially, these chunks must overlap slightly to ensure that context isn't lost at the boundaries.
- **Generating embeddings**: Each chunk is sent through an **embedding model** (like OpenAI's text-embedding-3-small or HuggingFace's BGE). This model transforms the text into a **vector**, a list of thousands of numbers (e.g., [0.12, -0.04, 0.89...]). This vector represents the *semantic essence* of the text.

- **The vector database**: These vectors are stored in a specialized database such as **Pinecone, Weaviate,** or **Milvus.** This database is optimized for *nearest neighbor* searches rather than traditional keyword searches.

Figure 11.2 illustrates the end-to-end ingestion pipeline, showing how raw data from various sources is parsed, semantically chunked, converted into vector embeddings, and stored in a vector database to enable efficient semantic retrieval:

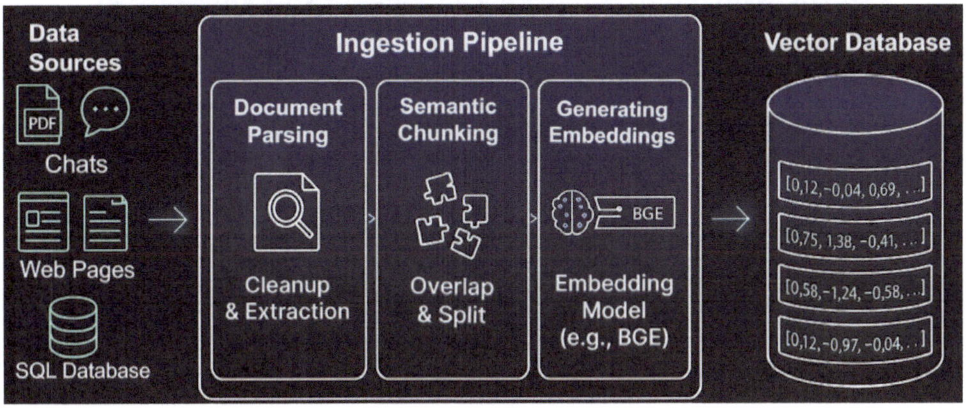

***Figure 11.2**: Data ingestion pipeline*

Retrieval and synthesis loop

When an SRE asks, *What is our failover procedure for the legacy SQL cluster?* The following technical process begins:

1. **Query embedding**: The user's question is converted into a vector using the exact same embedding model used during ingestion.

2. **Vector similarity search**: The system looks into the vector database to find chunks whose vectors are mathematically closest to the query vector. It uses metrics like **cosine similarity** to find text that *means* the same thing, even if the keywords are different.

3. **Prompt augmentation**: The system retrieves the top 3 or 5 most relevant chunks (e.g., the specific SQL failover runbook). It then constructs a *mega-prompt* for the LLM:

   ```
   You are an expert SRE. Use the following retrieved documentation to answer the user query. If the answer isn't in the documents, say you don't know. [Retrieved Documentation Chunks]... User Query: How do we failover the SQL cluster?
   ```

4. **LLM synthesis**: The LLM reads the retrieved text and the query. Its role here is not to *know* the answer from its training, but to **synthesize** a coherent, natural language response based *only* on the provided context.

Figure 11.3 illustrates the RAG workflow, showing how a user's query is converted into a vector representation, matched against relevant knowledge in the vector database, augmented with contextual information, and synthesized by LLM to produce an accurate and context-aware response.

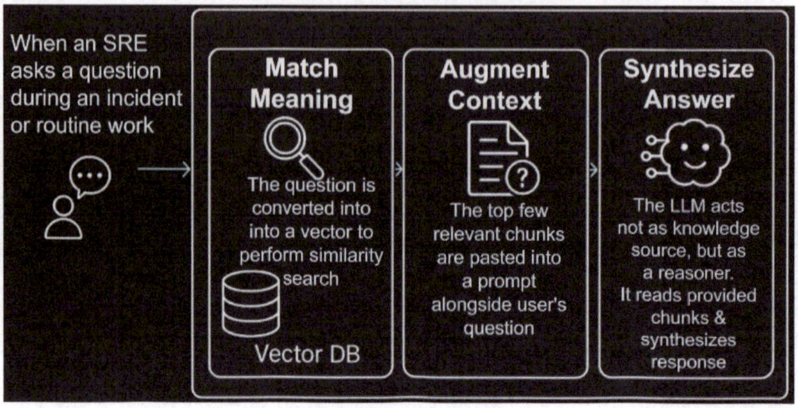

***Figure 11.3**: Data retrieval pipeline*

Importance of RAG for SREs

While RAG is useful in many domains, its application in SRE is particularly high-impact due to the nature of the work, as shown in the following examples:

- **Reducing mean time to recovery (MTTR)**: During a 3 AM incident, searching through Confluence, disorganized Slack threads, or 100-page PDFs for a *legacy SQL cluster failover procedure* is too slow.
    - **The RAG advantage**: The *semantic search* capability described means an engineer can ask *How do I fix the SQL thing?* and get the correct runbook even if they do not know the exact keywords used in the documentation. Instant access to the right runbook directly reduces downtime.
- **Democratizing tribal knowledge**: In many SRE teams, critical knowledge exists only in the heads of senior engineers or buried in ancient Slack conversations (which the ingestion pipeline specifically mentions targeting).
    - **The RAG advantage**: By ingesting Slack threads and post-mortems, tribal knowledge becomes instantly queryable by junior engineers without needing to interrupt senior staff.
- **Overcoming information overload and staleness**: SRE documentation is notoriously vast and quickly becomes outdated.
    - **The RAG advantage**: This is because the LLM synthesizes answers based *only* on retrieved context; the answers are as current as the last ingestion cycle.

Furthermore, *semantic chunking* ensures the model does not need to read the whole disaster recovery plan; it only needs the relevant three paragraphs to answer the immediate question.

- **Guardrails and accuracy**: A standard LLM might hallucinate a plausible-sounding but incorrect **`kubectl`** command that could worsen an outage.
    - **The RAG advantage**: The prompt augmentation step crucially instructs the LLM: **`Use the following retrieved documentation... If the answer isn't in the documents, say you don't know`**. This constraint is vital for operational safety, ensuring the chatbot relies on verified internal documentation rather than general internet training data.

AIOps Telemetry in the reasoning loop

A generative AI agent is only as intelligent as the context it receives. While RAG provides historical knowledge, real-time AIOps telemetry provides the present-state awareness that enables truly context-driven decision-making.

The two most critical telemetry signals for an SRE agent are error budgets and burn rates. An error budget represents the acceptable threshold of unreliability for a given service, for example, a 99.9% SLO allows 43.8 minutes of downtime per month. The burn rate measures how quickly that budget is being consumed relative to normal. A burn rate of 1.0 means the budget is being consumed at exactly the expected pace; a burn rate of 10 means it will be exhausted ten times faster than expected.

By injecting these signals directly into the agent's context window at query time, the LLM can shift from generic advice to operationally grounded decisions:

- If the burn rate for the checkout service is 14x and the error budget has 12% remaining, the agent escalates its response urgency and recommends immediate remediation over diagnostic investigation.
- If the burn rate is 0.5x and the budget is healthy, the agent may recommend a lower-priority investigation rather than a disruptive restart.

This transforms the agent from a reactive responder into a proactive reliability partner, one that understands not just what is failing, but how much that failure matters right now.

Rise of agentic AI and model context protocol

As we move beyond conversational assistants that merely respond to queries, we enter the era of **agentic AI**. While chatbot functions reactively by waiting for user input, an **agent** operates with a goal-oriented approach. It is given a high-level objective, such as *maintain a 99.9% availability for the checkout service*, and is empowered to autonomously plan, execute, and verify the necessary actions to achieve that goal.

This evolution follows a four-level automation maturity model:

1. **Manual operations**: Engineers respond to every incident through direct intervention.
2. **Assisted operations**: Tools like dashboards and alerts support human decision-making.
3. **Intelligent assistance**: Automated workflows and one-touch ops execute predefined remediation.
4. **Autonomous operations**: The agentic AI independently reasons, plans, and executes actions to maintain reliability goals without human intervention.

Organizations can use this model to benchmark their current state and identify the next step in their automation journey.

Agentic shift

The fundamental shift in SRE operations is moving from **instruction-based workflows** to **objective-based autonomy**.

- **Instruction-based (Chatbot)**: Restart the pod if the memory exceeds 80%.
- **Objective-based (Agent)**: Ensure the service remains stable during the flash sale. Use your discretion to scale, throttle, or restart components based on real-time cost-benefit analysis.

Agentic AI utilizes a **reasoning loop** (often called a ReAct pattern). The agent perceives an anomaly, forms a hypothesis about the root cause, selects a tool to test or fix the issue, observes the result, and iterates until the objective is met. This is not a linear script but a continuous loop that mimics the human SRE's diagnostic process, as shown in the following example:

- **Perception (Observation)**: The agent monitors the *short-term memory* of telemetry. It notices a 200ms increase in latency in the North America region.
- **Reasoning (Thought)**: Instead of just alerting, the agent forms a hypothesis. *I see latency is up, but error rates are stable. This suggests a saturated connection pool or an underlying network congestion, rather than a code-level crash.*
- **Planning (Action generation)**: The agent identifies the necessary *tool calls*. It decides to check the RDS connection count and run a traceroute between the application layer and the database.
- **Execution (Tool calling)**: The agent invokes the deterministic tools (the *hands*) to gather more data.
- **Reflection (Observation and iteration)**: The agent receives the data. *The traceroute shows high latency at the NAT Gateway. My initial hypothesis about the DB was wrong. I will now pivot to checking the VPC endpoint configurations.*

Multi-agent orchestration

As systems grow, a single monolithic agent becomes a bottleneck. The future of autonomous operations is **multi-agent systems** (**MAS**). In this architecture, specialized agents with distinct *personas* and *skillsets* collaborate to solve complex problems:

- **The network agent**: Specialized in BGP routing, VPC peering, and load balancer configurations.
- **The database agent**: Master of query optimization, indexing strategies, and replication lag remediation.
- **The chaos agent**: A proactive entity that constantly hunts for *weakest links* by running controlled experiments (as seen in *Chapter 10, Chaos Engineering and Reliability Testing*).
- **The orchestrator agent**: The *team lead* that delegates tasks to the specialists and synthesizes their findings for the human **decision architect**.

This collaborative approach reduces the cognitive load on any single model and allows for specialized *system prompts* that keep each agent focused on its domain of expertise.

The following figure is an architecture diagram that visualizes the transition from reactive scripts to autonomous operations, illustrating how a specialized **multi-agent system** (**MAS**) utilizes a **ReAct reasoning loop** to transform high-level human objectives into self-healing infrastructure actions. By delegating domain-specific tasks to specialized agents coordinated by a central orchestrator, the system maintains 99.9% availability while allowing the human SRE to step into the role of **decision architect**.

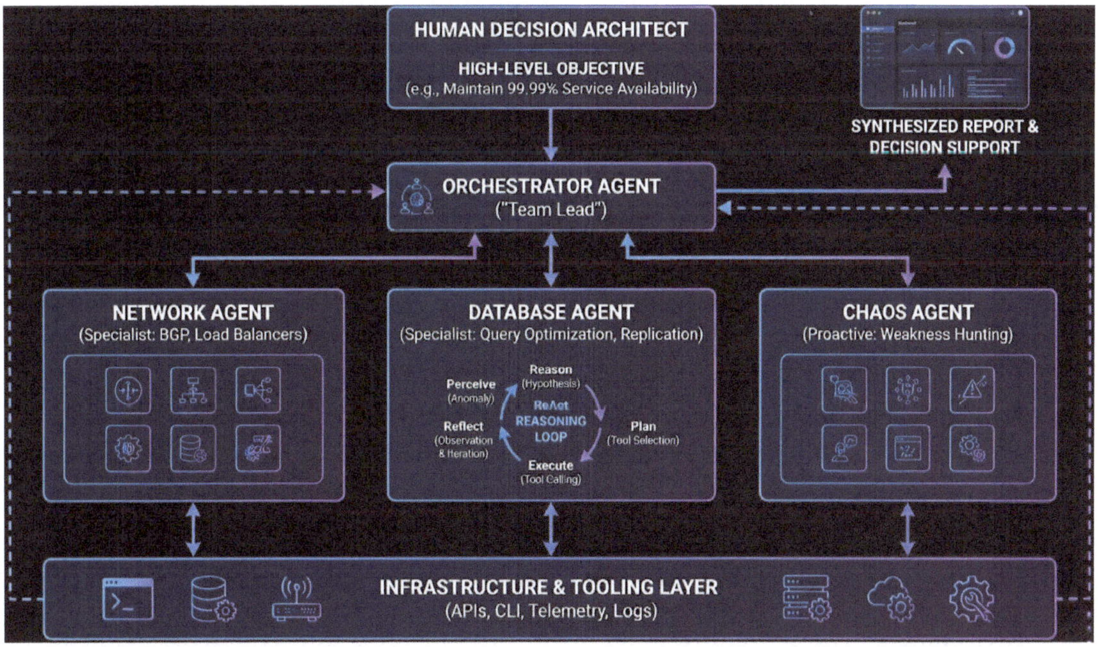

***Figure 11.4**: Agentic AI architecture*

Model context protocol

For these agents to move from theoretical *brains* to practical *operators*, they need a standardized way to interact with the world. Without a universal language, every SRE team would have to write custom code to connect their AI to AWS, Jira, GitHub, and Prometheus. This integration tax led to the development of the **model context protocol** (**MCP**), the universal interface that allows our autonomous agents to connect to enterprise infrastructure through a standardized interface.

While a chatbot is reactive, waiting for a human to provide a prompt, an agent is goal-oriented. One of the greatest hurdles in building autonomous SRE agents is the effort required to connect LLMs to disparate infrastructure systems. Each integration historically required custom *glue code*.

The MCP, an open standard, fundamentally changes this. MCP provides a universal interface that allows AI models to connect to infrastructure data and operational tools through standardized servers without the need for bespoke connectors for every new tool.

The MCP architecture consists of two primary components that enable secure and standardized interaction between the AI agent and enterprise infrastructure:

- **MCP servers**: These act as secure gateways to enterprise infrastructure. An SRE team can deploy an *AWS MCP Server* or a *Datadog MCP Server*. These servers expose specific *resources* (like log files or architecture diagrams) and *tools* (like restart instance or `update_security_group`) to the AI.
- **MCP clients (The agent)**: The AI agent acts as the client. It can query any MCP-compliant server to gather context or execute an action. This decoupling allows SREs to swap LLMs (e.g., moving from *GPT-4o* to *Claude 3.5* Sonnet) without rewriting their entire automation stack.

Agentic AI architecture powered by MCP

To understand how the MCP delivers a true agentic AI architecture, we must view it as more than just an API. It is the connective tissue that allows an LLM to transition from an *isolated brain* to a *plugged-in operator*. In an SRE context, MCP provides the standardized framework for **capability discovery**, **context injection**, and **deterministic execution**:

- **Capability discovery**: The handshake:

  In traditional automation, tools are *hard-coded* into the bot. If you add a new monitoring tool, you must rewrite the bot's code. In an MCP-based agentic architecture, the agent performs a **dynamic handshake** at startup.

  When the AI SRE agent initializes, it queries the MCP servers connected to the environment. The servers respond with a **list of tools and resources** defined in a machine-readable format. This allows the agent to learn its capabilities at runtime. For example, a *Cloud-Janitor* MCP server might suddenly appear, offering a tool to **`clean_orphaned_snapshots`**. The agent immediately incorporates this into its reasoning loop without a single line of the core AI logic being changed.

- **The separation of sensors (resources) and actuators (tools)**: MCP provides architectural separation between data retrieval (resources) and operational execution (tools) :
    - **Resources (The sensors)**: These are data-centric. MCP provides **resource templates** (e.g., **`sre://{service_id}/metrics`**) that the agent can *subscribe* to. When the agent reasons, *We need to see the current error budget*, it does not have to know the **structured query language** (**SQL**) query for the database; it simply requests the resource from the MCP server.
    - **Tools (The actuators)**: These are action-centric. They are deterministic functions with strict input validation. The MCP server ensures that when the agent decides to *scale a cluster*, the parameters passed (e.g., **`min_nodes`**, **`max_nodes`**) conform to the infrastructure's requirements.
- **Contextual grounding through sampling**: One of the most advanced features of MCP that enables agentic behavior is **sampling**. This is the inverse of a tool call. It allows the MCP server to ask the model for help.

For example, MCP server monitoring a deployment pipeline notices a failure. Instead of just sending an alert, the server can use the sampling interface to ask the agent: *I see a 'Permission Denied' error in this log. Based on our current RAG-retrieved policies, should I attempt a retry with elevated credentials or halt the pipeline?* This creates a **Bi-directional Intelligence Loop** where the infrastructure and the brain are in constant dialogue.

- **The safety proxy**: Governance in the protocol:

  MCP acts as a **security air gap**. It is because the LLM never communicates with the backend APIs (like AWS or K8s) directly, the MCP server serves as a *deterministic safety proxy*:
    - **Redaction**: The MCP server can automatically strip PII or secrets from logs before they reach the LLM's context window.
    - **Approval gates**: The protocol supports a *human-in-the-loop* workflow. When the agent initiates a high-impact tool call via MCP, the protocol can pause the request and wait for a signed-off JSON response from a human operator before the server actually executes the command on the backend.
- **Technical implementation**: The tool definition:

  To see how this works in practice, consider the following schema definition for an automated remediation tool hosted on an MCP server. This is what the LLM *sees* and uses to understand how to interact with your *hands* (from *Chapter 9, Intelligent SRE Assistant*):

```
{
  "name": "execute_one_touch_failover",
  "description": "Triggers a regional failover for a specific service.
Requires verified RPS > 70.",
  "inputSchema": {
    "type": "object",
    "properties": {
      "service_name": { "type": "string", "description": "The target
microservice" },
      "target_region": { "type": "string", "enum": ["us-east-1", "eu-
west-1"] },
      "safe_mode": { "type": "boolean", "default": true }
    },
    "required": ["service_name", "target_region"]
  }
}
```

By providing this structured *contract*, MCP allows the agentic AI to bridge the gap between a human's natural language intent: *The database in Virginia is struggling, move traffic to Ireland*, and the precise, API-driven execution required to maintain reliability. The SRE of the future doesn't write scripts to fix things; they build and govern the MCP servers that allow their AI partners to maintain the *steady state* of the world.

Natural language for incident automation

In the traditional world of site reliability engineering, an incident is a race against time characterized by high-velocity context switching. When a *P0* alert fires, an engineer is often forced into a state of **command-line paralysis**. They must navigate a fragmented landscape: one tab for Grafana metrics, another for Splunk logs, a terminal for `kubectl` commands, and a Slack channel for coordination. During a high-pressure crisis, the human brain's *working memory* becomes a bottleneck. The *cognitive load*, the mental effort required to recall syntax, find the right dashboard, and correlate disconnected data, directly inflates the MTTR.

The transition to **natural language-driven automation** transforms the SRE from a *manual operator* into a **strategic orchestrator**. By using a conversational interface, we replace the mechanics of *how* to find data with the logic of *what* the data means.

Keyword hunting to semantic summarization

In a manual response, an engineer might spend 15 minutes grepping through millions of lines of logs to find a pattern. A generative AI agent, powered by the architecture we have discussed, performs **semantic summarization**. Instead of presenting the logs, the agent presents the *insight*:

- **Traditional**: `kubectl logs -n prod | grep ERROR | tail -n 100` (Followed by manual parsing).
- **Conversational**: `Analyze the logs for the 'Payment' service in the last 10 minutes and tell me the top three unique error signatures.`
- **AI response**: `I found 4,200 errors. 92% are 'Timeout to DB-Primary,' 5% are 'Auth Token Expired,' and 3% are 'Memory Limit Exceeded.' The database timeout started exactly at 14:02 UTC.`

This shift allows the engineer to immediately bypass the *data gathering* phase and move directly to *hypothesis testing*.

Multi-tool synthesis

The most significant reduction in cognitive load comes from the AI's ability to act as a **universal interface**. An SRE often has to run a command in Kubernetes, check a configuration in Terraform, and verify a deployment in GitHub. Each requires different **command line interface** (**CLI**) tools and authentication contexts.

A natural language-driven agent uses its MCP connections to bridge these silos. An engineer can issue a single compound request:

```
Check the last three deployments for the 'Auth' service, compare the CPU usage before and after, and tell me if any feature flags were changed.
```

Behind the scenes, the agent queries GitHub, Prometheus, and Launch Darkly simultaneously. It synthesizes this disparate data into a single, coherent narrative, shielding the human from the underlying complexity of multiple APIs and syntaxes.

Operational mentor

During an outage, the *human-in-the-loop* often struggles with **decision fatigue**. Should we restart the pods or roll back the deployment? The AI agent acts as an **operational mentor**, utilizing RAG to cross-reference the current state with historical post-mortems (long-term memory).

Instead of a blank terminal screen, the agent provides a **guided decision path**:

```
I see the 'Inventory' service is failing. In the March 2024 outage, a similar signature was resolved by a 'Cell-Level Failover.' Would you like me to validate the traffic distribution or proceed with a 'One-Touch' failover to the standby region?
```

The engineer is no longer guessing; they are validating a recommendation based on institutional knowledge. By moving to a natural language interface, we are not just making things *easier*; we are making them **safer**. By lowering the cognitive load, we free the SRE to think critically about architectural resilience rather than struggling with terminal commands. The interface becomes a *Glass Box* where the agent's reasoning is transparent, its actions are governed by MCP-enforced safety guardrails, and the human's intent is the primary driver of reliability. The crisis is no longer a chaotic scramble for data; it is a structured, intelligent dialogue between an expert engineer and a system that understands its own state.

Post-incident lifecycle automation

The resolution of an incident is rarely the end of the reliability lifecycle; rather, it is the beginning of the most critical phase: learning. Historically, the post-incident process, drafting postmortems, and updating runbooks is the *weakest link* in SRE. After a high-pressure outage, engineers are often exhausted, leading to documentation that is either sparse, biased by recency, or delayed until the context is lost.

Generative AI transforms this *administrative burden* into an automated, data-driven feedback loop. By utilizing the agent as a 24/7 **digital scribe**, organizations can capture the nuance of a failure in real-time and translate it into permanent institutional knowledge.

Automating the paperwork

One of the most cognitively taxing parts of an incident is the administrative requirement to document the timeline while trying to fix the problem. This *dual-tasking* often leads to poor documentation and lost insights.

The generative AI agent serves as an **automated scribe**. This is because the entire incident response is occurring within a conversational thread, the agent can:

- **Generate real-time summaries**: Provide a *stakeholder update* every 15 minutes automatically.
- **Capture the timeline**: Tag every action, metric spike, and decision point with a timestamp.
- **Pre-fill the post-mortem**: By the time the incident is resolved, the agent has already drafted 80% of the post-incident report, including the **root cause analysis** (**RCA**) based on the diagnostic logs it analyzed during the incident.

Pattern recognition and causal analysis

Generative AI excels at finding needles in the haystack of high-cardinality data. By comparing the current incident's signature against the **vector database** (**RAG**) of previous years' outages, it identifies recurring **failure patterns**.

This pattern recognition capability enables the AI agent to perform several key analytical functions that support incident classification, root cause identification, and remediation planning:

- **Failure taxonomy mapping**: The agent categorizes the incident according to defined taxonomies (e.g., dependency poisoning, resource exhaustion, or configuration drift). It can tell the team: *This incident bears an 85% semantic similarity to the March 2023 outage, suggesting that our previous fix for the NAT Gateway was a workaround rather than a root-cause solution.*

- **Hypothesis validation**: In the postmortem draft, the AI does not just state what happened; it provides the data to prove it. It can automatically embed the specific Grafana panels or log snippets that validate the identified root cause, ensuring the report is grounded in evidence.

Transitioning from dead to living runbooks

The most significant impact of AI on the post-incident lifecycle is the automated update of recovery logic. Traditional runbooks are *dead* documents, static Wikis that quickly become obsolete. This transformation is enabled through the following automated mechanisms:

- **The delta analysis**: After an incident is resolved, the agent compares the actions taken by the SRE with the existing documented runbook. If the engineer found a more efficient way to recover, or if the runbook steps failed to work, the AI identifies this *delta*.

- **Automated PR generation (docs-as-code)**: The agent then drafts a **pull request** (**PR**) to the documentation repository. This PR contains the updated Markdown for the runbook, incorporating the new recovery steps discovered during the heat of the moment.

- **Synthesizing new remediation logic**: If a *one-touch* automated fix (from *Chapter 9, Intelligent SRE Assistant*) was used, the AI updates the script's metadata to include the new failure context, ensuring that the next time this pattern occurs, the **intelligent assistant** has the most up-to-date *vaccine* ready for injection.

Closing the loop by feeding the RAG

Every postmortem drafted by the AI is immediately indexed back into the vector database. This ensures that the *long-term memory* of the organization is always current. In the next incident, the agent's RAG retrieval will include this latest failure. This creates a compounding intelligence effect: the system becomes more resilient with every failure, as the AI's reasoning continuously improves based on high-fidelity documentation from previous incidents.

By streamlining the post-incident lifecycle, generative AI eliminates the reliance on tribal knowledge, the undocumented expertise held by experienced engineers. The post-incident phase shifts from a chore to an automated engine of growth. We no longer just *fix* systems; we use the generative SRE brain to ensure the organization never makes the same mistake twice, turning the scars of past outages into the blueprint for future reliability.

SRE bot implementation framework

Moving from theory to practice requires a framework that can orchestrate the interaction between LLMs, external data sources, and computational tools.

LangChain has emerged as a widely adopted framework for building agentic workflows. In this section, we will walk through a *Hello World* implementation of an SRE bot, a system that can *reason* about a latency alert, *retrieve* documentation from a vector store, and *act* by querying a monitoring tool.

Components of the SRE bot

To build this bot, we utilize four primary modules within the LangChain ecosystem:

- **The LLM (The brain)**: A model like GPT-4 or Claude 3.5 Sonnet that handles reasoning.
- **Tools (The hands)**: Python functions wrapped in LangChain's `@tool` decorator that allow the bot to interact with APIs (e.g., Prometheus or Kubernetes).
- **Vector store (The memory)**: A database like Pinecone or ChromaDB containing your indexed runbooks.
- **The agent executor (The orchestrator)**: The logic loop that decides which tool to use and when.

The implementation of the SRE bot follows a structured workflow that progressively integrates tools, knowledge retrieval, and reasoning capabilities:

1. **Defining the SRE tools**: First, we define the deterministic functions the bot can call. In a real-world scenario, these would interface with your AIOps stack.

   The following shows an example of defining a deterministic SRE tool using LangChain's `@tool` decorator, enabling the agent to query service latency from the monitoring system:

```
from langchain.tools import tool
@tool
def get_service_latency(service_name: str):
    """Queries Prometheus for the P99 latency of a given service."""
    # Logic to call Prometheus API
    # For 'Hello World', we return a simulated value
    return f"The P99 latency for {service_name} is currently 450ms
(Threshold: 400ms)."
@tool
def restart_microservice(service_name: str):
    """Triggers a rolling restart of a Kubernetes deployment."""
    # Logic to call kubectl or an MCP server
    return f"Successfully initiated a rolling restart for {service_
name}."
```

2. **Setting up the knowledge base (RAG)**: We use LangChain to load a markdown file (a sample runbook) and store its semantic *meaning* in a vector database (refer to the following):

```
from langchain_community.document_loaders import TextLoader
from langchain_openai import OpenAIEmbeddings
from langchain_community.vectorstores import FAISS

# Load internal runbook
loader = TextLoader("runbook_latency_issue.md")
documents = loader.load()

# Create vector store for semantic search
vector_store = FAISS.from_documents(documents, OpenAIEmbeddings())
retriever = vector_store.as_retriever()
```

3. **Initializing the agentic brain**: The *agent* is initialized with access to both the tools (for action) and the retriever (for knowledge). We use a *chat* prompt template to give it a specific persona: **`You are an expert SRE. Use the provided tools and runbooks to diagnose and resolve incidents.`**

```
from langchain.agents import create_openai_functions_agent,
AgentExecutor
from langchain_openai import ChatOpenAI

llm = ChatOpenAI(model="gpt-4", temperature=0)
tools = [get_service_latency, restart_microservice]

# Combine LLM and Tools into an Agent
agent = create_openai_functions_agent(llm, tools, prompt)
agent_executor = AgentExecutor(agent=agent, tools=tools, verbose=True)
```

Hello World execution scenario

When we run the agent with a natural language query, it begins its reasoning loop:

- **User input**: The checkout service is slow. Check the latency and suggest a fix from the runbook.
- **The agentic reasoning trace**:
  - **Thought**: The checkout service latency needs to be measured precisely.
  - **Action**: Call **`get_service_latency(service_name="checkout")`**.
  - **Observation**: The P99 latency for checkout is currently 450ms.

- **Thought**: The latency is above the threshold. The runbook for high latency procedures should be consulted
- **Action**: Query the vector store for *checkout high latency*.
- **Observation (Retrieved Text)**: If P99 exceeds 400ms, first verify the DB connection pool. If connections are normal, a rolling restart of the pod is the standard mitigation.
- **Final response**: The checkout service P99 is at 450ms. According to the internal runbook, **`a rolling restart is the recommended mitigation. Shall restart_microservice be executed?`**

- **Moving toward production**: While this *Hello World* example is simple, it demonstrates the core architectural shift. We have moved away from writing if-then-else scripts and toward intent-based operations.

To scale this framework, you would integrate the MCP discussed earlier, allowing these tools to be hosted on remote servers and shared across multiple agents. By using LangChain as the orchestrator, you ensure that every action the AI takes is grounded in your specific telemetry and guided by your verified institutional knowledge. This is the implementation of the *brain* that finally connects the hands of your automation to the *senses* of your observability stack.

Conclusion

The evolution from rule-based automation to generative, retrieval-augmented, and agentic AI marks a fundamental shift in site reliability engineering. In this chapter, we established the architectural blueprint for an autonomous SRE agent capable of reasoning about incidents, grounding decisions in enterprise knowledge, and executing deterministic remediation through governed interfaces. By integrating RAG, real-time telemetry, and structured tool-calling frameworks, the agent transforms static documentation and fragmented observability data into a unified, actionable intelligence layer.

This architecture redefines operational workflows. Instead of manually navigating dashboards, runbooks, and command-line tools, SREs can interact with a conversational system that understands context, retrieves institutional knowledge, and executes validated remediation actions. The incorporation of agentic reasoning and the MCP enables secure, standardized integration with infrastructure, allowing the agent to move beyond passive assistance toward autonomous, policy-aware operations.

Equally important, the agent closes the post-incident learning loop by automatically generating postmortems, updating runbooks, and continuously enriching its knowledge base. Each incident strengthens the system's diagnostic capability, creating a compounding cycle of operational intelligence.

In the next chapter, we will explore advanced deployment patterns, governance strategies, and real-world production considerations required to operationalize autonomous SRE agents at enterprise scale.

CHAPTER 12
Scaling AIOps Across the Enterprise

Introduction

In earlier chapters, we evolved from *hands* (automated workflows and one-touch ops) to the *immune system* (chaos-hardened resilience) and the *brain* (a generative, agentic SRE capability). At a small scale, these capabilities accelerate a single service. At enterprise scale, they must function as a digital nervous system that can sense, correlate, and act across global, fragmented infrastructure: hybrid and multi-cloud estates, mainframes and **software as a service** (**SaaS**), data centers and edge, product lines and business units.

This chapter explains how to operationalize that transition from local optimization to enterprise-wide coordination. We move beyond app-tier RCA to multi-domain correlation, we balance central standards with federated AIOps, we extend **role-based access control** (**RBAC**)-aware safety across hundreds of squads, and we elevate **service level objectives** (**SLOs**) from a single service to portfolio-level error budget management. Finally, we confront the human system: trust, explainability, guardrails, and skills, because scaling AIOps is as much a cultural transformation as it is an architectural one.

Structure

In this chapter, we will cover the following topics:

- Scaling AIOps via a federated model
- Change management for intelligent operations
- Organization design and cross-team collaboration
- Training and upskilling SRE teams
- Measuring enterprise-wide impact and ROI

Objective

By the end of this chapter, you will be able to architect a federated AIOps model that balances localized team agility with global enterprise governance and visibility. You will design a change management framework that uses **AI Explainability** (**XAI**) to improve transparency and stakeholder confidence. You will also establish an AIOps Center of Excellence that standardizes models, safety guardrails, and prompt engineering across the enterprise, and implement a measurement framework that translates technical reliability gains into high-level business value and ROI for leadership.

Scaling AIOps via a federated model

Scaling AIOps across an enterprise requires more than replicating a successful pilot. It demands a deliberate architectural shift that can accommodate diverse technology stacks, regional compliance requirements, and the organizational complexity of hundreds of teams operating simultaneously. The following subsections explore the core pillars of this transition.

Scaling a technology involves more than just *adding more servers*. At the enterprise level, AIOps must solve problems that are invisible at the department level. The *global fleet* introduces a level of entropy that simple automation cannot handle.

Multi-domain correlation

In a small-scale pilot, the causality chain is usually short. In a global enterprise, the *root cause* of a customer-facing outage in one region might be a silent network configuration change in another or a schema update in a shared legacy environment. To address this challenge, enterprise AIOps platforms rely on two key capabilities:

- **Federated context engine**: To scale, the AIOps platform must ingest and correlate telemetry from disparate domains, such as network, security, hybrid cloud, and application tiers. It must understand the *shared fate* of infrastructure.
- **Pattern recognition across silos**: Enterprise AIOps identifies recurring cross-domain issues. If multiple business units are all experiencing intermittent API timeouts, the AI can correlate these to a shared internal library or a specific cloud-region dependency that no individual team could see.

Federated AIOps architecture

As an organization moves from a single pilot to enterprise-wide adoption, the *monolithic AIOps* model, where one central brain attempts to manage every server, database, and network switch, often becomes difficult to manage due to increasing complexity. A single **large language model** (**LLM**) or heuristic model cannot maintain the deep, specialized context required to troubleshoot a 30-year-old **Common Business-Oriented Language** (**COBOL**) based mainframe system while simultaneously optimizing a cutting-edge, serverless GraphQL **application programming interface** (**API**).

The solution is a federated AIOps architecture. This approach mimics the structure of a modern global organization; it provides localized autonomy for specialized tasks while maintaining a central intelligence layer for global coordination and governance.

Architectural blueprint

In a federated model, the intelligence is distributed across two primary layers: the LocalEdge agents and the central enterprise orchestrator. Each layer serves a distinct purpose in the federated model, as described in the following:

- **The specialized edge agents (The domain experts)**: Instead of one generalist assistant, each business unit or technology domain (e.g., payments, logistics, cloud infrastructure, legacy systems) deploys its own specialized AI Agent:
    - **Context-specific training**: The *payments agent* is grounded in the specific documentation, transaction logs, and causal graphs of the payment processing stack. It understands that a 50ms delay in a database query is a *Category 1* emergency, whereas the *marketing analytics agent* might treat the same delay as negligible.
    - **Low latency and data sovereignty**: This is because these agents live closer to the data (at the *edge* of the department), and they can perform inference and remediation much faster. They also ensure that sensitive data stays within the department's boundaries, only sending anonymized metadata to the core.
- **The central enterprise orchestrator (The global brain)**: The central layer acts as the *connective tissue* of the enterprise. It does not manage individual servers; it manages the relationships between the edge agents:
    - **Cross-domain correlation**: If the payments agent reports an anomaly and the network agent reports a routing flap at the same time, the orchestrator correlates these signals to identify a *multi-domain incident*.
    - **Global knowledge propagation**: When the *web store agent* learns a new way to mitigate a specific type of **distributed denial-of-service** (**DDoS**) attack, the orchestrator captures that logic and pushes the *immune memory* to all other edge agents in the federation.

The following is the step-by-step workflow on how this architecture works. To understand how this functions in a real-world crisis, let us follow the lifecycle of a global failure:

- **Local detection**: The database edge agent in the *retail BU* detects an unusual spike in lock contention. It immediately performs a local **retrieval-augmented generation** (**RAG**) query against the retail-specific runbooks.
- **Autonomous local response**: The agent attempts a localized fix, perhaps increasing the connection pool size, and monitors the results.
- **Signal propagation**: Simultaneously, the agent sends a *health signal* and a *summary metadata* packet to the central enterprise orchestrator. It does not send the raw logs (to save bandwidth and maintain privacy); it sends a summarized *Intent and Action* report.

- **Global correlation**: The orchestrator receives similar signals from the identity management agent. The orchestrator's *higher-order reasoning* realizes that the retail DB issue is actually a side effect of a global authentication service failure.
- **Orchestrated resolution**: The orchestrator sends a command to the identity management agent to initiate a failover to the backup region while instructing the retail agent to put the database into *Read-Only* mode to prevent data corruption.

Multi-tenant governance and RBAC-aware execution

When an agent moves from suggesting to executing, security becomes the primary scaling bottleneck:

- **Policy-as-code integration**: Every autonomous action must be checked against the enterprise policy engine. Can the AI restart this server during a *Black Friday* freeze? Does it have RBAC to access the production database?
- **Compliance and sovereignty**: In an enterprise, AIOps must be *region-aware*. Data processing must follow specific regional guidelines (e.g., **General Data Protection Regulation** (GDPR)), requiring the AIOps construct to respect data sovereignty boundaries.

To illustrate how enterprises can balance centralized intelligence with decentralized operational autonomy, the following figure presents a federated AIOps architecture. This model highlights how a centrally governed *global intelligence* layer collaborates with distributed, domain-specific edge agents. Together, they form a unified operational framework in which local environments act independently while continuously contributing signals and context to a global reasoning engine, enabling scalable, resilient, and self-improving enterprise operations. The following figure illustrates how the federated AIOps architecture operates across the enterprise:

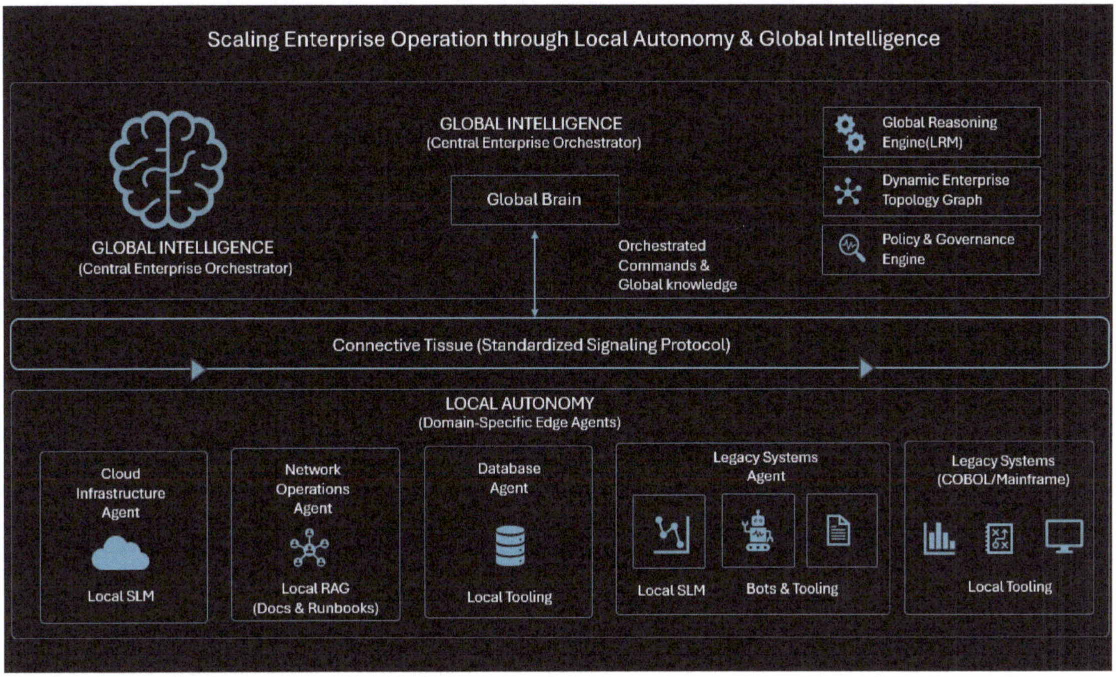

***Figure 12.1**: AIOps federated architecture*

Change management for intelligent operations

Transitioning an enterprise to AIOps is not a *software upgrade;* it is a fundamental shift in the organizational trust model. In traditional operations, change is managed through human-led **change advisory boards** (**CABs**) and manual checkpoints. In intelligent operations, the *decision engine* moves from a boardroom to an algorithm.

To scale successfully, leadership must implement a change management framework that addresses the psychological, technical, and procedural barriers to autonomy.

Trust ladder and phased maturity framework

The primary inhibitor of AIOps adoption is the *Black Box* fear, the anxiety that an autonomous agent will make a catastrophic decision in milliseconds. We resolve this by implementing a Trust Ladder, where automation *earns* its right to act based on verifiable performance. The Trust Ladder progresses through five distinct phases:

- **Phase 1**: **Observation and shadowing (Non-intrusive)**:

  The AI Agent observes human SREs during an incident. It generates *shadow insights,* internal logs that state what the AI *would* have done. Humans review these logs post-incident to validate the AI's logic against human intuition.

- **Phase 2: Advisory mode (The co-pilot):**

  The AI surfaces its reasoning in real-time via the SRE Chatbot (e.g., *I recommend failing over to US-East-1*). The human remains the sole executor.

- **Phase 3: HITL execution:**

  The AI prepares the remediation script and the *rollback plan*. The human engineer simply clicks the **Approve and Execute** button. This builds confidence in the agent's ability to handle the *Hands* of the system safely.

- **Phase 4: Supervised autonomy (The safety harness):**

  The AI executes low-risk remediations (e.g., clearing logs, scaling clusters) automatically but provides a *10-second pause* during which a human can hit a *kill switch*.

- **Phase 5: Full autonomy:**

  The AI manages the entire lifecycle of known failure patterns, reporting only the outcome and the **chain-of-thought** (CoT) reasoning for audit purposes.

The following figure illustrates the five phases of the progressive Trust Ladder and how automation earns increasing levels of autonomy over time:

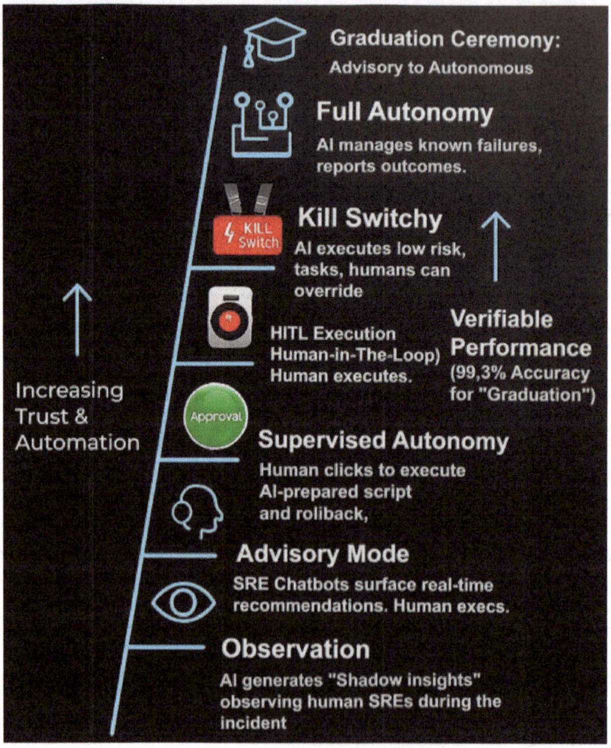

Figure 12.2: *Progressive Trust Ladder for AI automation*

Implementing chain-of-thought explainability

In a traditional enterprise, *why* is as important as *how*. If an AI agent restarts a mission-critical database, stakeholders need to know the rationale. We replace *Black Box* logic with explainable AI using CoT reasoning.

Every autonomous action must be accompanied by a structured rationale:

- **Observation**: I detected a 15% increase in latency on the checkout service.
- **Hypothesis**: Causal Inference (*Chapter 8, Causal Inference and Efficient Root Cause Analysis*) suggests the root cause is a connection leak in the payment DB.
- **Risk assessment**: Blast radius analysis shows that a restart will take 12 seconds with zero data loss risk.
- **Action**: Initiating connection pool reset.

This level of transparency transforms the AI from a mysterious entity into a peer engineer whose logic can be audited and improved.

Shift from gatekeeper to guardrail architect

Change management in the AIOps era redefines the SRE role. Traditionally, SREs acted as *gatekeepers*, manually reviewing PRs and change requests to prevent failures. In the intelligent operations construct, the SRE becomes a guardrail architect. This role shift manifests in two primary responsibilities:

- **Policy-as-code (PaC)**: Instead of manually approving a change, the SRE writes the code that defines the boundaries of the AI. For example, *The AI may autonomously scale the frontend, but it may never delete a production database without two-factor human authorization.*
- **Managing the safety governor**: SREs focus on tuning the sensitivity of the AI's *safety governor*. They define the error budget thresholds that, when crossed, automatically strip the AI of its autonomous powers and return the system to manual control.

Overcoming automation anxiety and cultural friction

Leadership must address the human element: the fear that AI will replace the engineer. Two cultural strategies help address this anxiety effectively:

- **Toil rebranding**: Change management focuses on the **reclamation of creativity**. We communicate that AIOps is not replacing the engineer; it is replacing the *toil*. By automating the *3:00 AM wake-up calls* for routine issues, the SRE is freed to focus on **decision architecture,** designing the next generation of resilient systems.

- **The no-blame AI culture**: Just as SREs practice blameless post-mortems for humans, the organization must adopt a blameless approach to AI failures. If an agent makes a mistake, the *fault* lies in the training data or the guardrails, not the *machine*. This encourages engineers to participate in improving the model rather than resisting it.

AIOps steering committee

For a multi-year transformation, change management requires a governance body that bridges the gap between technical teams and business stakeholders. This governance body operates through two core mechanisms:

- **The review loop**: A monthly AIOps governance meeting reviews the autonomous success rate.
- **The graduation ceremony**: When a specific remediation workflow (e.g., auto-remediation of disk full errors) achieves 99.9% accuracy over 100 instances in the *advisory phase*, the committee officially graduates it to the *autonomous phase*. This formal process ensures that leadership and compliance teams are aligned with the increasing velocity of the operation.

Therefore, change management for intelligent operations is the process of scaling trust. By moving up the Trust Ladder, insisting on explainability, and repositioning SREs as architects rather than firefighters, the enterprise creates a culture where humans and AI co-evolve. The goal is an organization that does not just tolerate automation but relies on it as the foundation of its global reliability.

Organization design and cross-team collaboration

The transition to enterprise-wide AIOps necessitates a shift from a *support* mindset to a *platform* mindset. When AI begins to handle the low-level orchestration of infrastructure, the traditional boundaries between development, operations, and data science begin to blur. To succeed, the organization must be redesigned to support **decision architecture** as a primary function.

AIOps Center of Excellence

In a multi-year transformation, a centralized AIOps **Center of Excellence** (**CoE**) acts as the architect of the *operational brain*. Unlike a traditional **Network Operations Center** (**NOC**) that reacts to fires, the CoE builds the tools that prevent them. The CoE is defined by three core attributes:

- **Composition**: A hybrid squad consisting of **machine learning** (**ML**) **engineers** (to tune models), **platform engineers** (to manage the RAG pipelines and vector stores), and **principal SREs** (to define the operational logic and guardrails).

- **Core responsibility**: The CoE does not *own* the incidents of every business unit. Instead, it owns the **global model lifecycle**. It ensures that the LLMs are grounded in the most recent architecture diagrams and that the *safety governor* logic is standardized across the company.
- **Standardizing the nervous system**: The CoE provides the API contracts that allow different departments to *plug in* their telemetry. This ensures that whether a team is using a legacy mainframe or a modern serverless stack, the central orchestrator can understand their Health Signals.

The organizational structure of the CoE is best visualized through a 6-layer model that defines the lifecycle of AI within the enterprise, as listed in the following table:

Layer	Primary function	Core responsibility
Layer 1: Strategy and vision	AI Ambition	Defines 12-month roadmaps, prioritization criteria, and success metrics
Layer 2: Governance	Responsible AI	Manages data or model governance, risk assessment, and regional compliance
Layer 3: Infrastructure	Enablement	Creates data pipelines, vector DB strategy, and model hosting platforms
Layer 4: Use case factory	Repeatability	Manages the progression from discovery workshops and **proofs of concept** (**PoCs**) to pilots and production
Layer 5: Delivery and integration	Actionability	Ensures AI plugs into workflows via agentic loops and monitoring dashboards
Layer 6: Upskilling and adoption	Literacy	Focuses on change champions, **Standard Operating Procedure** (**SOP**) redesign, and workflow training

***Table 12.1**: AIOps COE operational framework*

AIOps as an internal service product

One of the most common reasons AIOps fails is that it is *pushed* onto engineering teams as a mandatory tool rather than *pulled* in as a valuable service. To scale, you must treat your AIOps platform as an **internal product**. This product mindset is operationalized through two key practices:

- **Self-service onboarding**: A development team should be able to *subscribe* their microservice to the AIOps agent via a simple configuration file. The agent then automatically crawls their documentation, ingests their logs, and begins shadowing their incidents.

- **The feedback loop (reinforcement learning from human feedback)**: When an SRE interacts with the agent and corrects its reasoning (e.g., *No, that database latency is normal during the Monday batch job*), that feedback must be captured. The CoE uses this human-in-the-loop data to *fine-tune* the enterprise model, making the AI smarter for everyone.

Cross-team collaboration

In most large enterprises, the *network team* uses one set of tools, the *database team* uses another, and the app teams use a third. This creates a *semantic silo* where teams literally speak different operational languages. Enterprise AIOps resolves this fragmentation through two mechanisms:

- **Unified semantic memory**: The AIOps construct provides a **shared knowledge layer**. When the network team updates a firewall rule, the AI records that event in the global vector database. Ten minutes later, if the app team sees a connectivity error, the AI can immediately link the two events.

- **The global post-mortem**: Traditionally, post-mortems stay within the team that experienced the outage. With AIOps, the agent synthesizes the *lessons learned* from every incident across the company and proactively updates the runbooks of *other* teams that share similar architectural patterns.

Decision architect vs. siloed specialist

Organization design must evolve to create a new career path: the **decision architect**. This evolution in the SRE role is characterized by two key shifts:

- **The shift**: In the old model, an SRE was a specialist in a specific silo (e.g., *The Linux Guy* or *The Oracle Expert*). In the AIOps model, the SRE's value is their ability to **architect decisions**.

- **New workflows**: SREs from different business units collaborate on model tuning sessions. They meet to review the AI's CoT logic and decide which automated actions should be promoted from manual approval to full autonomy. This transforms collaboration from a reactive war room into a proactive strategy room.

Managing the shared fate of hybrid teams

In a scaled AIOps environment, teams are no longer responsible just for their code; they are responsible for the context they provide to the AI. This shared responsibility manifests in two collaborative practices:

- **Contextual responsibility**: Collaboration now means ensuring that your service's metadata (**service level indicators (SLI)**, **service level objectives (SLO)**, and dependency maps) is accurate. If a team provides dirty data or outdated runbooks, the AI will make poor decisions for the whole enterprise.

- **Joint error budgets**: Advanced organizations move toward **joint error budgets** for interconnected services. If Service A and Service B are tightly coupled, the AIOps platform manages their reliability as a single unit, forcing the teams to collaborate on stability rather than finger-pointing during failures.

Therefore, redesigning the organization for AIOps is about moving away from vertical silos and toward a horizontal intelligence layer. By establishing a CoE, treating the platform as a product, and empowering SREs as decision architects, the enterprise creates a structure where knowledge flows at the speed of the network, and reliability becomes a shared, automated asset.

Training and upskilling SRE teams

The shift toward AIOps and autonomous operations does not render the SRE obsolete; rather, it elevates the role from a practitioner of scripts to a decision architect. As we scale these systems across the enterprise, the gap between success and failure is often defined by the *cognitive readiness* of the engineering team. Upskilling for this new era requires a departure from traditional systems administration toward a specialized competency in AI orchestration.

New SRE tech stack

The modern SRE must move beyond Python and Bash to master a new layer of the stack. This *AI control plane* requires three core technical competencies:

- **Prompting for Ops (intent-based engineering)**: In previous chapters, we used **command line interface** (**CLI**) commands to interact with systems. In the scaling phase, the SRE must master **operational prompt engineering**. This is not just about asking questions; it is about defining **system instructions** that guide an agent through a high-stakes incident.
  - **Skill shift**: Learning to write *few-shot* prompts that provide the agent with examples of successful past remediations.
  - **Constraint design**: SREs must learn to prompt for safety, ensuring the agent always checks the *error budget* before executing a restart or a traffic shift.
- **Model observability (monitoring the machine's mind)**: Just as we monitor CPU and RAM, SREs must now monitor the health of the AI models. The two key skills underpin this capability:
  - **Detecting drift**: Training teams to recognize when an agent's reasoning begins to deviate from historical norms (e.g., suggesting a database flush for a network issue).
  - **Latency vs. accuracy**: Understanding the trade-offs between a fast, small model (suitable for simple alerts) and a slow, large model (required for complex causal reasoning).

- **Managing RAG pipelines**: RAG is the short-term memory of the AIOps agent. SREs must understand how data flows from a Jira ticket or a Slack thread into a **vector database**.
    - **The SRE's role**: Teams must be trained to manage the *indexing* of their own runbooks, ensuring that the AI is not pulling outdated or conflicting information from three-year-old documents.

    The following figure illustrates the new SRE tech stack pyramid, showing the layers of competency required in the AIOps era:

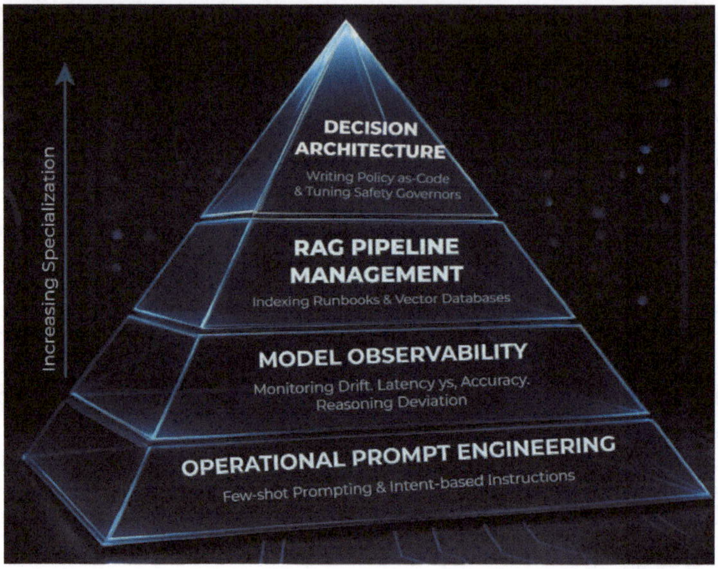

Figure 12.3: *New SRE tech stack pyramid*

ML literacy for pragmatic RCA

We do not expect SREs to become PhD data scientists, but they must achieve **ML literacy**. This is the ability to interpret the *probabilistic* outputs of an AI rather than the *deterministic* outputs of a script. This literacy encompasses three practical areas:

- **Probabilistic reasoning vs. Boolean logic**: Traditional scripts return *Success* or *Failure*. An AIOps agent returns a **confidence score**:
    - **Training focus**: SREs must learn how to handle an agent that says, *I am 82% sure the root cause is a connection leak.*
    - **Threshold management**: Teams are trained to set *Threshold-based Guardrails*. If the confidence is >90%, the agent can act. If it is <90%, the agent must escalate to a human.

- **Causal vs. correlative intuition**: As discussed in *Chapter 8, Causal Inference and Efficient Root Cause Analysis*, the *Brain* of our system relies on **directed acyclic graphs** (**DAGs**).
    - **The skill**: SREs are trained to audit these graphs. When the AI suggests a root cause, the SRE must be able to trace the *reasoning path* to ensure the AI is not being fooled by a *spurious correlation* (two things happening at once that have no causal link).

Curating the institutional brain

In the autonomous enterprise, **documentation is code**. If the documentation is poor, the AI's *brain* is essentially starved of oxygen. SREs must be upskilled to become **knowledge engineers**. This upskilling focuses on three core practices:

- **Knowledge curation as a Tier-1 task**: Upskilling involves shifting the culture so that writing a post-mortem or updating a runbook is seen as a *training event* for the AI.
    - **Semantic labeling**: SREs are trained to write documents in a way that is easily consumable by LLMs, using clear headings, structured **JavaScript Object Notation** (**JSON**) snippets for commands, and explicit *cause-effect* statements.
- **Grounding the agent**: Teams must learn to curate the **grounding data**, the specific, verified facts that prevent the AI from hallucinating.
    - **The gold standard library**: SREs curate a library of *perfect incident responses*. When a new incident occurs, the AI looks at this *institutional brain* to find the most reliable path forward. This turns every senior engineer's tribal knowledge into a permanent, digital asset for the entire company.

AI Game Day

To put this training into practice, organizations must evolve their **Game Days** (introduced in *Chapter 10, Chaos Engineering and Reliability Testing*) into **AI-human teaming drills**. These drills take two primary forms:

- **The red-team drill**: One group of engineers injects chaos, while another group uses the AIOps agent to diagnose and fix it.
- **The feedback workshop**: After the drill, the team reviews the AI's transcript. They identify where the AI's reasoning was flawed and immediately update the institutional brain (documentation) or the system prompt to fix the error. This creates a compounding cycle of learning where the human and the AI get smarter together.

Upskilling the SRE team is the final critical enabler in scaling AIOps. By mastering the new SRE stack, embracing ML literacy for root cause analysis, and taking ownership of the institutional brain, engineers move from being *victims of the alert storm* to being the architects of autonomy.

The goal of this training is to create a symbiotic relationship where the machine handles the complexity of the data, and the human provides the wisdom of the decision.

Measuring enterprise-wide impact and ROI

As AIOps transitions from a technical pilot to an enterprise-wide *operational nervous system*, the metrics of success must also evolve. For leadership, the value of AIOps is not found in CPU utilization or database active connections, but in the reclamation of human capital and the acceleration of business velocity.

To sustain a multi-year transformation, organizations must move beyond traditional operational metrics and adopt a framework that quantifies the financial and strategic impact of autonomous operations.

From technical KPIs to strategic value drivers

In a manual environment, we measure the speed of the human, expressed as MTTR. In an AIOps environment, we measure the **efficacy of the system** and the **cognitive relief** of the engineer:

- **Toil avoidance (TA) and reclaimed capacity**: The most significant **return on investment (ROI)** of AIOps is the elimination of *low-context decisions*, repetitive tasks that require human intervention but zero human creativity. This is measured and expressed in two ways:
    - **The metric**: We track the volume of automated remediations (e.g., auto-scaling, log rotation, automated failovers) multiplied by the average human time required to perform those tasks manually.
    - **The impact**: This is expressed as **FTE-hours reclaimed.** If AIOps handles 5,000 routine incidents per month, each taking 15 minutes, the organization has reclaimed 1,250 hours, essentially adding a squad of digital engineers to the workforce without increasing headcount.
- **Cognitive load index**: High cognitive load is the leading cause of SRE burnout and attrition. AIOps acts as a *noise filter*, ensuring that humans only engage with high-stakes, novel problems. This is tracked through two specific measures:
    - **The metric**: The ratio of raw alerts to actionable Incidents.
    - **The goal**: A 90% reduction in alert volume. Success is measured by the decrease in context switching events for engineers during their on-call shifts.

Cost of intelligence vs. cost of failure

To justify the investment in LLM tokens, vector databases, and the AIOps CoE, leadership must perform a specialized cost-benefit analysis. This analysis is structured around two key calculations:

- **The prevention premium (Avoided loss)**: The ROI of AIOps is often invisible because it is the cost of the outage that *never happened*. This is quantified through the following approach:
  - **Calculation**: Using historical data, we calculate the average cost per minute of downtime for a Tier-1 service. We then track **early warning events**, incidents where the AIOps platform identified a causal trend (*Chapter 8, Causal Inference and Efficient Root Cause Analysis*) and mitigated it before it breached an SLO.
  - **Example**: If AIOps detects a memory leak and initiates a proactive rolling restart 30 minutes before a crash, the ROI is the full cost of that avoided 30-minute outage.
- **Innovation velocity (The opportunity cost of firefighting)**: When SREs are trapped in reactive firefighting, they cannot work on architectural improvements. The impact of this constraint is measured in two ways:
  - **The metric**: The percentage of time spent on feature support vs. technical debt.
  - **The impact**: As AIOps scales, we look for a measurable shift in the *project-to-support* ratio. If teams move from spending 60% of their time on operations to 20%, the ROI is the 40% increase in the organization's ability to ship new products.

Operational maturity metrics

Beyond financial gain, the maturation of the autonomous construct is tracked through three operational metrics:

- **The automation graduation rate**: This tracks how many manual runbooks are converted into one-touch ops (*Chapter 9, Intelligent SRE Assistant*) and eventually into fully autonomous workflows each quarter.
- **The false positive and false negative ratio of causal graphs**: Measuring the accuracy of the AI's *brain*. A high accuracy rate (95%+) reduces the *Trust Gap* and accelerates the move up the **Trust Ladder** (discussed in the change management section).
- **Mean time to benefit (MTTB)**: How quickly can a new microservice be onboarded into the AIOps platform and start benefiting from autonomous guardrails?

Visualizing impact for executive leadership

To maintain momentum for a multi-year effort, the data must be synthesized into a **leadership ROI dashboard**. This dashboard should avoid technical jargon and focus on three key pillars:

- **Risk mitigation**: Total downtime prevented and error budget protection status.
- **Efficiency**: Total hours of manual labor replaced by autonomous agents.
- **Agility**: Improvement in deployment frequency facilitated by automated safety checks.

To provide a clear executive overview of the multi-year transformation, the following table summarizes the enterprise AIOps ROI framework across five key dimensions, such as efficiency, financial impact, organizational health, agility, and maturity:

Dimension	Primary metric	Description	Business value
Efficiency	**Toil avoidance** (**TA**)	Volume of low-context incidents (restarts, disk cleans, scaling) handled autonomously	**FTE-hours reclaimed**: Equivalent to adding virtual headcount without increasing budget
Financial	Avoided loss (prevention premium)	Cost of downtime saved by proactive causal mitigation before an SLO breach occurs	**Direct bottom-line protection**: Preserves revenue during peak events (e.g., Black Friday)
Organizational health	Cognitive load index	Reduction in the alert-to-incident ratio and context-switching events	**Talent retention**: Dramatic reduction in SRE burnout and turnover costs
Agility	Innovation velocity	Percentage shift of engineering time from Firefighting to feature development	**Market competitiveness**: Faster time-to-market for new products and services
Maturity	**Mean time to benefit** (**MTTB**)	The speed at which new services inherit the autonomous safety harness	**Reduced operational debt**: New business units become reliable by default instantly

Table 12.2: Enterprise AIOps ROI framework

Conclusion

Scaling AIOps from a localized pilot to a global enterprise standard is a significant shift from reactive troubleshooting to proactive digital resilience. By architecting a federated AIOps model, organizations can resolve the tension between the deep, specialized context required by individual technology domains and the high-level orchestration needed to manage a global fleet. This architecture ensures that specialized edge agents maintain local autonomy and data sovereignty while the central enterprise orchestrator provides the global brain necessary for cross-domain correlation and shared institutional memory.

However, the transition is as much a cultural shift as an architectural one. Success depends on building a Trust Ladder that systematically moves from human observation to supervised autonomy, ensuring AI earns its right to act through verifiable performance. Equally important is insisting on explainability, implementing chain-of-thought reasoning that transforms Black Box algorithms into transparent peer engineers whose rationale can be audited and refined. This must be accompanied by a redefinition of the SRE role, elevating engineers from gatekeepers of manual changes to guardrail architects and decision architects who design the policies that govern autonomous systems. Finally, institutionalizing intelligence through an AIOps Center of Excellence ensures the global model lifecycle is managed and that AIOps is treated as an internal product that engineers actively want to adopt.

Ultimately, the impact of this transformation is measured not just in technical uptime, but in strategic business value. By reclaiming thousands of FTE-hours from routine toil and reducing the cognitive load on engineering teams, the enterprise transforms its operational cost center into a primary driver of innovation velocity. In this mature state, the organization no longer just manages its infrastructure; it possesses a self-improving, autonomous nervous system capable of navigating the complexity of modern, global scale.

In the next chapter, we move beyond enterprise scaling to explore the future of SRE and AIOps, examining the emergence of autonomous ops and self-healing systems, predictive governance and risk modeling, the rise of AI agentic swarms, and the ethical responsibilities that every SRE must navigate as intelligent systems take on greater autonomy in the next decade.

CHAPTER 13
Future Trends in SRE and AIOps

Introduction

As established in *Chapter 1, SRE Principles Driving Modern Operations,* the journey began with an engineer confronting a wall of red alerts at 2 AM, attempting to reconstruct the architecture of a system that had grown beyond individual comprehension. In *Chapter 3, AIOps Knowledgebase,* we introduced the foundational tools that strengthened this engineer's operational capabilities. In *Chapter 10, Chaos Engineering and Reliability Testing,* the system's resilience was expanded through a more adaptive and fault-tolerant immune system, while in *Chapter 11, Generative AI-powered SRE Chatbot,* we added a reasoning layer that enabled intelligent interpretation of complex telemetry. By this chapter, the engineer is no longer reacting to incidents but shaping the architecture itself. This transformation, from reactive operator to strategic decision architect, captures the central evolution explored throughout this book.

Throughout this journey, we have traced the evolution of SRE from its manual, *toil-heavy* origins to the sophisticated, AI-augmented discipline it is today. We have built the *hands* of automation, the *immune system* of chaos engineering, and the *brain* of generative AI. We have seen how AIOps transforms a sea of telemetry into a surgical diagnostic path. Each chapter added a layer of intelligence to what was once a purely reactive discipline.

Yet, as we stand on the precipice of a new era, the nature of *scale* is changing once again. We are moving beyond microservices into the realm of *infinite complexity,* where systems are so distributed, ephemeral, and interconnected that no single human mind can fully grasp their state at any given moment. In this landscape, the goal of SRE is no longer just to *fix* what breaks, but to architect systems that possess an inherent, autonomous intelligence.

This final chapter serves as your strategic roadmap for the next decade. We will explore the emergence of autonomous ops, where self-healing is the default, not the exception. We will dive into predictive governance, moving from reactive audits to proactive risk modeling. We will examine the ethical boundaries and risks of autonomous systems, the questions no responsible SRE can afford to ignore. Finally, we will define the new role of the SRE in a world of agentic swarms and **large language models (LLMs)**. We are transitioning from being the *mechanics* of the digital world to being its *navigators* and *decision architects.*

Structure

In this chapter, we will cover the following topics:

- Autonomous ops and self-healing systems
- Predictive governance and risk modeling
- AI agents for reliability engineering
- Role of LLMs in SRE Workflows
- Ethics and risks of autonomous systems
- Preparing for the next reliability frontier
- Core pillars of your new roadmap

Objectives

After reading this chapter, you will be equipped to define the Architecture of Autonomy by understanding the shift from human-in-the-loop to closed-loop systems and building the trust-based guardrails required for autonomous remediation. You will learn to implement predictive risk modeling to move beyond reactive post-mortems toward a proactive governance model that quantifies the reliability risk of code changes while mastering the orchestration of agentic swarms within a multi-agent ecosystem where specialized AI agents collaborate to resolve complex, cross-domain incidents. Furthermore, you will be able to leverage LLMs as reasoning engines to bridge the gap between institutional tribal knowledge and real-time operational data, reason through the ethical boundaries of autonomous action, and ultimately evolve your career into a decision architect by identifying the cultural and skill-based shifts needed to lead an enterprise-level AIOps transformation.

Autonomous ops and self-healing systems

In earlier discussions, we examined the mechanics of one-click operations where human intervention served as the final gate for any remediation activity. The future of SRE represents a departure from this supervised model toward fully autonomous operations. In this paradigm, the system functions as a digital nervous system capable of sensing a deviation from the steady state and initiating a correction without any human prompt. This evolution requires a fundamental shift in how we perceive the role of automation, moving away from scripted sequences toward intelligent feedback loops that possess deep context and situational awareness.

Closed loop autonomous engine

The core of autonomous operations is the closed loop feedback system, which integrates observation, orientation, decision, and action into a single unified cycle. In a traditional setup, an alert might trigger a notification for an engineer who then logs into a console to execute a rollback. In an autonomous world, the AIOps platform identifies failure, correlates it with the most recent deployment, and triggers the rollback automatically. The sophistication of this system lies in its ability to verify its own success. After the remediation is applied, the engine continues to monitor the service level indicators to ensure that the system has returned to its healthy state. If the fix fails to resolve the issue, the engine proceeds to the next most likely solution based on historical data and causal probability. This cycle happens at machine speed, resolving incidents in seconds that would traditionally take hours of human investigation.

Building such a system requires a high level of mathematical certainty. We utilize three primary concepts to ensure safety within these loops. First, we establish deterministic guardrails, which are immutable rules that define what the system is never allowed to do, such as deleting a primary database or modifying security groups. Second, we rely on probabilistic confidence scores where the AI only acts if the likelihood of a correct diagnosis exceeds a specific threshold. Third, we implement automated verification cycles where the system must prove that its action improved the service level before it marks the incident as resolved.

Transition to intent-based reliability

The landscape of modern operations is witnessing a profound shift from imperative scripts toward intent-based reliability. In an imperative world, an engineer writes a script that says if memory exceeds 90%, then restart the service. This approach is inherently brittle because it cannot adapt to new or unforeseen failure modes and often leads to flapping, where the system enters a cycle of endless restarts. In an intent-based world, the engineer defines a desired outcome or a set of constraints rather than a specific procedure. This methodology relies on a reconciliation loop where the autonomous engine constantly compares the observed state of the environment against the target state defined by the engineer.

Consider a scenario where the engineer states that the checkout service must always remain available with a latency of less than fifty milliseconds while maintaining a specific cost efficiency. The autonomous engine then takes this high-level goal and determines the optimal way to achieve it using real-time constraints. It might decide to scale up the infrastructure, rebalance traffic across regions, or throttle low-priority background tasks such as reporting or logging. By focusing on the what instead of the how, the autonomous system gains the flexibility to navigate the immense complexity of modern distributed environments. This represents the ultimate maturity of the SRE discipline, where the human focuses on defining the policy and the business value while the machine manages the operational complexity required to sustain that value.

Industry examples and best practices

Leading technology organizations are already implementing these concepts through advanced orchestrators. For example, large-scale cloud providers use intent-based networking to reroute traffic automatically around fiber cuts or hardware failures without human intervention. In the world of software delivery, progressive delivery tools utilize intent-based gates to pause or rollback deployments if service-level indicators drop below a predefined threshold.

To succeed with intent-based systems, organizations should follow three critical best practices. First, ensure that the target state is defined using measurable metrics that the engine can observe with high fidelity. Second, implement a staggered roll out of autonomous actions, starting with read-only suggestions before granting the engine write permissions. Third, maintain a comprehensive audit log of every decision made by the autonomous engine to ensure that human operators can reconstruct the logic during a postmortem. These practices transform the autonomous system from a black box into a transparent and reliable partner.

The following figure illustrates how these three safety concepts, such as deterministic guardrails, probabilistic confidence scores, and automated verification cycles, integrate into a single, self-correcting closed-loop engine that operates continuously at machine speed:

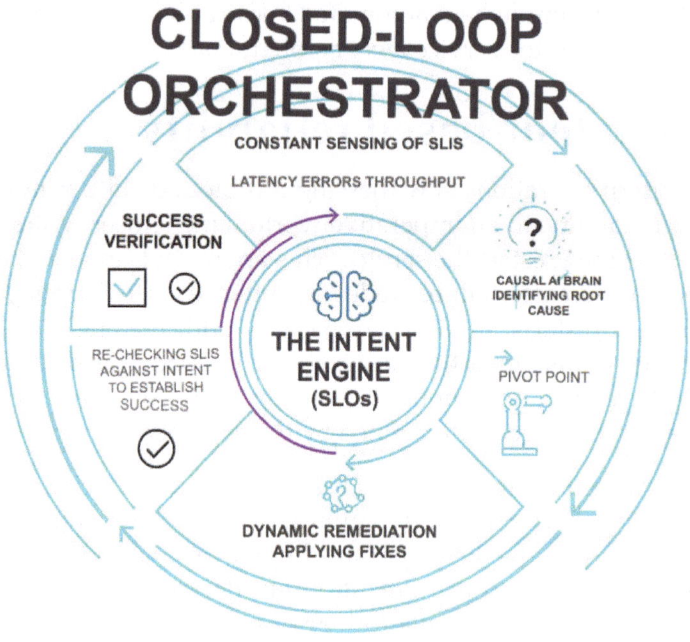

Figure 13.1: Closed loop automation engine

Predictive governance and risk modeling

Historically, *governance* has been a friction point, a series of manual gates, compliance checklists, and **change advisory board** (**CAB**) meetings that slow down innovation velocity. In the era of AIOps, governance evolves into a predictive service. Instead of looking backward at what went wrong, we use AI to model risk before a single line of code is deployed. This transition shifts the SRE from being a *gatekeeper* to a *risk architect*.

Reliability CI/CD gate

The future of the CI/CD pipeline is an intelligent, risk-aware orchestrator. Every **pull request (PR)** is no longer just checked for syntax and unit tests; it is assigned a reliability risk score. This score is generated by an AIOps engine that performs a multi-dimensional analysis:

- **Code sentiment and history**: AI analyzes the complexity of the change and compares it to historical *hotspots* in the codebase where previous incidents occurred.
- **Causal dependency mapping**: Utilizing the causal graphs discussed in *Chapter 8, Causal Inference and Efficient Root Cause Analysis*, the system identifies if the change impacts a *critical bridge* in the architecture, a component that, if failed, would cause a high-impact cascade.
- **Blast radius quantification**: The AI simulates the potential failure of the new code and calculates the percentage of users or revenue at risk.

If the risk score exceeds a predefined threshold, the pipeline does not just block the deployment; it triggers a pre-emptive verification loop. This might involve automatically spinning up a temporary environment to run a specific chaos experiment (*Chapter 10, Chaos Engineering and Reliability Testing*) targeted at the suspected weakness, effectively *vaccinating* the change before it reaches production.

Dynamic error budgets and adaptive SLOs

Predictive governance also extends to the management of error budgets, which traditionally remained static across long periods of time. In an intelligent operations model, the AIOps platform predicts periods of environmental volatility, such as major marketing events or seasonal traffic surges, and automatically adjusts the safety margins of the service level objectives. During these high-risk windows, the engine might tighten the error budget to enforce stricter deployment gates and require more rigorous automated testing.

Conversely, during periods of low activity, the system can relax these constraints to allow for faster innovation. This concept of adaptive governance ensures that the organization is always operating at the optimal intersection of speed and safety. The governance model becomes a living entity that responds to the actual state of the business and the technical environment rather than a static set of rules. This enables a state of continuous compliance where the system maintains a live ledger of every change and its associated risk score, providing a transparent audit trail that satisfies regulatory requirements while enabling high-frequency deployments without the need for traditional change advisory boards.

AI agents for reliability engineering

The transition from intelligent assistance to autonomous operations is catalyzed by the emergence of specialized AI agents that function as an integrated swarm. We are moving beyond the era of the monolithic chatbot toward a distributed ecosystem of intelligent actors where each agent possesses a specific domain of expertise. These agents do not merely respond to queries but actively collaborate to solve problems that were previously beyond the cognitive reach of a single engineer. This swarm architecture allows the site reliability engineer to function as a high-level conductor who orchestrates the actions of a digital workforce.

Architecture of the agentic swarm

In a multi-agent ecosystem, the collective intelligence of the swarm arises from the interactions between specialized personas. Each agent is equipped with a unique set of tools and a specific cognitive mission:

- The observer agent serves as the sensory organ of the swarm by constantly scanning high-cardinality telemetry and logs to identify the first sign of a steady state deviation. It does not just report anomalies but uses semantic understanding to distinguish between a harmless spike and a critical failure cascade that requires immediate attention.
- The historian agent is activated once an issue is identified to search the long-term memory of the organization. It crawls vector databases containing years of incident reports and past conversations to find similar failure patterns and previously successful remediation strategies that can ground the current investigation.
- The architect agent constructs a real-time model of the infrastructure topology by utilizing the causal discovery techniques discussed in previous chapters. Its mission is to map the blast radius and identify which upstream services or downstream dependencies might be impacted by the current failure mode.
- The executor agent takes the insights gathered by its peers and formulates a step-by-step remediation plan. This is not a static script but a dynamic sequence of actions that adjust based on the live feedback of the system as the remediation is carried out.
- The communicator agent translates the technical maneuvers and findings of the swarm into natural language summaries for the human stakeholders. This ensures that the entire organization remains informed of the incident status and progress without being overwhelmed by low-level technical noise.

The following figure depicts this multi-agent architecture, showing how collective intelligence emerges through shared context, structured reasoning loops, and human-defined policy boundaries:

***Figure 13.2**: Agentic swarm architecture*

Collaboration protocols and reasoning loops

The true power of the swarm lies in how these agents communicate and resolve conflicts. They utilize a shared blackboard architecture where agents post their findings and hypotheses for other agents to review. For example, the architect agent might propose that a database bottleneck is the cause of latency, but the observer agent might counter with data showing that the network throughput is actually the limiting factor.

This internal dialogue mimics the reasoning process of a team of human engineers during a war room session. The swarm uses chain-of-thought reasoning to arrive at a consensus, ensuring that the final decision is grounded in a holistic view of the system. This collaborative reasoning loop reduces the risk of false positives and ensures that the remediation action is surgical and precise. The human SRE oversees this process, providing high-level guidance and intervening only when the swarm reaches an impasse or when a high-risk action requires a final human authorization.

From reactive swarms to proactive agents

While much of the focus is on incident response, the agentic swarm also operates in a proactive mode to prevent incidents before they occur. The optimizer agent constantly analyzes resource utilization and service level indicators to suggest architectural improvements. It might identify that a specific microservice is consistently overprovisioned or that a particular database query could be optimized to reduce latency. The curator agent works to maintain the quality of the organizational knowledge base by identifying outdated runbooks and suggesting updates based on recent system changes.

This continuous proactive engagement transforms the SRE workflow from a cycle of firefighting to a journey of continuous improvement. The agents handle the repetitive and data-intensive tasks of optimization and documentation, leaving the human engineer to focus on the strategic direction of the reliability product. This represents a fundamental redefinition of the relationship between humans and machines in the operational domain, where the AI handles the complexity of scale while the human provides the intent and the ethics.

Role of LLMs in SRE Workflow

In previous chapters, we explored the use of LLMs for generating human-readable summaries and providing conversational interfaces. However, the future of SRE leverages these models not merely as text generators but as high-fidelity reasoning engines that sit at the core of the operational workflow. By treating the model as a cognitive processor, we can bridge the gap between static technical assets and the dynamic reality of production environments. This shift transforms the LLM from a passive librarian into an active logical validator that can reason through the implications of architectural choices and operational events.

Reasoning engines for code analysis

The most profound impact of LLMs in the SRE domain is their ability to perform deep semantic reasoning over the relationship between source code and production behavior. Traditional observability platforms are excellent at showing that a specific function is consuming excessive CPU cycles, but they lack the cognitive context to explain the logic that necessitated that consumption. When an LLM acts as a reasoning engine, it can ingest the application source code alongside high-cardinality telemetry and explain the causal link between a specific code change and a runtime anomaly.

This enables a new paradigm of code-to-cloud traceability where the model identifies logic branches that were intended for low-volume scenarios but are now being triggered by unexpected production traffic patterns. The model can reason about race conditions or lock contention issues by simulating the code execution logic in the context of the observed system state. This turns the LLM into a virtual peer engineer capable of providing an instant deep dive into the internal mechanics of a failing service. The SRE no longer spends hours navigating through unfamiliar codebases during a crisis because the reasoning engine provides a precise mapping of the failure logic and the specific lines of code that require attention.

Transition to dynamic runbooks and adaptive knowledge

The era of the static runbook is coming to an end as LLMs enable the creation of living knowledge structures that evolve in real-time. In the past, a runbook was a fixed set of instructions that quickly became irrelevant as the underlying infrastructure changed. By utilizing retrieval augmented generation and long-term memory architectures, the LLM ensures that the organizational knowledge is always synchronized with the current state of the production environment.

When an incident occurs, the reasoning engine analyzes the specific symptoms and pulls the most relevant historical patterns to generate a custom remediation plan. This plan is not a generic template but a context-aware guide that accounts for the latest software versions and deployment configurations. Furthermore, the model observes the outcome of the remediation and automatically updates the knowledge graph with any new insights or failures encountered during the process. This creates an adaptive feedback loop where the institutional knowledge matures every time the system experiences a disruption. The runbook effectively becomes a continuous stream of operational wisdom rather than a forgotten document.

Institutional memory as a strategic asset

Large engineering organizations frequently struggle with the loss of context as senior engineers depart or as teams grow more specialized. LLMs address this challenge by serving as the permanent custodian of the institutional memory by indexing every technical design document and every decision made during an incident. The reasoning engine allows anyone in the organization to query the rationale behind a legacy architectural choice or the specific tradeoffs made during a historical migration.

This capability ensures that the organization maintains a coherent narrative across years of evolution. The model can provide a synthesis of why a particular database technology was chosen or why a specific retry logic was implemented for a critical service. This prevents the recurrence of past mistakes and enables a more informed decision-making process for future architectural shifts. By providing a unified semantic interface over the entire history of the organization, the LLM transforms a fragmented collection of data into a powerful strategic asset that fuels the autonomous and agentic capabilities of the modern enterprise.

Advanced LLM applications in SRE

Beyond code analysis and documentation, the reasoning capacity of large language models is being applied to several high-impact operational domains:

- **Automated chaos hypothesis generation**: Instead of relying on manual brainstorming for chaos experiments, the LLM analyzes system architecture diagrams and historical failure logs to identify hidden vulnerabilities. The model can predict how a latency spike in a downstream dependency might cause resource exhaustion in the primary service and automatically propose a targeted chaos experiment to validate the resilience of the existing circuit breakers.
- **Policy-as-code generation and validation**: LLMs act as the bridge between natural language governance requirements and executable infrastructure policies. An

engineer can describe a new reliability standard in plain English, and the model will generate the corresponding code to enforce that standard across the entire cloud estate. Furthermore, it serves as an automated auditor that explains to developers why their infrastructure changes might be rejected based on the predicted risk to system stability.

- **Synthetic telemetry and simulation**: To test the robustness of monitoring configurations, the LLM can generate realistic streams of synthetic logs and metrics that mimic specific failure modes. This allows the SRE team to verify that their alerting logic and automated remediation workflows respond correctly to complex disasters such as slow memory leaks or subtle database deadlocks without having to experience a real production outage.
- **Semantic alert clustering and noise reduction**: Rather than relying on rigid rules for grouping alerts, the LLM performs semantic deduplication by understanding the underlying intent of different notifications. It can identify when fifty different alerts from various monitoring tools are describing the same core symptom and suppress the redundant noise, ensuring that the on-call engineer receives a single coherent situation report rather than an overwhelming storm of fragmented alerts.

Intent driven incident diagnosis

As SREs transition from *mechanics* to *decision architects*, the primary interface for managing production shifts from imperative command-line execution to intent-based dialogue. Vibe Debugging is the operational manifestation of this shift, mirroring *vibe coding* by allowing engineers to troubleshoot complex incidents through natural language prompts rather than manual toil. In this paradigm, the SRE navigates *infinite complexity* by providing the high-level *intent* while a reasoning engine orchestrates an agentic swarm to perform the investigation.

The prompt as a diagnostic gateway

In a vibe debugging workflow, the engineer no longer manually parses logs or correlates metrics. Instead, they act as a high-level conductor, using prompts to activate specialized agents with unique cognitive missions:

- **Semantic initiation**: The SRE describes a qualitative symptom (e.g., *The payment gateway feels jittery for mobile users; investigate the latest canary release*), which the LLM-based reasoning engine decomposes into actionable sub-tasks.
- **Multi-agent delegation**: The engine automatically tasks the observer agent to scan high-cardinality telemetry and the architect agent to map the *blast radius* of the recent change.
- **Chain-of-thought triage**: The agents utilize a shared *blackboard* architecture to post findings, mimicking a human war room session to resolve conflicts between data points before presenting a synthesized hypothesis to the SRE.

Deep reasoning over digital vibes

The depth of vibe debugging lies in the ability of LLMs to bridge the gap between static technical assets and the dynamic reality of production:

- **Code-to-cloud traceability**: When an SRE prompts the system about a *bad vibe* in a service, the reasoning engine can ingest application source code alongside real-time telemetry to explain the causal link between specific code logic and the observed anomaly.
- **Contextual historical grounding**: The historian agent searches the organization's long-term memory to find past incidents that *felt* similar, grounding the current investigation in years of institutional wisdom.
- **Recursive refinement**: If the initial automated diagnosis is insufficient, the SRE uses follow-up prompts to pivot the investigation (e.g., *Ignore the database; look for lock contention issues in the caching layer*), allowing for rapid, machine-speed iteration.

Ethics and risks of autonomous systems

Every chapter of this book has championed the power of autonomous AI in operations. However, intellectual honesty demands that we also confront the risks and ethical boundaries that come with it. The transition to autonomous operations is not without its landmines, and the SREs who thrive in this era will be those who are as skilled at building guardrails as they are at building pipelines. Ignoring these risks is not optimism; it is negligence.

Confident misdiagnosis in autonomous systems

The most dangerous failure mode of an autonomous system is not when it is obviously broken but when it is confidently wrong. An executor agent operating on a high-confidence but faulty diagnosis can trigger a remediation cascade that transforms a minor service degradation into a full-scale outage. This is the AI equivalent of a surgeon operating on the wrong limb. Historical training data can encode biases that cause agents to systematically misdiagnose failure modes in underserved regions, minority services, or new infrastructure patterns that the model has not seen before.

The mitigation is not to distrust the AI, but to design for its failure modes from the start. Every autonomous action must have a circuit breaker, a human-defined boundary that prevents the system from compounding a bad decision. Blast radius containment must be a first-class architectural concern, not an afterthought. The organization should treat *confident misdiagnosis* as a category of incident in its own right, with its own postmortem template and learning loop.

AI bias in incident triage

Machine learning models trained on historical incident data inherit the biases of that history. If past engineers consistently resolved P1 alerts faster for core revenue services than for internal tooling, the model learns this priority implicitly. Over time, this can create a two-tier reliability system where certain services receive faster and more accurate autonomous attention than others. This is not a hypothetical concern; it is a documented phenomenon in algorithmic systems across industries.

Responsible AIOps requires regular bias audits of the autonomous triage pipeline. Teams should track **mean time to remediation (MTTR)** not just in aggregate, but segmented by service tier, geographic region, and user population. Where disparities emerge, the training data and confidence thresholds of the relevant agents must be reviewed and corrected. Fairness in reliability is not a soft aspiration; it is a hard engineering requirement.

Over-reliance and erosion of human expertise

There is a subtler long-term risk that deserves equal attention: the gradual erosion of human expertise as engineers delegate more cognitive work to autonomous agents. If the historian agent always retrieves the relevant runbook and the executor agent always formulates the remediation plan, what happens when both are unavailable during a novel, catastrophic failure? The answer, in many organizations, will be a team that has lost the muscle memory to operate without AI assistance.

The antidote is deliberate practice. High-performing SRE organizations of the future will conduct regular *dark mode* drills where the autonomous systems are intentionally disabled, and human engineers must navigate incidents using only fundamental observability tools and first principles. These drills serve two purposes: they preserve human expertise as a critical backup capability, and they reveal the gaps in human understanding that the AI has been quietly papering over.

Accountability and the question of ownership

When an autonomous agent makes a decision that causes harm, a misguided rollback that corrupts data, or a traffic rebalancing that violates a compliance boundary, who is accountable? This is not a philosophical question. It has legal and organizational consequences. The current answer, which must be encoded in every AIOps governance framework, is clear: the humans who designed, trained, deployed, and approved the guardrails of the autonomous system bear full accountability for its actions.

This accountability framework must be operationalized, not merely stated in a policy document. Every autonomous action must be logged with sufficient detail to reconstruct the chain of reasoning that led to it. Every guardrail must have a named owner who is responsible for its accuracy and currency. And every AIOps platform must have an easily accessible *emergency stop* mechanism that any authorized operator can engage without navigating multiple layers of tooling. The machine acts, but the human answers.

Preparing for the next reliability frontier

As we stand at the threshold of this new era, it is vital to recognize that the technological advancements we have discussed are only half of the journey. The transition to an operation model driven by AI requires a fundamental restructuring of the human system that supports it. We are not merely adding new tools to an old workflow but are instead redefining the very nature of what it means to be a site reliability engineer. This preparation involves a deliberate shift in culture and a focused evolution of the engineering skillset to thrive in a landscape of intelligent operations.

From hero culture to decision architecture

For decades, the hallmark of a successful engineer was the ability to perform high-pressure manual interventions during an outage. This hero culture celebrated the individual who could stay awake for thirty hours to fix a kernel panic or manually patch a hundred servers. In the next reliability frontier, this model is not only unsustainable but is a primary source of risk. The future engineer must move from being a manual operator to becoming a decision architect.

As a decision architect, your primary responsibility is the design of the policies and the guardrails that govern the autonomous agents. You are no longer the one pulling the lever, but the one who determines the logic that dictates when the lever should be pulled. This requires a deep understanding of business context and risk tolerance, as well as the ability to translate those high-level goals into the mathematical constraints that the AI can understand. The value you provide to the organization is measured by the quality of the governance you establish and the resilience of the systems you oversee, rather than the number of manual fixes you perform.

SRE skills evolution roadmap

This transformation is not abstract. It maps directly to a concrete set of skills that today's SRE must deliberately cultivate. The following table contrasts the skill profile of the traditional SRE with that of the decision architect who will define the next decade of operations:

Skill domain	Traditional SRE	Decision architect (2027+)	How to bridge the gap
Incident response	Manual log parsing and ad-hoc correlation	Prompt engineering for agentic investigation	Practice vibe debugging; build runbook-to-prompt translations

Skill domain	Traditional SRE	Decision architect (2027+)	How to bridge the gap
Automation	Shell scripting and runbook execution	AI agent orchestration and policy design	Learn multi-agent frameworks (LangGraph, AutoGen); design guardrail logic
Observability	Dashboard monitoring and alert tuning	Semantic telemetry curation and synthetic data generation	Study OpenTelemetry roadmap; experiment with LLM-based alert clustering
Governance	CAB participation and change approval	Predictive risk modeling and reliability risk scores	Build blast radius calculators; integrate risk scoring into CI/CD pipelines
Knowledge management	Writing and maintaining static runbooks	Curating LLM training data and vector knowledge bases	Implement RAG-based runbook systems; audit institutional memory quality
Career identity	Firefighter and system expert	Strategic reliability product owner	Define reliability as a product; track SLO health as a business KPI

***Table 13.1**: The SRE skills evolution roadmap*

Technology maturity and adoption horizons

The transition to intelligent operations will not happen overnight. Understanding the likely cadence of change helps teams prioritize their learning investments and avoid both over-engineering for the distant future and under-preparing for the near term. The following table provides a practical horizon map based on current adoption curves and technology maturity trajectories:

Horizon	What becomes mainstream	What SREs should be doing now
By 2027	AI-assisted triage in CI/CD pipelines becomes standard; reliability risk scores appear in major platform engineering tools; LLM-based runbook generation is widely adopted	Build familiarity with prompt engineering and RAG architectures; instrument services for semantic observability; instrument services for AI-readable telemetry

Horizon	What becomes mainstream	What SREs should be doing now
By 2030	Fully closed-loop autonomous remediation for P2 and P3 incidents in mature organizations; agentic swarms handle routine on-call duties; LLMs serve as primary institutional knowledge interfaces	Design guardrail frameworks and autonomous governance policies; lead organizational shift from hero culture to decision architecture; run regular dark-mode drills
By 2035	Intent-based reliability is the default operating model; humans govern policy and ethics while AI manages all operational complexity; the SRE role fully converges with product and platform engineering	Position yourself as a reliable product owner; develop expertise in AI ethics, accountability frameworks, and cross-functional reliability leadership

***Table 13.2**: Reliability frontier timeline*

Managing reliability as a product

In the intelligent enterprise, reliability is no longer treated as a byproduct of the engineering lifecycle but as a core product in its own right. This shift necessitates that SRE teams adopt a product management mindset where they are responsible for the entire lifecycle of the reliability engine. This includes curating the data that feeds the AI models, ensuring the accuracy of the institutional memory, and continuously auditing the performance of the autonomous swarms.

The SRE team must focus on building a reliability platform that other engineering teams want to pull into their workflows. This means providing self-service tools for predictive risk modeling and automated chaos testing that allow developers to own the reliability of their own services within the guardrails provided by the central SRE team. By treating reliability as a product, the organization can scale its operational maturity without scaling its headcount, ensuring that the human engineers are always focused on the most strategic and creative aspects of the digital landscape.

Cultivating a culture of trust and verification

The final and perhaps most important preparation for the next frontier is the cultivation of trust between human operators and their digital partners. This trust is not granted blindly but is earned through the implementation of rigorous verification cycles. The future SRE workflow is grounded in the principle of verify then trust, where every autonomous action is transparently logged, and every AI hypothesis is validated against empirical data.

To foster this culture, the organization must prioritize explainability in its AIOps platforms. Engineers should be able to interrogate the reasoning engine at any time to understand the logic behind a specific decision. This transparency turns the AI from a black box into a trusted peer that the team can rely on during high-stakes scenarios. As we move forward, the organizations that succeed will be those that strike the perfect balance between the speed of the machine and the wisdom of the human. This partnership is the true essence of the next reliability frontier and the foundation upon which we will build the most resilient systems the world has ever seen. The following figure illustrates the four stages of operational maturity, tracing the evolution from manual toil-driven practices to a fully autonomous, intent-based decision architecture:

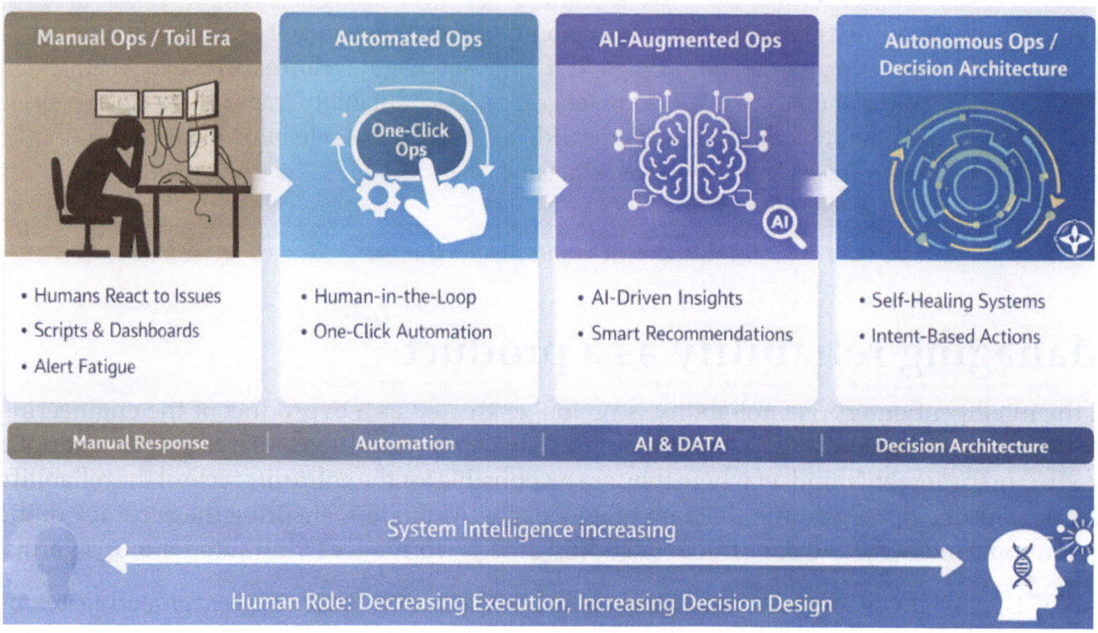

Figure 13.3: *Operational maturity evolution*

Recommended learning path and resources

The journey from SRE to decision architect does not end with the final page of this book. It is a continuous investment. The following are the communities, frameworks, and hands-on experiments that will accelerate your growth in the era of intelligent operations:

- **Communities and continuous learning**: The **Cloud Native Computing Foundation (CNCF)** TAG observability group tracks the cutting edge of open-source observability and AIOps tooling. SRE weekly curates the best thinking across the reliability discipline. The OpenTelemetry project roadmap is essential reading for anyone building the telemetry pipelines that autonomous agents will depend on.
- **Frameworks and papers to study**: The **reasoning and acting (ReAct)** prompting framework is the foundational model for how LLMs orchestrate tool use in agentic systems. Microsoft's AutoGen and LangChain's LangGraph are the leading open-

source frameworks for building multi-agent reliability workflows. The Google SRE Workbook chapters on toil elimination provide an essential baseline for measuring what autonomous systems should be eliminating.

- **Hands-on experiments to run**: Build a single-agent chaos hypothesis generator using a public LLM API and a sample service architecture diagram. Implement a simple reliability risk score for one CI/CD pipeline using code complexity metrics and deployment history. Run a *dark mode* drill with your team to measure baseline human performance without AI assistance. These practical experiments will teach you more about the real boundaries of autonomous operations than any theoretical framework.
- **Certifications and formal programs**: Platform engineering and reliability-focused certifications from major cloud providers (AWS, GCP, Azure) are rapidly incorporating AIOps modules. The Linux Foundation's SRE certification tracks are evolving to include AI governance and autonomous operations components. Supplement these with courses in machine learning fundamentals and AI ethics to build the cross-disciplinary foundation that the decision architect role demands.

Case study: The Zero-Touch Enterprise

To truly grasp the power of the *architecture of autonomy*, we must look at how these technologies converge in a real-world, high-stakes environment. The Zero-Touch Enterprise is an organization where the system functions as a digital nervous system, capable of sensing deviations and initiating corrections without human prompts.

Scenario: The seasonal surge

Imagine a global e-commerce platform approaching a massive, scheduled flash sale. Historically, this would require *hero culture* intervention, engineers on standby for 30-hour shifts to manually patch servers and monitor dashboards. In a Zero-Touch Enterprise, the workflow is fundamentally different. The following scenario illustrates the end-to-end operational sequence of a Zero-Touch Enterprise, where predictive governance, agentic swarms, and closed-loop verification eliminate the need for hero-culture intervention:

1. **Predictive governance and preparation**: Weeks before the event, the predictive governance model identifies the upcoming seasonal traffic surge. The governance model responds by initiating the following pre-emptive safeguards:
    - **Adaptive SLOs**: The AIOps platform automatically tightens the safety margins of SLOs to enforce stricter deployment gates.
    - **Automated chaos vaccination**: The optimizer agent analyzes historical failure logs and architecture diagrams to identify hidden vulnerabilities. It automatically triggers a *pre-emptive verification loop*, running targeted chaos experiments to *vaccinate* the system against predicted resource exhaustion.

2. **The autonomous incident response**: During the peak of the sale, a subtle race condition begins to cause a latency spike in the checkout service. Three agents activate in sequence to detect, diagnose, and remediate the issue:
    - **The swarm activates**: The observer agent detects a deviation from the steady state. It alerts the architect agent, which immediately maps the *blast radius* to ensure the failure does not cause a high-impact cascade to the payment gateway.
    - **Reasoning through code**: The historian agent crawls vector databases of past incidents, while the LLM-based reasoning engine ingests application source code to explain the causal link between the current traffic pattern and the failing code logic.
    - **Surgical remediation**: The executor agent formulates a dynamic remediation plan, not a static script, but a sequence of actions like rebalancing traffic and throttling low-priority background tasks.
3. **Success verification and knowledge maturation**: Within seconds, the system scales the infrastructure and resolves the bottleneck at machine speed. Once remediation is applied, the closed-loop engine validates success and preserves the outcome for future use:
    - **Verification**: The closed-loop engine continues to monitor SLIs to ensure the system has returned to a healthy state.
    - **Institutional memory**: The curator agent observes the outcome and automatically updates the organizational knowledge graph. What was once a *forgotten document* or a *tribal knowledge* fix is now a living piece of operational wisdom for the future.

Outcome:

In this Zero-Touch model, the SRE acted as a decision architect, providing the *intent* (the checkout service must remain available under 50ms) while the AI handled the *complexity of scale*. Critically, the autonomous response was constrained throughout by human-defined guardrails: the system could rebalance traffic and throttle background tasks, but it could not modify the payment gateway's security configuration or delete any persistent data without explicit human authorization. The result is a system that is not just *fixed* when it breaks, but is inherently, autonomously intelligent, operating within boundaries that humans defined and humans can audit.

Core pillars of your new roadmap

By mastering the concepts in this final chapter, you are now equipped with a strategic roadmap for the next decade of engineering:

- **The architecture of autonomy**: You understand the shift from human-in-the-loop to closed-loop systems, where intent-based reliability allows the machine to manage operational complexity while you define the policy and business value.

- **Predictive governance**: You have moved beyond reactive post-mortems toward proactive risk modeling, using AI to quantify the *blast radius* of changes before they are even deployed.
- **Agentic swarms**: You can now orchestrate a distributed ecosystem of specialized AI agents, such as observers, historians, and architects, that collaborate to resolve incidents that once sat beyond the cognitive reach of any single human.
- **LLMs as reasoning engines**: You see LLMs not just as chatbots, but as the institutional memory and logical processors that bridge the gap between static code and the dynamic reality of production.
- **Ethical governance of autonomous systems**: You recognize that the organizations that will lead this era are not those who move fastest, but those who move most responsibly, with transparent audit trails, bias-audited triage pipelines, and human accountability at every layer.
- **The decision architect career path**: You have a concrete skills roadmap, a tiered timeline of what to expect, and a recommended learning path to guide your continuous evolution in this field.

Conclusion

We started this book with a single engineer and a wall of red. We end it with a vision of a system that rarely produces red in the first place, one that anticipates, adapts, and heals itself while the engineers who built it focus on the questions only humans can answer: What does this system need to accomplish? What are we willing to risk to get there? What does *good enough* look like for the people who depend on us?

The premise we set in *Chapter 1, SRE Principles Driving Modern Operations* has proven true: complexity is outstripping human capacity. AIOps is not a luxury; it is a survival requirement for the modern enterprise. However, this chapter has added an essential caveat to that premise. The machines we build to manage complexity are only as trustworthy as the humans who design their boundaries, audit their decisions, and accept accountability for their actions. Autonomy without ethics is not progress. It is a risk at scale.

By embracing the trends of autonomy, predictive governance, and agentic reasoning, and by holding them accountable to the ethical standards we have outlined, you are not automating yourself out of a job. You are elevating yourself. You are shedding the *toil* of the past, the manual log parsing, the frantic alert storms, the repetitive post-mortems, and stepping into the role of the decision architect.

This book has provided the *hands*, the *immune system*, and the *brain* of modern operations. Now, the final piece of the puzzle is your leadership. In this new era, humans provide the intent and ethics, while AI provides the scale and speed. Together, we are building a digital world that is more resilient, innovative, and reliable than ever before.

The engineer who stared at that wall of red alerts in *Chapter 1, SRE Principles Driving Modern Operations,* did not need fewer alerts. They needed a system wise enough to need fewer engineers. You now know how to build that system. More importantly, you know how to lead the humans who will live inside it.

The frontier is open. You know the way. It is time to lead.

Join our Discord space

Join our Discord workspace for latest updates, offers, tech happenings around the world, new releases, and sessions with the authors:

https://discord.bpbonline.com

Index

A

B

C

P

R